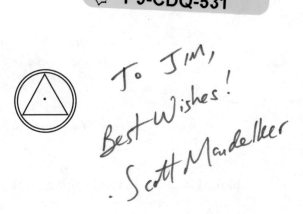

To Jim,
Best Wishes!
- Scott Mandelker

UNIVERSAL VISION

Soul-Evolution and the Cosmic Plan

by Scott Mandelker, Ph.D.

UV WAY

SAN FRANCISCO, CALIFORNIA

Universal Vision:
Soul Evolution and the Cosmic Plan

by
Scott Mandelker, Ph.D.
Author of *From Elsewhere: Being ET in America*

Published in 2000; Revised edition 2001.
Copyright © Scott Mandelker, 1999, 2001

COVER, LAYOUT, AND DESIGN BY SARA LYARA ESTES

ISBN# 0-9701985-0-7

Library of Congress CCN# 99-074546

UV WAY
SAN FRANCISCO, CA
USA

Printed in USA on acid-free paper

ᴄ Contents ᴄ

II. THE PRINCIPLES OF SOUL-EVOLUTION

A. HEALING AND SELF-TRANSFORMATION

B. BUDDHISM AND MEDITATION

— DEDICATION —

This book is dedicated to all my Teachers,
Both seen and unseen, appreciated and otherwise—
For all your patience, acceptance, and ever-streaming light
through the long cycles of all my Earthly dreaming. . .
With a special dedication to the Wanderers—

Pledged to universal service and comfort:
No need to worry—
Each day is Harvest.

— ACKNOWLEDGEMENT —

Sincere appreciation to my parents, grandmother, and uncle—
For all your love and trust, open-mindedness, and
Heart-felt desire that I be fulfilled in this lifetime.
Special thanks to the readers and subscribers to The ET Journal—
Your calling in the garden called forth the gardeners,
Tilling and re-tilling the ageless ground from which our book first grew.

And final thanks to RM—
For your selfless giving, kind support, and flawless generosity.
The resurrection of this book is due to you.

◆ OM MANI PADME HUM ◆

INTRODUCTION

IN THE FOLLOWING CHAPTERS, you will find a most unusual synthesis, a unique integration of many diverse traditions. On my own winding path I've met many sources of wisdom, and like you, I've relied on the inner voice to try to learn from each of them. Today, they're blended in all that I teach. Yet all these sources are, in fact, just elements of a single unified whole, what can be called the Path of Return, the Path to the Heart of Self, or *The Principles of Soul-Evolution*. The purpose of this book is to unite these different perspectives, and present a comprehensive and up-to-date guide to spiritual life on Earth at the dawn of a new millennium. As you might agree, it *is* a special time.

In my first book, *From Elsewhere: Being ET in America* (Dell paperback, 1996), I explored the personal world of those who consider themselves Wanderers, Walk-ins, or ET souls living in America. In it, twenty-five people from all walks of life described what it was like for them to realize that though they live on Earth, they are not from Earth. And in the final chapter I told my own story, including the fact that I, too, share their extra-terrestrial identity. I also consider myself a Wanderer, a soul *from elsewhere* here to assist the planet like millions of others among us. Perhaps the measure of how much things have changed in the years since release of that book is the fact that there my story was reserved for the end, placed inconspicuously in the second appendix. But here, I am telling you up front: the author of this book is an ET soul (Gosh!). Yet, despite dramatics, I don't think it's a big deal. As in all traditions of spiritual initiation, yesterday's grand revelation is just the floor for further growth today.

Once I was publicly out of the ET closet, I found myself launched upon the larger task of teaching and counseling throughout the U.S. and overseas. For the past few years, I've been speaking regularly at

UFO and New Age expos in the United States, Japan, and Israel, as well as giving seminars and personal counseling. Along the way, I've met hundreds of people who also consider themselves ET souls. In many cases, they had had spiritual or visionary experiences identical to the people I interviewed for my first book, and they also fit a distinctive profile, versions of which you'll find in Section I, Chapter 4 ("The Sleeping ETs Quiz"), as well as Appendix 3 ("The New ET Questionnaire").

I believe that the ET community on Earth—which includes the vast majority of "Lightworkers" as well as many of those who consider themselves spiritual seekers, in every nation—numbers close to 100 million. While a large part of my work has supported this particular community, this has become just the starting-point of my work—as well as the launch-pad for this book. To be ET or not ET, this is *not* the question: it is far more important that each of us find, and then proceed in balance upon our own unique (and universal) spiritual path. Ironically, for most Wanderers, it has almost nothing to do with ET matters! This is primarily due the fact that most of them are actually unaware of their cosmic identity—and they are also trying hard to fit into human society.

I certainly affirm the legitimacy, and even the perfection of each of our paths. While it is my guess that if you were drawn to this book you may also be a Wanderer or ET soul, it is certainly **not** my intention to try to persuade you. In my counseling, I often tell people, "if it is true, you might as well know it." But if you honestly don't feel that exploring your possible ET roots is important to where you are today, then of course leave it alone. In writing this book, it is not my main goal at all to spark your ET awakening, though that may happen, and millions of Wanderers will surely awaken to their identity in the next few years. My primary goal is to present the essential teachings of benevolent extraterrestrial groups and enlightened beings, as far as I have realized them in my own life. To help you grasp their relevance and value, I have set these principles in the context of the world today, so they become practical to you on your own path.

Let me explain the structure here. The first two sections of the book are divided into two parts each. In the first, I explore the metaphysics and cosmic purpose behind global UFO/ET visitation and the presence of Wanderers among us. From this foundation, you'll see that a vast cosmic drama of inter-galactic evolution is the essential context in which all our personal growth and world service occurs. In the second section, I will connect some spiritual traditions that are rarely presented together, though their relationship is so close that they should never have been parted in the first place. In particular, I will discuss the fundamentals of self-healing and love, Higher Self and the chakras, Buddhism and meditation. I'll stress the practical application of these ideas in daily life.

Some of the approaches I will integrate include Western integral psychology (healing body, mind, and spirit), Eastern mystic traditions (Chinese and Japanese Zen, Theravada and Tibetan Buddhism, Indian Vedanta and Chinese Taoism), the ageless wisdom of Theosophy as presented by Alice Bailey, and the channeled teachings of an ET group named "RA." This last body of teachings, taken from the five volumes of question-and-answer sessions entitled *The Law of One* (also called *The RA Material*), is considered by many Wanderers, including myself, to be the finest source of channeled information in English. You'll find many quotations from this important source, and I believe that by the end of this book you will also come to appreciate their view. I am planning to make available a study guide to their first volume on my home page later on.

Though my own spiritual path led me to years of formal training in U.S. and Asian Buddhist temples, and then onto earning a Master's degree in Integral Counseling and a Doctorate in East-West Psychology, it was only when I could unite all these studies with those of my more "cosmic teachers" that the light of greater wisdom shone on all these paths as one. Through prolonged study and quiet meditation, I realized that the major teachings of all these diverse traditions were in fact scattered portions of a single unified whole. All real paths reveal the One Path.

This was also stated by RA in their first contact with the group in Louisville, Kentucky that received their teachings in the early 1980s. They hinted that what is of most value is **not** some new-fangled, fast-track weekend-workshop, processed New Age spirituality. Before imparting their grand vision of cosmic unity, they stated their intentions most simply:

> *We hope to offer you a somewhat different slant upon the information which is always and ever the same.*[1]

This book, *Universal Vision*, offers yet another "somewhat different slant" upon the essential principles of the Path which are always and ever the same. In fact, over the course of many years I have learned that this is the **only** measure of the purity and potency of true spiritual information: *its durability over time*, which is why it is rightly called "ageless" wisdom.

In the fall of 1995, at about the same time *From Elsewhere* was released, I also began writing and publishing a 10-page bi-monthly newsletter called *The ET Journal*. Almost immediately, it became a forum for dialogue on UFOs and ET souls, cosmic plan and global change, and the principles and applications of spiritual teaching for personal growth. In the last three years, it became a forum for Wanderers around the country, and a few dozen around the world, who shared their letters, questions, and personal stories. In the *Journal* we've been able to explore our connections with one another, our relationship to Earth and humanity, the purpose of our presence, and the ways of deepening love and wisdom. *The ET Journal* forms the matrix upon which this book is built, and most of the chapters here are drawn from its pages.

Thus, the first part of Section I concerns the specific issues of Wanderers on Earth: achieving harmony within ourselves and human society, then offering love and light in world service. It also explores, in depth, the mind and intentions of the major ET groups now visiting

---

1. Elkins, Rueckert, McCarty, *The RA Material* (*The Law of One, Vol. I*), p. 65. Schiffer Publishing, West Chester, PA, 1984.

the planet—in other words, UFO methods, means, and ultimate agendas. The second part of Section I explores the social implications of such cosmic forces, Earth Changes, humanity, and the current global shift. After a chapter of *Q and A*, we will then proceed to Section II, where you'll find "the heart of the matter." Here we will explore the timeless principles of the evolution of body, mind, and spirit, as well as some of the essential tools available to us on the ageless path to healing, enlightenment, and union with the Higher Self—what the Buddhists call non-duality, and the Hindus call Godhead, *Atman* (true Self), or *Sat-Chit-Ananda* (Being-Consciousness-Bliss).

Before going further, perhaps a little background on RA (my main source) will be helpful. Although I was already familiar with the teachings of many traditions, discovering *The Law of One* books was like finding a deep vein of pure gold. It quickly became the philosophical basis for *The ET Journal*, my personal learning, and all my teaching. I hold it in the highest esteem, and to be honest, I've lost interest in most other sources of channeled information in print. In the four main volumes I found answers to my most pressing questions about life on Earth and Wanderers; about positive and negative ET groups; and about the principles of balance, healing and service.

This material has proven to be a potent catalyst to my own body-mind-spirit activation, which is also a measure of its value. My process of studying, assimilating, systematizing, and finally conveying this information to others has been extremely transformative, as powerful as 20 years of Buddhist breath meditation. Together with the principles of ageless wisdom and Eastern religion, these have become the pillars of my own self-learning.

For those unfamiliar with this source, it is useful to understand how *The Law of One* was born. For twenty years, Don Elkins, a former airline pilot and University of Louisville physics professor, conducted experiments in communication with disincarnate intelligence. His work began in 1961 with a small group of interested students and academics. After years of trial and error, they finally learned how to accurately receive and assess telepathic information. Eventually, Don was joined by Carla Rueckert, who later became the "instrument" or full-trance channel for RA. Carla also wrote *A Channeling Handbook*, which is available from her organization, L/L Research (see the "Information for Seekers" in Appendix 4).

Despite the efforts of Don and Carla, it was not until a third person, James McCarty, arrived in Louisville and joined their ongoing work that the circle was complete. Soon thereafter, they were contacted by a source that called itself "RA," and at that point, the quality of the information they were receiving changed dramatically. As if a circuit had finally been looped and a greater energy voltage could at last be delivered, abruptly and almost overnight, the clarity and potency of their material took a quantum leap forward.

In contrast to most other channeling, their procedure was formal, solemn, and precise. It was never done in public, never done without prescribed ritual protection, and never intended for the widest possible audience. To maintain the RA contact, Carla had to be in full-trance absorption—lying supine on a bed, swathed in blankets with special neck support, hooked up to microphones and no less than three tape recorders (due to repeated malfunctioning). Don sat nearby asking the questions, while Jim remained in constant prayer, sending only love and light. Few outsiders ever sat in on their sessions, and RA often cautioned them about the need to keep their desire to "serve the Creator" as pure as possible. In my experience, I have never met a more rigorous contact than this one. They never hit the New Age circuit, for many years never charged for their books, and never sought to build a following. Yet, over the years, many people have come to appreciate the gems they uncovered. In the "List of Resources," you will also find some Web sites devoted to their networking.

From 1981 through 1984, Don, Carla and Jim dedicated themselves full-time to maintaining the RA contact, which identified itself as a "social memory complex," an oversoul group-consciousness in which all members have shared awareness. RA claims to have provided the basic teachings on healing, pyramids, crystals and initiation to the ancient Egyptians, and to have had direct contact with Pharaoh Ikhnaton (also considered a Wanderer) around the year 4000 B.C. (for more on this, see Section I, Chapter 8, "ET-Earth History: An Overview"). They can be considered one of the major ET groups responsible for assisting the growth of humanity through the ages.

Originally, the RA group came from Venus, but now they claim to dwell in what is called "sixth density," a state of unified being in which they "no longer seek light, but rather have become light." This state corresponds to the awareness of Higher Self, associated with the 6th chakra in the human subtle body. Their real name, that is, whatever they called themselves before they came to Earth, is probably not "RA" at all. I imagine they simply chose the name because it symbolized Unity to the Egyptians, personified as the Sun-God that they worshipped as the One Creator. In other words, the name suited RA's nature and their basic purpose: offering what they call "The Law of One," the teachings of cosmic unity. This is the main perspective I'll be sharing in this book.

The four main volumes of *The Law of One* consist of over 100 question-and-answer sessions, using the same format each time. Don formed the questions, Carla was the trance receiver or voice channel, and Jim was the scribe whose task was to take notes and support the other two in myriad ways. Each session began with a precisely formulated invocation for protection, and ritual items that held special significance for Carla (such as the Christian Bible, censer, and a chalice of water) were carefully placed behind her head on a special table—to empower their state of mind and remind them to be meticulous and vigilant. Understandably, RA called their contact "a narrow band transmission," and in fact, it was *so* narrow that RA often corrected the group regarding the proper orientation of the ritual items, suggesting, for example, that they move the censer .4 degrees northeast. I have never seen this degree of extreme care in other channeled works, and it is a cosmic law that the purity of calling determines the purity of response. The late Dr. Andrija Puharich, friend and colleague of the psychic Uri Geller, called it "the best cosmic connection I have seen in my lifetime." I believe it is one of the most important spiritual transmissions in print.

From the beginning, RA emphasized that they were merely "a humble messenger of The Law of One," offering the truth of non-duality, which they defined succinctly in the first session. In relation to Self and the Universe, our true self-nature and spiritual identity, they said:

> *You are not speaking of similar or somewhat like entities or things. You are every thing, every being, every emotion, every event, every situation. You are unity. You are infinity. You are love/light, light/love. You are. This is the Law of One.*[2]

In the contact with Elkins, Rueckert, and McCarty, RA's goal was to "lessen the distortions" in human consciousness inspired by their previous, somewhat naive attempts to help us. These efforts, primarily in Egypt, were later distorted for elitist purposes and co-opted by the selfish priestly caste around Ikhnaton. Today, we can get an idea of RA's commitment to the work from a statement they made. They note, in no uncertain terms, that *"the fidelity of RA towards the attempt to remove distortions is total."*[3] Of this, I have no doubt.

Therefore, they firmly emphasized "essential principles," and never devolved into more sexy information to satisfy curiosity. When the receiving group asked questions that strayed into matters of "transient importance," such as UFO cover-ups and conspiracies, facts and figures on ET races and galactic history, RA noted time and again the limited value of such knowledge. Throughout the entire contact, they stressed the importance of seeking only that level of truth which can lead to genuine self-transformation, centered on the timeless principles of body-mind-spirit. Even the language they used was carefully chosen. For maximum precision, they often used archaic words and concepts far removed from the conscious vocabulary of anyone in the room. In this book I will also stay tuned to the timeless principles of spiritual growth.

RA never intended their contact to be abstruse: they hoped simply to reveal the splendor of cosmic unity in a pure, undistorted form.

---

2. Ibid., p. 67.
3. Elkins, Rueckert, McCarty, *The Law of One*, Vol. IV, p. 27. Schiffer Publishing, 1982.

Nevertheless, many readers do find their material quite challenging in its original presentation. And that's where this book comes in. The following chapters will integrate a great deal of their teachings, adapted to present conditions and blended with my own practice and background in Eastern traditions. RA even stated that "very few [readers] can harmonize their vibrations" with them, but nonetheless, I have found over the years many people can understand what they taught. My role is like a transducer or medium through which their universal vision can be made more personal, more relevant to modern life.

If you have read my first book, my own story is familiar. It is a journey that began with confusion and existential angst as a teenager (a condition extremely common among ET souls), progressed to intensive monasticism and Buddhist meditation in my twenties, went on to academic study and later work in counseling and East-West psychology, and finally arrived at my own ET roots. Only then could I integrate the lessons of this journey in my own teaching and counseling. Yet, the heart of my path has been Buddhist meditation and wide spiritual study—which is probably why I am not content to be boxed in the role of "Spokesman" for the ET Souls. That job is far too narrow, and in fact, these days I have less and less interest in UFO matters at all.

For those who are Wanderers, realizing ET identity is just the first step—and after you know it's true for yourself, you need to move onto more universal concerns. ET or otherwise, the greater work is developing our full potential, the body/mind/spirit, which leads inevitably to greater self-fulfillment and greater ability to be dynamic and centered in service to others. This book is offered in just that spirit—centered on the essentials as much as possible, integrating the practical concerns of life on Earth at the start of the 21st Century, and directed towards the major spiritual goals of soul evolution: blossoming the flower of balanced love-wisdom, and moving towards joy in union with All That Is. In other words, full enlightenment. On the eternal path, we all walk together. There is no high or low, no right or wrong, and the total power of the Infinite Creator is always here. Filled with this Light, there is glory everywhere.

SECTION I

THE COSMIC PLAN

PART A:

ET SOULS AND THE UFO PRESENCE

» *Chapter 1* «

DOORS AND DEFINITIONS

As in the classic TV show "Let's Make A Deal," we face three choices when considering our approach to UFOs and ET life. First, there is *Door Number 1*, through which we find nothing more than facts and figures on sightings, material evidence, cover-ups and conspiracies. Inside this box, we find endless debates between those with secret information and those who deny it, UFO researchers of various stripes and professional debunkers, the so-called scientists who guide public opinion of cosmic truth (the late Carl Sagan having been foremost among them). These two groups, strange bedfellows indeed, have been locked in mortal combat for the past 50 years. Each side claims to hold the truth, but neither is convinced by the other. One says yes, the other cries no.

To be honest, die-hard skeptics will never cry defeat, while UFO researchers, no matter how professional (such as Dr. John Mack of Harvard University, who specializes in abduction research), cannot produce indisputable proof of alien life, cover-ups or secret deals. I guess it is to be expected, but what really seems sad is that this whole battle actually does quite little to improve humanity. Like nomads fighting over sand dunes in the desert, arguments between skeptics and believers are fruitless, and in any case, the human spirit can never be nourished by physical ET proof or evidence of cover-ups. Material evidence is mute for speaking to soul.

Although *Door Number 2* is a bit more exciting, it is also a dead-end street. Choose this one and you'll find spooky grays, bizarre experiments and genetic tinkering by shadowy intruders. While I acknowledge the reality of abduction contact and negative beings, I have no doubt these are but one small piece of a much larger puzzle. To try to grasp the mind of ETs by living in this box is like trying to judge national character by visiting jails: we will suffer from a severe sampling bias.

Furthermore, in my opinion, most people who have had traumatic experience, including the experts on the front-line trying to help them, are unaware of the deeper issues involved. Unfortunately, they usually have scant metaphysical understanding of the powers of Self, the laws of interdimensional contact, the ways of spiritual healing, and the means of accessing Divine Power. Instead, this community is fed a steady diet of horror tales, left in the dark helpless and confused, expecting the worst—with no recourse to inner God. Yet, all this represents just one chapter in a much larger book, and there **are** answers and solutions. Nevertheless, the ET-abduction research community does not seem to have answers nor solutions. If we get stuck to the ET-criminal element, we will miss the Greater Light that stands behind them.

But there is still *Door Number 3*, through which you will find an integrated spiritual perspective, a vision of the metaphysics of cosmic plan in which ET Walk-ins, Wanderers, and world servers operate. With a different view of UFO reality and a focus on *soul-evolution*, the emphasis here is wholly spiritual: love, wisdom, and purpose. Here we talk about cosmic unity, transformation of consciousness, the two paths, and trust in Higher Self. While skeptics and researchers are locked in endless debate, while anti-conspiracy activists rail against the system (which, by the way, is going to collapse soon anyway), and while abduction researchers either lament or happy-spin their tales of negative ET contact—we can go a whole lot deeper by considering the spiritual view.

Behind this third door we can find inspiration, purpose and meaning, as well as real people who have been awakened by rare experiences. They're not arguing; they don't predict doom; they are not trying to convince you of anything (and nor am I). They affirm that the cosmos is filled with intelligent life, and they say that love is the key. But most importantly, their message reveals a more balanced picture of Universal Life—a picture in which UFOs and ETs make perfect sense.

BASIC DEFINITIONS

In describing ET Souls, I use often the terms Walk-ins and Wanderers (this second group is also called Star People, Star Born, or Star Children). Although their higher-dimensional origins and life-purpose may be the same, what distinguishes them is how they took birth in human form:

Walk-in: This term describes a process of inter-dimensional, inter-planetary *soul exchange*, as well as the individuals who experience it. In this process, a soul from an older ET or Angelic civilization (or a more evolved Earth soul) enters the voluntarily surrendered body and personality-system of a human being, to better serve humanity and Earth. Interestingly, some Walk-ins do not consider themselves ET souls and have little interest in such matters. In my view, however, most so-called Walk-ins are actually Wanderers, as I believe that genuine Walk-ins are far more rare than people imagine (see Chapter 3, "Extraterrestrials Living on Earth," for one story).

Wanderer: This poetic term, used by George Hunt Williamson and other UFO contactees in the 1950s, describes a process of inter-dimensional, inter-planetary *soul transfer*—in which a higher-dimensional ET soul incarnates in the normal way (e.g. as a baby), and agrees to forget their own memory of ET identity and purpose, to aid the evolution of humanity and the planet. This process of cosmic soul-wandering has occurred since the beginning of human experience on Earth and is common throughout the Universe, and expresses of the basic Law of Service in which elder souls roam freely the many worlds in need.

Chapter 2

ET Souls and the New Age

As you probably know, there's been a lot more human-ET contact behind the scenes than most people realize. In my view, one of the most important elements of this drama is the claim that extraterrestrial (ET) souls have taken birth among us for tens of thousands of years. Using the terms "Walk-ins" and "Star People," the existence of this group was first brought to wide public attention by the books of Brad Steiger and Ruth Montgomery. However, this phenomenon, no matter how strange it seems, is just part of a greater cosmic plan. From this angle, inter-dimensional soul transfers to Earth are just the vanguard of a more spectacular and rare event—no less than *planetary initiation.* It's for this reason, and to witness such an event, that our galactic family has now come to call. The desire to aid this world process is the main reason why Wanderers and ET Walk-ins are here.

A prediction is made in some New Age circles that after the transition to fourth density (a condition of higher energy and consciousness, predicted to occur around 2010—2013 A.D.), human society will be transformed into a culture of kindness and compassion. Many people are predicting that Earth will soon be accepted into a benevolent Confederation of Planets, a galactic union of various worlds. It's said that many more ETs will then come live among us—fully conscious of their identity and still holding their higher-dimensional powers. Working side by side with humanity, they will build, teach, and offer their technologies for reconstruction. Other channeled sources state that our planetary mother, the long-suffering Gaia, will soon be liberated from her role as schoolhouse for destructive, immature souls. In the main, I agree with all these ideas.

Clearly, wonderful things are expected. Despite the panic and pain of abduction experience, the tangled threads of conspiracy, endless cover-ups, and the debunkers' shrill cry, the basic tone of UFO/ET matters is really one of optimism. To broaden our understanding, we must consider the ultimate purpose of benevolent ET groups and those who've chosen to take human form: the Wanderers and Walk-ins. In esoteric terms, what's really happening is the birth of a new planet.

Yet, how can we believe this is so, seeing such glaring social ills around us, the cultural decay of nations, and the arrogant hubris and deceit of geopolitics? From a worldly perspective, things look pretty bad indeed, and to my eyes, they are actually getting worse. However, I consider this just the death of the old king: the surfacing, at last, of the many evils of confused humanity, and ultimately, the final futile power-grab of a self-serving elite. Could it be that the galactic energies now streaming into Earth's energy-grid actually amplify the power of both polarities—amping up both kindness and self-centered aggression? Could it be that within this charged clime, humanity's deep-seated corruption is fast rising to the surface like a breaking fever, a kind of collective healing crisis? As it is always darkest before dawn, I believe Earth's long suffering nightmare is coming to a close. And among the Wanderers and lightworkers that I know, the consensus is that it's not a moment too soon! Many of us, and perhaps you too, are eager for the new dawn.

In the midst of the planetary birth, with labor pains, nausea and social cramping, there's definitely a need for some kind of stability. Many ET channeled sources agree that intensified *heart-center energy* is now streaming into Earth, and must be integrated into the changing grid of the planet itself. However, this process is hindered and distorted by the accumulated force from centuries of human disharmony, both individual and collective. The planet itself is weakened and requires a resonant core of *awakened, love-infused beings* to anchor the cosmic energies coming in. This radiant group, the true world servers, actually circulate, channel and harmonize the absorption of such light energies. It sounds esoteric, and it really is.

And so we arrive at the role of Wanderers: to receive, amplify, and transmit the cosmic heart-energies of love to balance and assist world initiation. It doesn't matter if such Star People or Star Born teach, organize, go public, or even recognize their own ET identity—because their very presence, to the extent they are living from the heart, offers a crystallized force that actively supports global transformation. Of course, this is not to say that those who are not (or who think they are not) ET souls, are themselves not helping Earth. Service to others is rendered by love, ET or otherwise.

These are subtle matters, but I think they need to be explored for two reasons: first, to provide a larger window through which we can see the meaning of the present time; and secondly, to support those of us who actually are from elsewhere. Extraterrestrial souls really do come to help the planet, and our work doesn't really depend on the extent of public acceptance. The planet itself can use the harmonized energies that stream from awakened and balanced ET souls, as well as from all those who live in love. Like an elementary school that is about to become a high school, I believe that very soon this Earth will no longer house destructive young souls who don't appreciate loving-kindness. They'll simply need to go elsewhere.

For the past 75,000 years, beginning in the long-lost civilizations of Atlantis and Lemuria, this planet has been a "schoolhouse" for souls who have not yet learned to love. In the future, in what is considered "Fourth Density," it will become a school for those who are already based in love, and are in the process of developing wisdom. This spiritual winnowing process is the true meaning of the Christian terms of "rapture…apocalypse…judgment day" and "the kingdom of Heaven." The meek (those who are loving, kind, gentle and generous) will indeed inherit the Earth.

As living souls evolve freely throughout an infinite cosmos, there are countless places to go for people who keep their hearts shut and deny inner love. It is the task of those from elsewhere, the Wanderers and Walk-ins, to simply provide an energy boost for Earth in its time of need, and to unconditionally support those who come our way and call for help. We are simply here as catalyst.

And remember, nothing is carved in stone. If we are committed to spiritual growth, our work begins with clearing the personal haze of thinking and feeling, and continues on to further service that can radiate the clear light of love, wisdom, and Unity. If you want to help, you will make a difference by giving whatever you can when you can, being sensitive to those around you, and living an open life with kindness and intelligent goodwill. ET souls on Earth, not special or grandiose, are simply here to support humanity's growth into a more conscious race.

In the next chapter, we will look at the stories of three people who came to realize their own cosmic roots, and how they have gone on from there.

» *Chapter 3* «

Extraterrestrials Living on Earth

Now that we have covered the basic groundwork, it's time to hear from some people who consider themselves Walk-ins and Wanderers. In the research I did for my first book, I found most of them intelligent, reasonable, and quite willing to share their stories and the details of their awakening. To simply label them kooky and far-out ignores the subtlety of what they're saying, and the intensity of what they have gone through. Here are a few stories.

Jonathan: As a child, Jonathan (or Jody as he likes to be called) says "I often left my body at bedtime, to meet and travel in other dimensions with friends," and was fully conscious during these strange experiences. He remembers looking down at his body as he floated upwards—and while awake, as a child, he couldn't understand why he couldn't fly as easily! He said that he often communicated with ETs and wrote down what they told him. Naturally, his favorite TV program was *My Favorite Martian* and he found the special abilities of the main character totally natural. He also drew spaceships in his elementary school art class, until a teacher forbade him to indulge his special interest. Actually, this kind of youthful fascination with space is quite common among those who later come to realize themselves as ET Wanderers (for some other traits, see the next chapter, "The Sleeping ETs Quiz").

At the age of sixteen, Jody had a near-drowning accident while surfing, during which he was trapped underwater until he began to lose consciousness. Interestingly, at a certain point he no longer felt the need to struggle towards the surface, and was aware of himself as a golden ball of light, able to see in all directions. After losing consciousness, he later found himself still in his Earth-body, floating on the surface of the sea. This experience changed his thinking forever.

During later adolescence and into his twenties, he felt extreme anguish about the state of the world, experiencing deep alienation and longing for some sort of spiritual connection. In a moment of crisis, he called out with all the intensity he could muster, *"How do I contact other life?"*—and suddenly, as if the center of his being had been struck like a bell, he heard, saw, and knew the words "WE ARE GATHERING," as if all the voices in creation spoke as One. Actually, many other Wanderers have since told me that they've heard this same phrase.

He saw the Earth as if from space, and viewing the globe along with him were gathered a multitude of beings, both in UFO ships and also formless, all of whom he realized were his true spiritual family. From that point on, his awareness of being an ET soul has grown clearer and clearer, so that today Jody is an articulate teacher who has helped many people understand their own unusual experiences, and works extensively on the Internet[1] assisting Wanderers around the world.

Zaradia: The woman who calls herself Zaradia has been a spiritual teacher and organizer in Southern California for many years. She told me that Zaradia is "an extraterrestrial and captain of a starship" and is actually one of her multi-dimensional selves with whom she has become a *soul braid*, by which she means that their awareness is blended together. The story of how she came to this conclusion is quite interesting.

She first became aware of Zaradia in 1986, after an unusual contact experience. Having prepared herself through meditation with a close friend, she lay on the floor and became aware of a beam of light from a distant ship, shining on the middle of her chest. The next thing she knew, she was in a different body on a star ship, a foot taller and quite comfortable in her new body—because she realized it was her own! Surrounded by friends and ET companions, she realized her connection to the constellation Arcturus and also her purpose for living on Earth. She later began channeling Zaradia regularly.

One day soon after, all this became clearer. Feeling extreme

---

1. To contact Jody Boyne at his e-mail and web-site addresses, see *Appendix 4.*

alienation during the day, she went outside at night, looked up at the stars, and asked for help because she couldn't understand what was happening and why she felt so uncomfortable. This kind of heartfelt longing for the stars is very common among Walk-ins and Wanderers. That night she dreamt of being in a strange town, in a different house, wearing clothes she had never seen before. She had no idea who she was.

Friends and family noticed that she became more sensitive and emotional for days, and out of the blue, a psychic said she had a telepathic mind-link with an ET group. Soon after this, a woman she had never met before told her she actually was the UFO captain that she met in a vivid out-of-body experience! Her connection with Zaradia became stronger as the years passed, so that today she says that she knows it is her identity at "a core level." She told me that "by becoming a soul braid and acknowledging my higher self and becoming it, I can help others do the same." Today, she helps other "earthbound extraterrestrials" in the process of discovering who they are.

Timothy: Living in the Southwest, Timothy is a counselor, network organizer, and educator deeply involved in the global peace movement. He has extensive background in hospital administration, corporate management, and has even coordinated a vice-presidential campaign. There can be no doubt that he is someone who's been actively engaged in society for years.

Yet, behind the surface, Tim considers himself an ET Walk-in, and in 1985 he had a miraculous transformation that changed all aspects of his life. At the time, he was facing tremendous physical, emotional, financial and interpersonal challenges, and felt like he was at the end of his rope. In many ways, he had lost all hope. But through a series of events, he felt that a new soul entered his body (literally, "walked-in") and replaced the soul which he had been for 31 years. Unlike the stories of the two Wanderers Jody and Zaradia, Tim had not requested any help from above—it simply came to him like a blessing showered from heaven.

The central experience that changed everything occurred during this period of intense personal crisis. At a restaurant with his friends, feeling desperate and depressed, he had a strange feeling of sensing several different streams of thought coming into him at the same time; he then became dizzy and collapsed. Everyone with him, who knew how bad he had been feeling, thought this was his death-knell, but in the ambulance on the way to the hospital he heard another voice in his head telling him to go home. Without understanding it, he simply followed the guidance. At home, surrounded by terrified friends, he went into an out-of-body altered state of awareness, and says he experienced indescribable peace, joy and stillness. He was told in no uncertain terms: *"If you want to live, you have to breathe!"*—and feeling renewed vigor for life, he did just that.

For several months afterward, he regularly heard in his mind the phrase: *"I have given you a new spirit."* From the way things turned out, Tim knows it really did happen. After the experience, everything in his life improved—including personal relationships, self-esteem, and his feeling of commitment to serving society. Today, Tim is as active, enthusiastic, and helpful as he's ever been, although—like most other ETs I've met—he rarely talks about his cosmic identity, even though he actually accepted the ET-name that came with his Walk-in experience. Indeed, most of those from elsewhere realize that while being ET is certainly important, it is far more important to be a productive, loving member of society. Timothy is a perfect example of this.

Some Conclusions: What conclusions can we draw from these stories? Well, wherever I lecture about the experience of being from elsewhere, I find many people who say "this fits me exactly!" It seems there are far more Walk-ins and Wanderers among us than we know, though it's certainly not trendy to say you come from another planet! It's not much of a popularity-grabber, and of course, many people greet these ideas with disbelief, scorn, or even contempt. How could anyone be eager to share such strange ideas?

Certainly, there are some people, I imagine, who say they're ET to make themselves feel special, but the psychological origin of this claim for some people doesn't mean that everyone is just "making it up." At the same time, no one can argue that Earth-human science already knows everything about the universe and soul-evolution. What about all the paranormal experiences of those who claim to have been out-of-body, had near-death journeys, or contacted non-human intelligence? Can we reasonably write them all off as mere hallucinations? Frankly, this kind of blithe dismissal is most immature. In the very near future, I think the scoffers and UFO debunkers will find themselves in the minority, struggling to play catch-up and understand what they denied for so long, the obvious reality of non-human ET life. With some degree of confidence, I predict that within the next decade (before 2013 A.D.), the reality of human-ET interaction will be widely accepted. If you are feeling some inner movement beginning to stir at this point, please read on…

» *Chapter 4* «

THE SLEEPING ETS QUIZ

B EFORE YOU READ THE FOLLOWING PROFILE of the qualities and experiences that are clues to a possible ET identity, you might want to ask yourself one simple, important question:

Can I really know for sure I am an ET soul?

In my opinion, yes!—but only if you ask yourself sincerely and really want to know the truth at a core level, beneath all the conditioned notions of who you think you are. To make this kind of recognition, it takes a process of subjective knowing, and it requires a quiet receptive mind in which you focus your question again and again—and then wait patiently. With an open mind, free from haste, welcoming and accepting whatever inspiration comes and then seeking its meaning— this is the way to allow subjective knowing. You can apply your critical reason later.

The profile below shows some of what I look for when I'm trying to figure out if someone is an ET soul. As you read each of the following clues, remain sensitive to any feelings, memories, or images that arise. Even if you don't understand what they are, what they mean, or where they come from, just be with your experience. Remember, to be ET or not ET is *not* a big deal—but if it's true, you really ought to admit it. Keep an open mind and a receptive heart, and then listen to the clues that arise from the deep. The balance here is between reason and intuition.

✦ Were you often lost in daydreams of UFOs, ETs, other worlds, space travel and ideal societies as a child? Your family may have thought you were a bit odd, without knowing quite why.

✦ Did you sometimes feel like your parents were not your true parents, that your real family was far away or hidden? Perhaps you thought things around you were somehow not the way they ought to be, or you had faint recollections of another way of life, entirely different. These beliefs may have caused you a great deal of discomfort. You felt out of place. (Perhaps you were!)

✦ Have you had one or more vivid UFO experiences, whether in dreams or during waking hours, which dramatically changed your life? They helped resolve doubts, inspired confidence and hope, or gave you meaning and a greater sense of purpose. You may have felt a subtle shift in consciousness, an increase in spiritual presence, or a fundamentally altered outlook on life, all connected with that experience. It really changed your life: you became a different person.

✦ Are you are genuinely kind, gentle, harmless, peaceful, and non-aggressive (not just sometimes, but almost always)? If someone must do without, does it usually end up being you? Acts of human cruelty, mindless destruction and global warfare may seem really strange (shall we say, *alien?*) to you. Killing off one's brothers and sisters, destroying the environment that is our home, and so on—all this anger, rage, and violence just doesn't compute.

✦ Do you have a hard time recognizing evil and trickery? Do some people call you naive? When you do perceive real negativity, perhaps you recoil in horror and feel somewhat shocked that people *really do* things like that. You may actually feel confused, perhaps sensing that life doesn't have to be this way, or that you've known a place or a life free of such conflict.

✦ Is the essence of your life serving others, be they family, friends, colleagues or clients? You hold great ideals, which may also be somewhat innocent and naive in worldly terms, but you sincerely and truly hope to help the world. You've probably experienced a lot of disappointment and frustration when your hopes and dreams are not realized...

✦ Could you be described as having a scientific temperament, with a cool, reasonable and measured approach to life? Human passion and red hot desire seem strange; when you find these traits in others, you feel somewhat baffled. Romantic love and the entire world of feelings are far removed from your logical, analytical way. Perhaps people say you are "in your head"—and it's probably true! (*Note:* Wanderers of this type are not common, and most of them wouldn't even be reading this book! They are often skeptics to the UFO issue and even hardened debunkers, such as the late Dr. Carl Sagan. They may also be great scientists, "odd birds," brilliant inventors, New Science enthusiasts or wild-eyed eccentrics.)

✦ Can you quickly lose yourself in science fiction, medieval epic fantasy (such as the works of J.R. Tolkien) and visionary art? Your dreams of the past or future may seem more real than life in the present, and sometimes you consider your Earth life boring and empty, and long for an exciting life of adventure. Such yearnings have been with you many years.

✦ Do you have a strong interest in UFOs, life on other worlds, or previous Earth civilizations such as Atlantis or Lemuria? Sometimes you feel like you've been there, and may even go back someday. Perhaps you've amassed an extensive home library on such subjects. (*Note:* This is really a give-away, since only Walk-ins and Wanderers have profound curiosity about worlds beyond—and for good reason, since they just recently left them!)

✦ Do you have a strong interest in mystic spirituality, either in theory or practice, with a sense that you used to have greater powers but somehow lost them? When you begin to get involved in their practices you may feel it is unnecessary to discipline yourself since you've already been there, even though you seem to have forgotten what you used to know. Others may doubt your sincerity and resolve, but you know it's not that simple.

✦ Are you a conscious channel for ETs or some other non-Earth source of spiritual teaching—and you already realize that the purpose of your life is to help others grow and evolve? If you answered "yes," you are probably no longer sleeping, *Wanderer*!

✦ Do you feel—and perhaps *all* your life have felt—great alienation and a sense of never quite fitting in? Maybe you hope to be like others, try your best to be normal, or sincerely imagine that you are really not different, but all of your mental tricks never quite work. You simply *feel* different, and you always have. (Time to be honest here!) You have a very real fear you may never find a place in this world. (*Note:* This is the classic trait of Wanderers.)

The truth is, some Wanderers do *not* find a comfortable place down here. Of all the different indicators in the profile above, you should know that the last one (i.e. feeling different) is the most common trait among those from elsewhere. Of course, not everyone who feels alienated from human society is an ET soul, but among those who do, many are (especially if you are reading this book!).

If you have some kind of inner knowing that you might be a Wanderer, then it is critical to use discernment when deciding with whom of your friends and family you'll share your ideas. As I discussed in *From Elsewhere*, many marriages have not weathered the storms of the ET "coming out" phase, and in some cases, merely raising the possibility of cosmic belonging was sufficient to destroy a partner's trust. One man told me his wife felt betrayed when she learned he had a separate ET family in the stars. It was as if he had a second wife in another state!

Besides grappling with who to tell, how to tell, or how much to tell your significant others, you may also have to deal with hostility from friends and acquaintances. Some of those I interviewed in my first book were not self-sufficient enough to keep quiet, and were then flooded by negativity and ridicule from those in whom they had confided. While it's certainly hard, you can try to use such criticism as a mirror to clarify your own thinking. It's best to give every opinion a hearing, compare all the views and possibilities, let it all settle down in your mind—and then listen to what *you* think! As in the process of subjective knowing that helped many Wanderers clarify their spiritual experiences, identity, and purpose on Earth, you can use the same self-validation process to figure out which opinions to trust, which to hold, and which to discard. Interacting with people who question our beliefs is a fine way of deepening our familiarity with exactly what we do believe.

The title of Robert A. Heinlein's sci-fi classic, *A Stranger in a Strange Land,* is the perfect description of being a Wanderer on Earth. In some sense, each of the indicators in the ET profile above are simply variations on a theme: they are leads and pointers that can help you get clear if indeed you are such a "stranger" down here. In fact, with Planet Earth looking more and more like Planet Hollywood every day, a lot of people would agree that this is indeed "a strange land." If you are still lost in doubt, I recommend you learn how to *relax into your natural mind* (which may, however, require a lot of disciplined meditation), and then listen for the quiet, inner voice. I assure you, with time, all doubts fall away and only the *real* will remain. Have faith in yourself: we all have the resources we need to understand and integrate what is truly essential to our life on Earth.

Again, if you are a Wanderer or ET Walk-in, you really ought to know it. If not, it's fine with me if you leave it alone. For another version of this ET Quiz, check out Appendix 3.

In the next chapter, we will zero in on the most common experience of ETs living on Earth: *not fitting in!*

» Chapter 5 «

The Wanderers' Alienation

After a recent lecture in Minnesota, I was asked a special question by the wife of a man who knew he was an ET Wanderer. Sounding concerned, she told me her husband is sure he is from elsewhere and now has no more doubt. But after this momentous discovery (which he had suspected for years), his life became more difficult, not less. His wife explained that it's been very hard for him to find something worthwhile to do on Earth, since he feels overcome by a deep sense of aimlessness. In fact, she said, he had to "develop an interest in something here and train his mind to get excited about it!" Obviously, the knowledge of being an ET soul severed his interest in human involvement, and dissolved any sense of meaning he previously gained from being in society. As I told his wife, this experience is actually quite common. It's simply an early phase of emotional re-adjustment.

Almost every Wanderer I interviewed in my first book had a powerful sense of alienation at some point in their life. Usually, it marked the beginning of their path towards ET identity. Many people felt a strong sense of differentness during childhood, despite friends and loving family. It usually accompanied a vague longing for the stars, for true family, for a long-forgotten home. When the person reached adolescence, their ongoing alienation was further compounded by a very real terror: *"How will I ever fit into this world and find something I like?"* Despite the pain and confusion of such feelings, the issue at stake here is easily defined: it is the need for meaningful social engagement. However, the issue is not so easily resolved.

How do you fit into a world which you feel is not your own? And more than that, how do you participate in a society that might call you *insane* if you shared your ideas, then label you a victim of delusion? This mis-fitting is far more complex than simply some kind of cross-cultural adjustment or living far from home, as with cross-border immigration. The Wanderer's alienation is like an identity badge pinned to the heart, part of the very substance of all his or her experience on Earth. It is not easily dismissed, nor should it be. This alienation is like a flashing light above the gateway to our remembrance, as well as the cross we've chosen to bear as a responsibility for the honor and privilege of serving on a planet in such dire need of love-light. Discomfort is just part of the job.

When I first discovered that this kind of extreme personal alienation and differentness was common among those who claim to be Wanderers and Star People, I knew it would set off alarms among the so-called experts. As the conventional explanation for this most unconventional sense of identity, the standard psychological response runs something like this:

> "Yes, of course, they obviously call themselves ETs because it gives them comfort and self-importance, making their painful feelings of social maladjustment easier to bear."

If you agree with this interpretation, you'll probably also believe "there's no such thing as ET souls, only ordinary humans with ordinary emotional problems, trying to make something special out of it." This opinion is at the core of the skeptic's position, and it certainly does have some merit. In *some* cases, I certainly agree.

Yet, despite their merit and clear mental logic, such psychological interpretations cannot ever be proven. First of all, not everyone with social alienation claims to be an ET, and not all those who claim to be ET souls feel such alienation. Just because a radical belief brings comfort and self-esteem does not prove that the notion was cooked-up to bring comfort and self-esteem. Just because we feel better knowing that Earth revolves around the Sun doesn't mean it's not true; just because people seek meaning in life, and find meaning in a belief in God, doesn't mean that their belief is but fantasy. It may seem inane to say, but human belief in God does not prove there is no God! As we reason this way and draw out their argument, the logic of die-hard skeptics becomes folly.

Furthermore, not all Wanderers are comforted by their recognition of being ET. As in the story above, some people feel more disoriented by this self-discovery. This so-called "compensatory delusion" (apparently compensating for some sort of emotional deficiency or palliating an assumed psychological conflict) often brings more life challenges and inner conflict. So, then we cannot argue that it is an emotionally based notion designed to quell inner discontent. Actually, all the many psychologizing arguments really don't take us that far.

It's just the old chicken-and-egg question: does childhood alienation *create the need to imagine* being from elsewhere, or does the *reality* of being an ET soul since birth naturally generate feelings of alienation? I'll be the first to admit that believers can't prove their point; but to be fair, neither can the skeptics. Oh, well…

Now that we've finished that little game, let's get on to more important questions:

Can psychological dynamics **co-exist** with transcendental reality?

Does the field of human psychology explain all facets of human experience?

Without going too far into the approaching dense thicket of debate, let me simply say this: more and more people are telling me that the knowledge they have gained from their subjective spiritual process has far greater value to them, than the current beliefs of so-called experts. On anyone's scale of mental health, the majority of those who say they're ET souls will be judged stable, intelligent, "high-functioning," and willing to listen to opposing views. Of course, psychological explanations have their place and import in understanding human behavior and motivations, but they don't tell the whole story. Our presumably advanced civilization should be enlightened enough by now to realize that human beings are far deeper than human psychology…

As a teenager, I often consulted the *I Ching* or *Book of Changes*, an ancient Chinese oracle and fortune-telling system. In my innocence I plainly asked, "Who am I?"—since at the time I actually imagined such a deep query could be answered by a book! Nevertheless, my innocence was well-received: the book did point me towards deeper self-understanding—a vision that did, however, take many years to grow. The answer I received from the *I Ching* was *Hexagram #56, Lu,* "The Wanderer"! Are you surprised? You should already know God works in strange ways. Anyway, here's one translation of that answer:

"**THE WANDERER.** Success through smallness. Perseverance brings good fortune to the Wanderer. The meaning of the time of The Wanderer is truly great."

"Whatever greatness may exhaust itself upon, this much is certain: it loses its home… He who has few friends: this is The Wanderer."[1]

What the *I Ching* says about *Lu* (which is just one of 64 six-lined images or symbol-hexagrams in the book) is relevant to that other type of wanderer: the ET kind. They too have "lost their home." (And some psychologists would add they've lost their minds as well!) Moreover, Wanderers have also lost their greatness, which is much harder to accept: like sad eagles with clipped wings, they are full of vigor but unable to fly. The husband unwilling to return to "normal society" after discovering his ET roots was probably suffering this same type of "exhaustion of greatness": the dull pain of knowing he is not who he used to be, and that the glory of Spirit he once knew is apparently beyond reach. No wonder he and his wife had to train his mind to get excited about social engagement! He was suffering spiritual deflation, which is common to both Wanderers as well as those who return from deeper states of meditation, near-death experiences, and vivid out-of-body journeys. It is simply the pain of interdimensional re-adjustment, re-entering a more disharmonious vibratory environment.

So what's a good ET to do about all this? Really, the best advice would be to meditate every day—but how many of us are really willing do it? Short of this, it seems important to realize that *alienation is normal* and just part of the landscape. I admit the reality and the influence of various psychological factors, and I agree that counseling can be useful.

1. *The I Ching: Book of Changes*, p. 675, Wilhelm/Baynes translation; Bollingen, 1967.

Wanderers, like everyone else, often have a difficult childhood, and usually have emotional conflicts of one sort or another.

But dealing with alienation goes far beyond the analysis and healing of childhood wounds. It is really part of a subtle process of making peace with living at a lower density of light than that to which we are accustomed. Our adjustment is thus *psycho-spiritual*—both psychological and spiritual, not one or the other. It is also a matter of increased self-acceptance—taking responsibility for our spiritual longing and confusion, then having the will to forge constructive activity in this world. And by the way, moving beyond spiritual deflation usually leads to greater dedication to some form of service on Earth.

If you do consider yourself a visitor, then realize that *you chose to be here*—it is neither an accident nor your prison. Then ask yourself this: *Why did I choose to be here, and what might now bring me fulfillment?* It is useless to try to force yourself to get in step with society—it's far better to *learn your own steps*. And don't be afraid to feel different. If you really are, then that's just the way it is.

» *Chapter 6* «

WHERE IS HOME?

SPEAKING OF ET SOULS on Earth, let me tell you another story. Recently I was asked a second interesting question: "Where, for you, is home?" Instead of my usual answer, which seems mature enough and runs something like this: *"I'm not sure where I'm from in physical terms, and it's not such a big deal,"* another thought came into my mind. This answer seemed to drive deeper to the essence of the question and the heart of the answer—capturing the *feeling* of home far better, and offering a much different perspective on the whole issue (which is often quite important for Wanderers on their path of discovery). After really absorbing the thought that came to me, I felt a kind of breakthrough, an epiphany or revelation, which led me to write this chapter.

Instead of giving my standard answer, I listened to the deeper roots of mind and answered:

"My real home is a state of unbounded awareness in tremendous unity; this is the place from which I am estranged during my life on Earth.

My homesickness is the pain of having lost this beautiful, open state of being…"

After I said this, a mild image and soft feeling came over me, like a tiny window opening to a long-forgotten landscape of rare beauty. It was not dramatic, not intense, not a peak experience—perhaps I have become too buried in human life! But there was a familiar, sweet scent like roses in mid-summer bloom, and it struck like a bell that my real Home was truly a state of consciousness, not some place nor constellation in the sky.

Today, when I look within to sense the process that brought this insight, all becomes dark. It is not the darkness of sorrow, however, but rather the darkness of space, in which invisible energy lines criss-cross in great fullness—yet, without eyes to see, we can't normally perceive this vitality. And so, I can only return to my original state of awareness with heightened, piercing vision—a vision that knows I am not *seeking* a place, but rather a state of being, always available. *True self is the true home*; dwelling in boundless mind is the real homecoming; the entire spiritual path leads to the Original Home. This understanding is not ET-related at all, and it is really the goal of all mystic traditions. When a Wanderer's seeking goes far enough, it strikes the center of what has been called "the infinite way"—the timeless path of union with All That Is.

Where is home? It is the clear reality of the individual mind I call my own, fully merged with countless other beings, the most intimate family I know. *This is my true Group.*

Where is home? It is the unbroken memory and ever-present vivid experience of all past lives, countless rich experiences on myriad worlds—learning in joy and sorrow, passing from ignorance to enlightenment. *This is my Self.*

Where is home? It is the fluid embrace and grandeur of being, a transcendent passion of union with the One Creator whose body is the entire Universe. This is my world. True home, for all of us, is realizing endless awareness, endless meaning and endless value in each iota of matter, thought, and circumstance. *This is Godhead.*

And yet, if we choose to return to modes of ordinary perception, we could say: "I am Zoron from the Pleiades," but doesn't this sound silly? Yes indeed, Mr. or Mrs. ET soul—Mr. or Mrs. Walk-in, Wanderer, or Star Person—this may be so, but who were you *before* you were Zoron from the Pleiades? Who is the Initiator who gave the spark of consciousness which formed your Spirit? Who is the Inner Master and Voice from which you, so-called ET visitor, draw the breath of Life itself? *Full awareness of the bright light* at the core of our being is the *real* home, even while our body sits on Earth, in the Pleiades, or anywhere else.

Now, I certainly don't mean to be disrespectful. I, of all people, have great regard for the enormous sacrifice of ET Walk-ins and Wanderers living on Earth, serving humanity towards its own New Age home—which is, nevertheless, yet another time/space illusion if you forget eternity, no matter how lovely fourth density is. As you know, I based my doctoral research on the lives of those who say "I am from such-and-such planet," and I too consider myself an Wanderer. Nevertheless...

Who are we really, and where are we really from? In the final analysis, spiritual maturity is measured by the quality of our awareness, sensitivity, love and wisdom—certainly not by the religion we follow, the dogmas we hold, the beings we channel, nor the quantity of books we've read. Genuine illumination of the Real, the emergence of Self, entry into clear mind luminosity is *"a revelation of burning veils,"* a shattering of old forms of thought and countless mis-identifications with the "unreal." What is Real is what is eternal, which is, in fact, the Creator of heaven and earth and all things in between—the Creator of all time-space realms, densities and dimensions, as well as all the beings within them. Essentially, we ourselves are not different or separate from this Eternal Creator—**we are the Infinite Creator**. And if we identify ourselves with anything less, it's simply another illusion, which must be shattered on the final path Going Home. (For more on these matters, see Section II, Chapter 1: "Self and God.")

» *Chapter 7* «

A MATTER OF PURPOSE

By looking for a "should" and a "supposed to," we're starting from an incorrect premise...

Of course, in time and space, ET souls are not quite home. So how can we tell who might indeed be a Wanderer? One simple way is to find the person who's worrying about finding their purpose on Earth. As I continue my own wandering travels around the world, I'm continually meeting people who ask me, *Why am I here?* They often feel great anxiety as they struggle to uncover some kind of pre-ordained path or social role, and the question they usually ask is this:

What am I supposed to be doing?

I tell them I honestly don't know if they're supposed to be doing anything, and if they are still listening (since some people turn off at that point, disappointed I didn't do a psychic reading), I then add that it is this kind of thinking that keeps them from finding their purpose! To settle the matter of purpose, which is essential to the life and well-being of Wanderers (as well as anyone else who cares about personal growth), you must recall the awareness you had before you were born—which certainly can not be done by typical human reasoning! One needs to return to a more primordial consciousness, a state of mental quiet, purity, and simplicity.

The problem is that by looking for a "should" and a "supposed to," we are starting from an incorrect premise, which dooms our conclusions from the start. It is far better to ask this: How do you know there is anything you ***should*** be doing?

The needle-and-haystack approach, which says, "I could do anything but I must first find the thing I *have* to do," is both simplistic and dogmatic. The RA group offers an essential perspective here:

"It was the aim of Wanderers to [1] serve the entities of this planet in whatever way was requested, and [2] it was also the aim of Wanderers that their vibratory patterns might lighten the planetary vibration as a whole... Specific intentions, such as aiding in a situation not yet manifest, are not the aim of Wanderers. Light and love go where they are sought and needed, and their direction is not planned aforetimes." [1]

It seems to me this passage brings us a lot closer to the mind of self-sacrifice, which Wanderers (and all those who serve) knew quite well before taking birth. The sentence bears repeating: *Light and love go where they are sought and needed, and their direction is not planned aforetimes.* This is exactly the mind of a true server: giving what is needed when and where it is needed, without much personal agenda or personal goals. This attitude is epitomized in the simple title of a classic book by Ram Dass, *How Can I Help?*

After explaining this, RA added that there are three forms of service planned by ET souls, once the forgetting is penetrated (which for most ETs on Earth, usually is not!). Of course, these forms of service also apply to anyone who cares to make the world a better place:

"...in addition to [1] the doubling effect of planetary love and light, and [2] the basic function of serving as beacon or shepherd, [3] each Wanderer has its unique abilities, biases, and specialties... an array of pre-incarnative talents, which then may be expressed upon this plane..." [2]

In short then, Wanderers come to Earth to simply offer love and light—freely, openly, without consideration of reward or social role. At the levels of awareness upon which cosmic souls dwelled before their 3D veils, the great potential of rendering useful service to Earth and humanity was more than enough to merit the hazards and trials of direct incarnation (which is, by the way, somewhat like parachuting behind enemy lines, armed only with love). What is the grand purpose you are

---

1. Elkins, Rueckert, McCarty, The Law of One, Vol. III, p. 74–5. Schiffer Publishing, 1982.
2. Ibid., p. 7

here for, you the unknown visitor from realms beyond conception?

Just be kind and helpful. As the Dalai Lama says, "Kindness is my religion." Life-purpose is really that simple.

Esoterically, the radiatory effect of love and light is also more profound than we imagine. Why is it that great yogis, adepts, and Masters of the East stay in their lonely caves, when they profess such universal compassion? Simply because they know how to consciously radiate higher energies by mind, and they understand how thought influences physical reality. Serving the world, a task which seems to imply such a huge burden, really depends on the way we live each moment, day-by-day (for more on this practice, see "Moment to Moment" in Section II).

The three functions that RA notes are the primary means by which Wanderers are now serving Earth to fulfill their purpose. Of these, the first (i.e. "the doubling effect of planetary love and light") means simply showing up: to the extent you are balanced and living in kindness and clarity, to just that extent does your very presence radiate harmonious energy that aids the planet. Again, this form of service also applies to non-Wanderers. So what is the prescription for a sprained personal purpose? *Just be at ease in your self, and offer it freely to the world.*

The second function explained by RA—acting as a "beacon or shepherd"—also does not mean we must adopt some special social role. Literally, a beacon brings light and guidance to those traveling in the dark (sounds like Earth to me!), and a shepherd protects and shelters the innocent flock. The symbolism here is ripe; and again, it's just a matter of how we live day by day—the act of service is fulfilled by the mind of service in each moment of being.

It is only when we come to the third and final function that some degree of soul-searching and social placement is needed: in the expression of each Wanderer's unique talent. Yet, this simply tells us to do what we like and follow our heart! Since the true activity of service rests on attitude, you can drive a San Francisco limo, help the Ohio dentist, fix Seattle computers, sell ladies' clothing in Indiana, or paint alone in your New York basement—and *still* serve the whole world. It's all a matter of awareness: what is served to the planet is simply your state of being.

Of course, once you've found your niche, a line of expression compatible with your own skills and desires, then the work becomes a little more subtle. Then it's a matter of poise and skillful means (called *upaya* in the Buddhist tradition): serving fully and freely, wisely and well, all the while keeping balanced in mind/body/spirit. The questions at that point are more fine-tuned: what to give, how much to give, when to wait, how much you need, and how to embody universal consciousness in each particular situation. These are more subtle issues that demand self-reflection and an ample dose of honesty with oneself. Here's where meditation and some kind of group support are most helpful, since they provide the inner depth and outer structure within which our individual purpose can be developed in society. As we progress along the path, the needed balances become more delicate.

Last but not least, we should not underestimate the tremendous power that Wanderers generate by simply "waking up" to their unusual identity. Again, we can turn to passages from RA to get more insight on the potency of directed spiritual work on Earth:

> "The Wanderer, if it remembers and dedicates itself to service, will polarize much more rapidly than is possible in the far more etiolated [i.e. "made pale by excluding light"] realms of higher density catalyst..."[3]

> "This [accelerated learning available on Earth] is due to the intensive life experiences and opportunities of the third-density. Thusly, the positively oriented Wanderer chooses to hazard the danger of the forgetting in order to be of service to others by radiating love of others. If the forgetting is penetrated, the amount of catalyst in third-density will polarize the Wanderer with much greater efficiency than shall be expected in the higher and more harmonious densities."[4]

3. Elkins, op. cit., Vol. III, p. 7.
4. Elkins, op. cit., Vol. II, p. 67.

As you must realize by now, Earth is a "schoolhouse"—and for Wanderers, it is also an intensive training ground that holds the promise of accelerating evolution far more rapidly than if we simply "stayed home." It also bears noting that RA describes the higher realms as etiolated, an unusual and rarely used word that describes a plant deprived of sunlight or a person with a sickly hue! Of course, the group in Kentucky that channeled this contact had never heard the word before. Have you ever heard the so-called higher dimensions described this way? I certainly have not, and upon reflection, it makes me appreciate the RA contact all the more. But their point is clear: From the standpoint of useful catalyst that creates opportunities for developing consciousness, Earth life in this "lower-density" is far more useful and desirable than the blissful higher realms…

Wanderers should not feel so bad about being here. If evolution is your goal, you can relax in knowing you are definitely in the right place, even though your purpose may seem vague at times. If you already know your cosmic nature and the importance of service, appreciate both kindness and clarity and are truly sensitive to the needs of others in daily life, then everything is right on track just as planned. In fact, excessive worry and self-doubt will throw you off balance and impair the fullness of your offering, since they impair the wholeness of self-appreciation. Self-appreciation, a quality associated with the sixth chakra, the "third eye" that is a gateway to Higher Self, is essential to link us up to cosmic power. Just realize that what is offered in service is simply just you, Wanderer or not, which is why the very personal work of balancing mind/body/spirit and opening to total self-acceptance is so central to the path of service.

In the next few chapters, we will expand our focus to a more cosmic level, and see how ET groups themselves fulfill the mandate of universal service. But first, let's take a brief look at the last million years of ET-Earth history!

» *Chapter 8* «

ET-Earth History: An Overview

WHAT CAN I SAY about the entire history of ET-Earth contact in a few short pages? How can I be pithy about the long cycles of evolution of billions of souls? Well, the presentation depends on our perspective—which, as always, depends on our level of awareness. Looking at the woods, is it a forest or just trees, a panoply of inter-mixed colors or just the motion of atoms? Of course, any level of analysis can be chosen, and each yields an interesting story. For this discussion, we are going to target the inexorable growth of human consciousness, which just so happens to be what the whole drama here is all about! To fill in the details, please refer to the timeline at the end of this chapter: "Earth and ET Contact: A Brief History," taken from *The RA Material*. I assure you, it is one of a kind!

From a physical 3D perspective, we could fill vast libraries with tales of the rise and fall of races (including Mars and Maldek), and the development of technology from sticks and stones to laser surgery and particle-beam warfare. Indeed, there are such libraries, and many of us have been there (as in the typical "astral-plane academy" dream). There are also more than a few channeled books, which give details on the hidden history of Earth and galactic races.

Metaphysically speaking, the growth of material civilization is the out-picturing of subtle changes in consciousness, which is all that matters from the view of Higher Self. Souls can develop the basic trinity of *love*, *wisdom*, and *will*, with or without hi-tech culture (a concept not well appreciated on this world). The Earth-race fascination with gadgets and physicality is actually somewhat of an anomaly, universally speaking. Most 3D races are far more spiritual.

Furthermore, the history of empires spinning on the wheels of *samsara* (a Sanskrit word meaning "the cycle of birth and death") is not particularly important, in and of itself. As RA once commented, in speaking about the imminent Earth Harvest in 2010–2013 A.D., all such outer changes are simply aspects of "progressive cycles for experiential use." It is far better to turn our attention to the *quality* and *integrity* of how we *use* these cycles of life. If we look at history in this way, we'll start to form the big picture: cosmic purpose and cosmic plan.

Atop the banner-head of each issue of my *ET Journal,* I used another quote from RA:

> *"the original desire is that entities seek and become one…"*

It sounds nice enough, but how does it relate to the history of Earth and ET contact? Well, for starters, it puts a damper on techno-fascination (past, present, and future; human and ET). Just because they took you on a huge mothership does not mean they are enlightened. In fact, it says nothing about their virtue, compassion, or honesty; they have simply mastered material construction. Realizing Oneness is something entirely different.

More importantly, if the purpose of evolution is self-willed spiritual seeking that realizes *unity* (the joining of Self with self, others, and the Creator), then how well has Earth fared? Even before we step into the timeline, let's look at a few telling statistics.

From an economic newsletter I received in 1996, here are the startling facts regarding the present state of our advanced Terran Earth Culture:

✦ **50%** suffer from malnutrition;

✦ **70%** are unable to read;

✦ **80%** live in sub-standard housing;

✦ **50%** of the world's wealth is controlled by only **6%** of the people, all of whom are Americans; and

✦ Only **1%** have a college education…

As a snapshot of gross inequity and non-sharing, it is also a portrait of extreme disunity, a world of shards and splinters. Ours is a planet in which the left hand not only does not know what the right hand is doing, but it couldn't care less. Of course, I am not referring here to all the kind-hearted people trying to make the world a better place. Rather, I am talking about most people on the planet: they are either sinking in abject poverty fighting to survive, or paddling in relative ease trying to stay afloat—unaware of their shipmates drowning beside the boats.

With that sobering picture, let's take a more detailed look at human history to find out how these statistics came to be. Distilling what I consider to be the main points from the timeline that follows, several facts explain a lot:

✦ **Earth's rootstock soul population** comes from three main sources: **Mars** (its civilization self-destroyed); **Maldek** (its planet self-destroyed); and **Other 3D Races** (i.e. souls who have missed other fourth density harvests). This is not exactly a quick-learning bunch.

✦ **During the last 50,000 years of human evolution** (two major cycles of about 25,000 years each, in agreement with the Mayan calendar), only about 150 people were qualified to go on into fourth density (aside, I assume, from certain adepts). This is a condition of chronic global inability to love.

✦ **Both (positive) Confederation and (negative) Orion ET** groups have been actively working with humanity. Despite their ongoing efforts, humanity is still blind, in the main, to the reality of higher-dimensional life, and generally uninterested. This shows great spiritual apathy.

✦ **As a result of human disharmony**, the lifespan has steadily decreased, from 900 years at the beginning of Lemuria (which was considered normal at the time), to a low of 35 years during Atlantis. And modern science thinks that 80 is great! This echoes the notion of "a fall from grace."

✦ **Human soul-experience** includes the catastrophic destruction of several recent civilizations (Maldek, Mars, Lemuria, Atlantis); warfare and suffering have become habitual and commonplace. We can assume that deep scars of mistrust, fear, insecurity, and hopelessness remain in the collective human subconscious.

✦ **The story of Yahweh** and the ancient Hebrews, hatred and the modern Jews, and millennia of Middle East conflict is bound up with massive negative-ET Orion influence. In these nations we still see a region locked into the ways of warfare. Their failure to make peace reflects a global failure, and conditions are worsening.

✦ **Confederation and Orion** fourth-density ET groups have been engaged on inner planes in the real Armageddon for centuries, yet a great deal of physical 3D suffering has been averted due to this neutralizing "War in Heaven." As above, so below: Earth warfare is tied to cosmic polarity!

✦ **Commencement of the modern era** in the 18th century coincides with a heavy influx of Wanderers coming for Harvest in 2010–2013 A.D. Therefore, we should realize that the calling and need for love and light are far greater today than ever before.

So, there you have it: a brief synopsis of *the saga of light and shadow on SOL 3*, the human life of what is called "Sanat Kumara" or Gaia, the local Planetary Logos or Creator—a Being on its own Path. Realistically, we can imagine that this Logos has either got real some serious problems (at its own inconceivable level of consciousness), or rather, that it's chosen some real hard training.

As yet another 3D schoolhouse for souls who have not yet learned to love, the Being we call Terra or Gaia has chosen to work with some pretty tough cases: chronically insensitive souls with a long record of running in place—either fighting among themselves and remaining impoverished, supporting self-serving leaders who encourage their own self-destruction, or remaining apathetic to inner love and light in favor of self-distraction through indulgent materialism and meaningless entertainment. You will find lots of shadows down here on this ground.

As subjective forces give rise to objective events, and world history shapes the growth of personal experience, a feedback loop is born. Unfortunately, the soul groups who can truly call Earth their "home" (i.e. souls who have achieved third-density awareness, *not* Wanderers), seem relatively stuck in self-defeating patterns of body/mind/spirit. A good deal of healing is in order, yet *only Self can heal the Self* and those of us who seek to serve can only do so much.

To the vision of sixth density, elder ETs and the cosmic Guardians who guide the evolution of Light in our solar system, Earth's saga of polarity brings no regret. Through countless lifetimes, all souls learn their lessons and develop the divine equipment. Negatively-oriented souls (considered by RA to be of Orion, plus most human leaders) have their own path, and they are free to do their own work—just as you and I are free to fan the flames of love, wisdom, and will, living in the Light of Truth. As RA once said, "What your peoples' need is *orientation*," a need still unmet even today—just as it was a million years ago. These matters, which are no less than the history of developing consciousness on planet Earth, should be well understood by all of us—especially if we hope to render some kind of useful service in this corner of the galaxy.

The following timeline gives you the blow-by-blow details, compiled from the four main volumes of *The Law of One*.

EARTH AND ET CONTACT:

A BRIEF HISTORY

A. PRE-HUMAN CIVILIZATION

705,000 B.P.*—Extensive Maldek Wars (creates metaphysical-astral "knot of fear" for Maldek souls).

600,000 B.P.—Confederation spiritual healing of the Maldek population on inner 3D planes.

500,000 B.P.—Destruction of 3D Maldek (current "asteroid belt"), soul-transfer to Earth (Bigfoot).

✦ Earth hosting only 2D life (mineral, plant, animal kingdoms); no native 3D human groups

✦ Eventually, highest 2D animal groups become bi-pedal, gradually become 3D *homo Sapiens*

B. EARLY HUMAN CIVILIZATION (75,000–25,000 B.P.)

75,000 B.P.—Final destruction of Mars civilization/atmosphere, population soul-transfer to Earth.

✦ Beginning of human civilization/Earth human 3D life: 50% Martian, 25% native, 25% other 3D

✦ Confederation/Yahweh aid to Martian souls (genetic cloning to sharpen senses/strengthen mind)

✦ Light-Quarantine intensified around Earth (regarding Yahweh). Human lifespan approximately 900 years

60,000 B.P.—Orion group influence: (a) telepathic contact (b) power-charged stone-formations in Central America/Pacific Oceana (Nazca lines; Easter Island heads; unsuccessful attempt, no negativity achieved).

** **B.P.** indicates years "before present"*

58,000 B.P.—Confederation aid to early Lemurian/Mu civilization (prolonged contact).

53,000 B.P.—Lemurian civilization fully established (primitive group mind, spiritually advanced).

✦ Later destroyed by Earth tectonic-plate readjustment, flooding; survivors ⟹ Russia, North/South America (current indigenous groups; originally from 2D planet in Deneb star system).

50,000 B.P.—END OF 3D MAJOR CYCLE I/No harvest; life-span ~700 years.

46,000 B.P.—Spiritual calling from Maldek souls on Earth ⟺ Confederation aid (love/light sent).

31,000 B.P.—Atlantean civilization begins development (slow-growing, agrarian, conglomerate).

✦ Atlantean calling for guidance ⟺ Confederation telepathic information sent; life-span 70–140 yrs.

25,000 B.P.—END OF 3D MAJOR CYCLE II / No harvest; life-span 35–100 yrs. (pop. ~ 345,000).

✦ South American group (Elder Race; pop. 150; life-span 900 years) all 4D+ harvestable; all remain in 3D

C. LATER HUMAN CIVILIZATION (18,000–2,300 B.P.)

18,000 B.P.—RA contact w/Egyptians ("crystal-powered bell-shaped craft"); UFO sightings only.

15,000 B.P.—Beginning of rapid, intensified Atlantean technological development in society.

13,000 B.P.—Confederation information/aid to Atlantis (pyramids, healing); lifespan much reduced.

✦ Initial usage of intelligent energy for negative polarization (cloning for genetic superiority)

11,000 B.P.—RA contact w/Egyptians (landings, direct encounters for teaching); meaning distorted.

✦ First major Atlantean wars, approximately 40% population death, partial migration to North Africa

10,821 B.P.—Final destruction of Atlantis by nuclear/crystal-energy warfare; civilization ends.

✦ Triple migration to safe, mountainous regions: Tibet, Peru, Turkey (root of mystery schools)

9,600 B.P.—Final Earth Changes and sinkings of Atlantean land-masses (direct result of warfare).

8,500 B.P.—RA enters/returns to Earth inner planes, begins thought-construction of Great Pyramid.

7,500 B.P.—Confederation aid to South America (Amazon landings/ teaching, pyramids/hidden cities).

6,000–4,500 B.P.—Great Pyramid at Giza completed (by thought, instant appearance); Ikhnaton contacted. Additional pyramids constructed from physical, Earth-based materials.

3,600–3,300 B.P.—Major Orion influence in Middle East; distorted positive Yahweh actions.

✦ Confederation/Yahweh sexual/genetic intervention: strengthening Anak-group physical bodies

✦ Yahweh sends love/light, telepathic contact, manifests UFO thought-forms to inspire seeking

✦ Orion distorts Anak-intervention (establishes Hebrew-group elite); replaces/co-opts Yahweh telepathic contact w/ Hebrews (answers call: sends negative philosophy); reveals UFO as a fiery cloud

✦ Light-Quarantine around Earth strengthened in response to "serious inroads" made by Orion

✦ Begins "intense portion of Armageddon" in Earth's 4D inner planes; Orion vs. Confederation

3,000 B.P.—Orion group leaves Earth 3D skies; Confederation completes South America aid/contact.

✦ Armageddon 4D "thought-war" of light continues/intensifies (Confederation vs. Orion)

2,600 B.P.—Greek calling; Confederation aid leads to 4D+"philosophy (Heraclitus, Thales, Pericles).

2,300 B.P.—Confederation aid to Egypt only (telepathic contact, love/light).

D. MODERN TIMES (1700–2013 A.D.)

~1784 A.D.—Increased influx of harvestable 3D souls and Wanderers, increased Confederation aid.

✦ Generally telepathic aid, love/light sent; no planned UFO landings or direct contact-teaching

✦ Positive free will philosophy (freedom, liberty, justice, democracy, human rights) developed

>1945 A.D.—Increased Confederation UFO thought-form appearance, coincides w/ nuclear age

>1950 A.D.—Increased influx of Wanderers, 4D "double-bodied" children to support Harvest.

2010–2013 A.D.—Earth 3D Harvest: planetary Logos/surface human civilization fully in 4D+.

✦ Earth Changes complete, humanity 4D+ only, supplemental galactic ET-souls influx/support

In the next chapter, we will examine the major ET collective whose chosen task is to support the work that all servers perform: the growth of love and light on Earth. According to RA, this ET group is called "The Confederation of Planets in Service to the One Infinite Creator." Bear in mind that most Wanderers are actually members of this group, in one way or another.

» Chapter 9 «

INSIDE THE CONFEDERATION

If there is fear and doom, the contact was likely of a negative nature. If the result is hope, friendly feelings, and the awakening of a positive feeling of purposeful service to others, the marks of Confederation contact are evident.[1]

I AM SURE YOU REMEMBER those colorful episodes on the original *Star Trek* series in which the "Federation" had its governing meetings aboard the USS Enterprise. There were all sorts of strange-looking ambassadors speaking in weird tongues, chatting among themselves garbed in far-out cosmic costumes. Of course, that was just a story, wasn't it? And of course, since Earth is the only planet in the Universe hosting intelligent life there couldn't *really* be such a thing as this kind of intergalactic administration.

Fiction is fiction, right?

Well, according to 6000 years of Eastern mystic traditions, hundreds of channeled books worldwide, and millions of people who claim to have had paranormal experience, Earth is not alone, the Universe is teeming with intelligent life, and much of that life is far more intelligent than what we find here on Earth. Back in the 1950s, UFO study groups claimed to be in contact with the "Space Brothers." Today, thousands of people around the globe believe in or channel the "Ashtar Command" (a term also coined in the 1950s by contactees and groups who claimed to be in communication with a federation of benevolent ETs under the direction of a leader named "Ashtar").

In *The RA Material*, a great deal of information is presented on "The Confederation of Planets in Service to the One Infinite Creator"— not the most catchy title, but another reference to the same type of cosmic collective as the Space Brothers or Ashtar Command.

---

1. Elkins, op cit., Vol. III, p.12.

Apparently, the endless sightings of lone UFOs in night skies are just the tip of an iceberg—and we must seriously consider the possibility of a massively coordinated extraterrestrial presence on Earth. While the existence of such cosmic governance has not yet been empirically proven to the satisfaction of skeptics (and probably will never be), I believe their message has certainly been sent.

When we begin to examine the role of ETs in human history and their function on Earth at the present time, we have to raise questions of collective purpose and intelligently coordinated design. We cannot afford not to. The RA group also stated that they are an active member of this same Confederation. Taking some passages from the first volume of The Law of One will give us a better foundation for understanding this collective group and their work on Earth.

Who are the Confederation members?

"There are approximately 53 civilizations, comprising approximately 500 planetary consciousness complexes in this Confederation. [It] contains those from your own planet who have attained dimensions beyond your [own]... planetary entities within your solar system, and... planetary entities from other galaxies [i.e. solar systems]. It is a true Confederation in that its members are not alike, but allied in service according to *The Law of One*."[2]

Do some Confederation members appear as UFOs?

"There have been as many as fifteen of the Confederation entities in your skies at any one time. The others are available to you through thought... Their purposes are very simple: to allow those entities of your planet to become aware of infinity... the mysterious or unknown."[3]

What about cases of direct contact?

"The most efficient mode of contact is that which you experience at this space/time [i.e. their channeling sessions]. The infringement

---

2. Elkins, op. cit., Vol. I, p. 94.
3. Ibid., p. 95.

upon free will is greatly undesired. Therefore, those entities which are *Wanderers*…will be the *only* subjects for the thought projections, which make up the so-called "Close Encounters" and meetings between [the Confederation] and Wanderers… The feeling of being awakened is the goal of this type of contact… If the result is hope, friendly feelings, and the awakening of a positive feeling of purposeful service to others, the marks of Confederation contact are evident."[4]

These are provocative statements, and their implications are huge. Clearly, any such interplanetary federation is a serious matter which involves dozens of races from different solar systems, jointly responsible for hundreds of planets. I know it is a far more serious matter than the somewhat glib way in which it's been presented in most of the popular ET-channeled books.

As for those sneaky little UFOs, who dart away as soon as they are spotted and rarely stop to say hello, according to RA's understanding, it's not their agenda to prove their own existence. In fact, distant sightings of Confederation-member "ships" (in distinction to those of other, less benevolent ETs) have nothing to do with revealing their secrets—their sole purpose is to tease open our sleeping awareness. Their goal is simple: to help us become aware of infinity and jump-start our spiritual seeking. Many of the strange sightings are not ships at all, but rather *thought-projections*, which is another reason why they flaunt the known laws of physics. Confederation groups sincerely hope we open our eyes to galactic grandeur, but they will not force them open.

What are the chances of direct physical contact, the hope of many a UFO researcher, ET Walk-in and Wanderer? At present, it seems highly unlikely that large numbers of people will experience such contact (the so-called mass-landing scenario predicted by a few, somewhat discredited ET channels)—not because the Confederation is stingy with their time, but rather, because their duty is to safeguard our free choice, which in this case means the unstated opposition of most of humanity to open meeting and cooperation! Their freedom to sleep must not be broached (strange but true).

---

4. Elkins, op cit., Vol. III, p. 10–12.

Were the benevolent ET groups to openly walk among us (as some did in Atlantis, Egypt and South America), when today but a tiny handful of people truly desire ET contact, would most certainly be infringement upon free will. Of course, not the free will of the seekers, who fervently wait for physical contact—but rather, the will of the overwhelming majority, who follow normal Earth religions and recognize their own "higher power," in addition to the multitudes who could not care less about cosmic unity—many of whom are simply trying to stay alive. Such meticulous service, extending even to those who wish to remain unaware of greater Life, shows clearly how this Confederation operates. They are pledged to serve all beings. Unless the mass of humanity makes a major shift towards conscious cosmic calling, I believe that the hope for benevolent mass-landing will remain unrequited. Any channel who tells you otherwise should be asked to fully explain their understanding of the Law of Free Will.

Some people, however, will have sightings, dreams, visions, and other close encounters with benevolent ETs. According to RA, if the contact was inspirational, filled with good feelings, and resulted in a renewed desire for self-understanding and service to others, then it surely was Confederation contact. But it also means one more thing—it means you are an ET soul, since according to this view, Wanderers are the only ones who are now given this sort of meeting. Such extreme selectivity is not due to any kind of elite status of the so-called Star Born, but rather, it is yet another way to protect the natives whose spiritual development must not be hampered by what we could call "artificially-induced paradigm shift." If you have had this kind of profound ET contact, then you should really ask yourself if you could be from elsewhere.

Our discussion of ET Confederation provides us with a vision of vast interstellar cooperation and extreme purity of service. It points to a grand evolutionary design, coordinated and planned by beings from all reaches of the galaxy, standing behind the scattered UFO sightings and ET contacts we all read about. More than a few New Age teachers and seekers, myself included, believe Earth will soon become a member-planet in this galactic grouping. If it is to be, it must await our greater opening to inter-species contact, the intensification of human calling, and a clear consensus among the family of Terran Humanity that we need benevolent ET support. But not to worry: the Confederation can wait.

Next, our discussion will go even deeper into the cosmic laws that stand behind the Confederation's extreme reluctance to intervene directly in human affairs: *The Law of Free Will.*

» *Chapter 10* «

ETs and the Law of Free Will

Were there no potentials for misunderstanding and, therefore, understanding, there would be no experience.[1]

THOSE WHO KNOW they are on the spiritual path soon realize that Life is not random, that order and meaning surround us. At the personal level, mystic traditions around the world tell us we have seven energy centers or *chakras* (from Sanskrit, meaning "wheels"), which when fully developed, leads to total enlightenment. Likewise, religious teachers, seers and channels all claim there are universal laws that regulate evolution throughout the cosmos. We can safely assume that the extraterrestrials whom we would recognize as spiritual teachers (unlike those ETs such as the "grays" who abduct and terrify) are fully aware of such laws. According to benevolent ET groups and incarnate ET souls who say they are here to help, the most important rule they follow is called *The Law of Free Will.*

Not only does this rule set limits to their inter-dimensional involvement in human affairs, but it also forms the very matrix upon which the entire tapestry of cosmic life is spun. What was called the "Prime Directive" on the TV show *Star Trek* is no Hollywood concoction; there really is cosmic law that guides evolution. And silent beneath its outer shell, what is really going on in the UFO phenomenon is none other than the working of the Mind of God. As an essential universal pattern, if we delve into the design of global UFO contact we will proceed straight back to the source of all Life. The Law of Free Will is central to our cosmic drama.

In practical terms, you will find that many of our ordinary innocent questions, such as the old favorites—

Why don't the Space Brothers just land on the White House lawn (and give us a cure for cancer)?

1. Elkins, op cit., Vol. III, p.14.

Why don't the Greys just invade the Earth (and get it all over with)?

How could a loving God allow evil and cruelty?

—are quite easily answered if we understand that **free choice is the linchpin of evolution**. As you might expect, *The Law of One* speaks extensively about free will in the context of UFOs, cosmic plan, and human development. RA explains how it applies to both positive and negative ET groups—those who serve others in love, and those who serve themselves through control—and how individual decision drives the course of evolution. Freedom to choose is our divine birthright, and gives shape to all experience on all planes of existence.

However, the same universal mandate that preserves free will also ensures confusion. In fact, *The RA Material* is the only source in print I have ever read which makes this bold equation:

The Law of Free Will = The Law of Confusion!

It is no accident people are so confused; it's actually part of the plan. Here are some choice quotes from *The Law of One*. Bear in mind that RA considers *The Law of One* to be the awareness of essential, perfect, absolute unity of all things everywhere—and so they consider any presumption of anything less a "distortion," even The Law of Free Will itself:

"*The Law of One* has as one of its primal distortions the free will distortion, thus each entity is free to accept, reject, or ignore [others] about it and ignore the creation itself…" [2]

"In this distortion [Free Will] it is recognized that the Creator will know Itself… In your illusion all experience springs from The Law of Free Will or Way of Confusion." [3]

"The Law of Confusion offers a free reach for the energies of each [being]." [4]

---

2. Elkins, op cit., Vol. I, p. 113.
3. Elkins, op cit., Vol. II, p. 2–3.
4. Elkins, op cit., Vol. III, p.15.

"Were there no potentials for misunderstanding and, therefore, understanding, *there would be no experience.*" [5]

If you're now starting to doubt the old teaching that "God is Love," then just consider this: according to the will of the Creator, *all souls have the freedom to ignore the very basis of life—to deny the very reality of their own source*, if they so choose. To me, this is the epitome of unconditional love. Like parents who freely give their resources to children, who eventually reject them, the Law of Free Will offers "free reach" to all possibilities including stubborn, willful human ignorance (a condition I am sure we are all familiar with), as well as what we call "evil." And this is just the point: only from choice and free will comes vivid experience, which leads to seeking, learning, wisdom, and enlightenment. Misunderstanding is more than inevitable; it is built into the system. Confusion is absolutely integral to the process. It is the basic catalyst that leads to clarity.

Therefore, the denial and rejection of spiritual reality that we find in human society—bound up with atheism, rational-materialism, and an undue focus on the tangible world—is not really a mistake. While it may reek of arrogance and spiritual immaturity, such attitudes are fully within the scope of cosmic design, and they simply reflect soul-consciousness at one particular level of development. To be specific, this level can be considered as somewhere in between the non-self conscious animals and the junior members of the ET community, races such as the Pleiadians who acknowledge they're only several thousand years older than Earth humanity.

So why doesn't the Confederation (otherwise called the good guys) just take us to paradise, and why don't the Greys (a.k.a. the bad guys) "just throw us to hell? Simply put, because the human freedom to choose has potent protectors, whether we choose to believe in them or not.

And yet, a certain degree of direct ET influence on Earth continues: thousands of people worldwide claim to have been either inspired or

---

5. Ibid., p.14.

terrorized by non-human contact. Even to the most diehard UFO researchers (those still lobbying for the government's Roswell files, who also think channeling is for the birds), deliberate ET contact appears to be a measured response, and humanity is definitely not calling the shots. Their presence is on their agenda, not ours.

As you might expect, RA explains some of the larger dynamics, such as UFO influence on Earth, ET polarity (what we call "good and evil"), personal choice, and human evolution—all in the context of the Law of Free Will. You may find the following passages difficult upon first reading, but if you review them several times, you will see that they explain a lot:

> "The Guardians [cosmic elders who are beyond the Confederation] guard the free will distortion of [those] of third density on this planetary sphere [Earth]…
>
> Attempts of the so-called Crusaders [Orion-based negative ETs] to interfere with free will are acceptable upon the dimension of their understanding [acceptable to them]. However, the [beings] of this dimension [Earth]…are not able to…recognize in full the distortions towards manipulation.
>
> Thus… a quarantine, this being a balancing situation whereby the free will of the Orion group [the "Crusaders"] is not stopped but given a challenge. Meanwhile, the third group [humanity] is not hindered from free choice."[6]
>
> "Their [negative ET] purpose is conquest, unlike those of the Confederation who wait for the calling. The so-called Orion group calls itself to conquest… The Confederation is concerned with the preservation of the conditions conducive to learning. This, for the most part, revolves about the primal distortion of free will…"[7]

In terms of the notion of "quarantine," RA defines it as a net made

6. Elkins, op cit., Vol. I, p. 149.
7. Ibid., p. 102, 194.

of higher-dimensional light that surrounds the planet, established by cosmic intelligence (so-called Guardians, who are far beyond RA) to balance the negative ET influx. However, the purpose of this net is not to cancel out human evil, nor prevent all negative ET influence on humanity; the point is simply to ensure a level playing field. With the quarantine in place, the Confederation's positive influx of love and light, expressing what they consider the path of unity, gets equal air time with the teachings of elitism, greed and selfish domination offered by the Orion Crusaders (those who follow what is called "the path of separation"). Both groups can be seen as rendering their own form of service.

In this way, relatively naive humanity is not overwhelmed by the treachery of negative ETs, and souls here can choose which path to follow: *love* or *separation*. Remember, in the Boundless Love of the Infinite Creator, the Law of Free Will gives the power to choose. Although at higher levels of spiritual understanding (i.e. sixth dimension or the density associated with Higher Self) there is no more sense of duality, human souls in 3D must choose their path through time and space to return to this state of One. Such a path develops the total divine equipment, mind/body/spirit, and souls learn to fan the flames of either love or control. Believe it or not, either path does lead back to Source—although the path of separation lacks love, and must in the end be renounced.

To support the free choice of path, the Guardians generate "random windows" in the light quarantine which restrain, but do not prevent the onrush of negative ETs. UFO flaps or mass sightings (perhaps the New York Hudson Valley, or more recently, Mexico City sightings), often result from such temporary openings. These random windows, allowing some but not all negative influx, actually balance the positive and negative group influences on humanity, and preserve our freedom to choose between them. Humanity thus has full freedom to choose the path offered by each.

This is exactly the lesson of schoolhouse Earth: *the individual choice of polarity—service to self (separation) or service to others (unity)*. Negative

ETs hope to lure us into the darkness of ego-based separation, while the Confederation seeks to reveal the light of our essential God-Self. But it is completely our choice. However, unfortunately, most people have not yet made their choice.

Although there is a lot more to discuss regarding ETs and the Law of Free Will, perhaps this chapter will serve as an introduction, and perhaps it will get you thinking. After all is said and done, we are left with the time/space reality of cosmic polarity, so-called good and evil, as an integral part of the divine play. And *play* it is—just as the Hindu mystics consider the Universe to be the dance of Shiva, or an expression of *lila* (from Sanskrit, meaning "play"). RA makes the same analogy when they try to describe exactly why different souls choose one of the two paths (unity or separation):

"Some love the light. Some love the darkness. It is a matter of the unique and infinitely various Creator choosing and playing among its experiences as a child upon a picnic. Some enjoy the picnic and find the sun beautiful, the food delicious, the games refreshing, and glow with the joy of creation. Some find the night delicious, their picnic being pain, difficulty, suffering of others, and the examination of the perversities of nature. These enjoy a different picnic. All these experiences are available. It is the free will of each entity which chooses the form of play, the form of pleasure."[8]

---

8. Elkins, op cit., Vol. I, p. 181.

» *Chapter 11* «

The Last Lifetime

Better to handle your work in this body,
this society, on this Earth!

A deep remembrance came to me recently while working hard at home vacuuming: that is, *this is my last life on Earth*. All the many issues and conflicts brought with me into this birth, all the frustrations and conflicts of various situations, for all these I have got one last incarnation here to achieve some sort of balance—for very soon this life will be a memory, a vivid parade of images for healing and review on the other side. Of course, it is not quite accurate to say we have got only one chance to deal with all the non-healed experiences of past lives, because many aspects of Self that remain out of balance can be reconciled beyond physical 3D life. Nevertheless, many of the Wanderers will soon be going home after what is called "Harvest" (a separation of souls according to their awareness, widely predicted for 2010–2013 A.D.; see Section II for more details). But for ET souls in particular, this is a pivotal incarnation for balancing our karmic books.

Of course, to discover the unresolved issues carried over from previous lives, we do not have to look much further than our present-day conflicts. Much of what we consider painful, the areas of life where we feel stuck, the many points of strong emotion, upheaval, confusion, and stagnation—all these experiences point to old unresolved matters. Since the mind of enlightenment (which we seek) already has perfect love, light, ease, and all the virtues we admire—to the extent we do not live this daily we have got unresolved issues! Fears, doubts, petty irritations and blocked expression of all sorts point to baggage yet unpacked, dragging limply behind us. For most people, the origin of this is past life experience. For Wanderers, these difficulties may also include the residue of centuries of painful adjustment to human society, and this camel will certainly *not* pass through the eye of the needle on our return back to the home density and cosmic family. It is important to address as many of these issues as we can, NOW. Of course, it is easier said than done.

To continue the process of discovery, identifying that which demands "final-life healing," we can survey the broad field of our personality. We can try to acknowledge the various conflicts and confusions about ourselves that we have acquired from 3D life, most of which come from having forgotten the love/light with which we entered the human system. As we do this, our difficulty is probably not finding a particular set of problems, but rather finding those that are most pressing. How do you find your biggest challenge among a crowd of problems? If it is not right here in your face, draping a cloud over everyday life experience, then it's most likely out in the backyard, waiting for you when you can no longer avoid it. Since there are some common issues shared by Wanderers and others who follow the spiritual path and seek greater healing, a brief tour of some of these final-life matters might be helpful.

For many of us, the greatest conflicts are about **path**: finding our purpose, coming to define a sense of mission and purpose that we know is essential but cannot quite grasp. For others, it is about **relationship**—to stay or not to stay, to compromise or hold fast, take a risk or play it safe, trust or remain alone. In other cases the issue is a bit bigger: the challenge of **human society**, dealing with all the aggression, mistrust, competition, and materialism out there. And we cannot forget the many problems of **self-value**: moving beyond self-pity and self-judgment towards a more balanced knowing and appreciation of who we really are—both our strengths and our weaknesses.

Dealing with self-valuation, personal relationships, as well as human society usually challenges us to learn how to welcome others as they are. It requires us to work through and accept our expectations, hurt, blame, loss, and self-complaining. Life on Earth is anything but easy, and for both Wanderers and others who are sensitive to inner truth and outer obligation, simply following the line of least resistance is often not enough. If we try to remain in the comfort zone, we will most likely avoid the important conflicts within ourselves and in our relationships. Unfortunately, avoiding pain is *not* a solution to pain. It may work in the short run, but even then not too well!

A supervisor at my counseling center many years ago used to say, "If you can't see through it, you've got to see it through"—which are words to live by. He was pointing out the two basic options we have for dealing with psychological conflict, what can be considered the Buddhist way and the Western way, the mystic and the psychological. The first way demands spiritual vision and gnosis (which means direct realization of things as they are, beyond all conceptual labels—not easy!), while the second course calls for full emotional honesty and is more familiar to most of us.

In Theravada Buddhist meditation (especially in the forest traditions of Thailand, Burma, and Sri Lanka, the root-lineage of all Buddhist schools), the fundamental goal is *insight*—direct contact and knowledge of self and phenomena as-it-is, developing a clear vision of that which is beyond change. In Sanskrit terminology, this is considered awareness of *sunyata*, also called emptiness, impermanence, insubstantiality, and the illusory nature of all that is conditioned, all that arises and passes away. This emptiness can also be identified as "Reality"—the eternal and changeless Creator, the True Self, the One, or the Absolute— although most Buddhists would also say that all these conceptual terms are illusory, as well. Of course, this awareness is beyond all rational thought.

If you look long enough with the still vision of quiet mind, you will see that the only element that does not arise and pass away is the *mystery-source* of who we really are, the *root-source* or true Being which inspires our personal awareness. Whether you label it Higher Self, No-Self, True Mind or No-Mind is irrelevant. I promise you, label or no-label, this will be the only thing that remains after all else passes away. If you can sustain this type of awareness while dealing with the ordinary challenges of life (both inner emotional process and outer interpersonal affairs), then you are truly "seeing through it." If so, then no situation would be emotionally charged, and you would not even use the term "life-challenges." Everything would be seen as emptiness, God, sacred mystery, or energy-in-flux. If you are not seeing things this way, then you have got to see it through!

This second path of "seeing it through" is the road most often trod in therapy and personal counseling, a road that rarely approaches the mystic vision described above. It usually does not lead to the realization of emptiness or the illusory-nature of thoughts and emotions— nevertheless, it is still quite useful in dealing with personal affairs in daily life. In general, seeing it through requires consistent self-reflection— carefully observing, accepting, and understanding our habitual patterns of thought, feeling, and behavior. It demands vigilance and a degree of detachment-in-kindness.

An example of this can be found in situations in which we are normally avoiding something (in particular, so-called negative emotions). By seeing it through, we first acknowledge our feelings of fear and insecurity. In situations where we ordinarily get mad, we would recognize the particular thoughts of anger and confusion that usually come first. Nipping matters in the bud, we gain the ability to detach from habitual personality patterns through unconditional acceptance of our conditioned psychological process. We willingly suffer the brunt of their force, without blame or control, and allow ourselves to feel ourselves completely.

In this approach, we also learn the fine art of dialogue—sharing our process with others through greater self-expression, articulating thoughts and feelings in relationships to generate mutual understanding. From both inner and outer work, self-observation and discussion, we slowly become less reactive and our mind becomes more spacious. Events, situations, and people that used to trigger us into reflexive patterns become less charged. At last we gain a measure of ease.

While these two approaches are useful to anyone, they also relate to the challenges of a Wanderer's last lifetime. Actually, these two paths help us balance karma, clear dysfunctional patterns, accept our choices and forgive those of others—all of which lightens the karmic load and helps us regain the awareness with which we came to Earth. Returning to Jesus' metaphor of the camel that must pass through the eye of a needle: there are requirements for returning home!

This is because each density represents a certain intensity of light, and our ability to enter those realms depends on our ability to appreciate, enjoy, and integrate that frequency of light energy. The central determinant of who goes where (the "where" being a dimension or realm of experience in which we take some kind of body-form), is simply our state of consciousness. You've got to live the mind of heaven to go to heaven! If we are stuck in emotion or lost in clouds of confusion, we will probably need a bit of healing on "the inner planes" before going home.

Frankly, this kind of soul-delay for self-healing is not such a big deal, since life is eternal and we have more than ample resources for the task. But, better to handle our work in this body, this society, on this Earth. Incarnation here is a tremendous catalyst for growth, far more potent than the higher realms in which all is love and light—no challenge at all! "Giving Caesar his due" (another saying attributed to Jesus, referring to the difference between material idolatry and spiritual worship) can also mean healing our own humanity, taking full responsibility for dealing with the personality blockages we have created on Earth while still living on Earth. This is also world service.

For most of the Wanderers out there, quite soon you will be returning home. In less time than you think, this Earth life will become a dream, a vivid chain of experience rapidly fused in expanding awareness far greater than you've known for a long time. Considering this, reflecting on the many implications, what is your own course of faithful action, your own path of meaning here and now? Service to all begins at home, and our true home is the Kingdom of Self, a boundless Kingdom of Heaven in which we live, move, and have our being. (Dear *Kings* and *Queens*, do you still have some royal matters yet undone?)

» *Chapter 12* «

QUESTIONS AND ANSWERS

Discovering ET Identity

Q: *How can I really know if I am from another planet? Can I ever be 100% sure?*

A: Yes, you can be 100% sure, but only after developing a deep intuitive awareness, which would probably require some kind of meditation and consistent self-reflection. You need to acknowledge any fear, pride and doubt you have in your mind, and then be willing to accept the truth of your identity, whatever it might be. There is no glory in being an ET soul, and no shame in not. It is only the truth that really matters, plus the trust in yourself that is needed to uncover it. If you feel a sincere, burning need to know, then follow all the clues and listen to all your thoughts and feelings. Then relax. Over time, the answer will come by itself.

The Mission of Wanderers

Q: *I have always felt that I had a special mission on Earth, yet I've never been able to define it. Can you tell me how to figure this out?*

A: As I have mentioned before, all Wanderers had a definite reason for coming, but not all of us have some grand mission to perform on the world stage. The basic reason we are here is to give a boost of love and light to assist the planet itself in its own transformation, which is no less than a cosmic initiation. Just being here awake in human form is a kind of radiatory service, and it fully supports the planetary process of growth.

In terms of a particular form of service, it all depends on your inclinations and desires. Some people can heal, some write or teach, while others make wonderful parents or even limousine drivers (as I used to be a limo driver myself, I know it's true! In fact, our company had another driver who also confided that he too believed himself to be an ET). So you can do whatever you like, but I don't think many Wanderers come here to change the course of history with inventions, peace treaties, technologies, or medical breakthroughs (although it does happen sometimes). *The most profound service can really be done by offering kindness, compassion, and a bit of clear thinking to all those we meet.* Each of us has our own sphere of influence (such as family, friends, community and workplace) in which we can be available to help, and the most important place to make a difference is always *right in front of us.*

Universal Wandering #1

Q: *Is information available about the* **system** *by which extraterrestrials come to Earth? For example, how is this decision made? Who is selected, by whom, on what criteria, and for how long? Are there other possible destinations for them, or is Earth their one alternative?*

A: As you might expect of Wanderers whose origin and identity have been veiled by agreement, most ET souls cannot explain exactly *how* they came to Earth. Since there is little channeled information on these specific matters, we can only turn to subjective sources, intuition, and inner guidance to get something close to real answers on the background procedures of cosmic wandering.

In my understanding, there is no obligation upon anyone to "leave home," but rather it is a voluntary agreement between higher-density souls, their entire society, and those who oversee inter-dimensional soul transfers onto particular worlds. Individual souls must sincerely desire the opportunity to serve in this way, and through their unified consciousness (in the home society) it must be agreed upon by the entire group, since it affects them all. Indeed, many Wanderers sense that what they do on Earth is intimately known and felt by their home-density group. Of course, Earth is not the only site of incarnation. Any planet with souls calling for aid, consciously or otherwise, is eligible to get such assistance. "Call and you shall receive."

Since this type of intervention affects other solar systems, the influx of souls must also be okayed by those who oversee the evolution of life on the destination-world. In the RA books, it is said that the "Council of Saturn," a group of fully-enlightened beings (comparable to cosmic Buddhas) living in the rings of Saturn, has ultimate responsibility for this particular solar system. Therefore, they are also involved in the planning and oversight of Wanderer-groups coming here. The exact details of specific agreements (including the length of stay, number of incarnations, birth locale, and human family) are complex decisions which have to take into account many different factors. However, the primary factor that drives the entire process is the destination-planet's need for service (more esoterically, its need for love/light energies); other factors include the planetary Being's own point of evolution and Its cycles of growth, as well as the spiritual path of learning particular to each ET soul coming into that system.

In accordance with cosmic law, a planetary call for assistance can only be honored with respect for the basic preservation of free will. To protect souls on Earth who are not interested in developing higher vision, the Wanderers come in veiled—without free use of their home-density powers. For those humans who have yet to choose their own path of development (service to self or service to others, the paths of unity or separation), as well as souls who have already chosen self-service, there is also allowed some degree of incoming negative ET groups (which includes a few negative Wanderers as well), who are here solely to increase their power through domination.

The evolutionary concerns of all parties involved—humanity and the plant/animal/mineral kingdoms, planet Earth and the solar system, Wanderers and their own home races—must all be balanced according to needs, limitations, and the best opportunities for growth. While it may seem unfortunate to us, there are limits upon the number of incoming positive Wanderers, and limits upon the influx of love/light from elsewhere. Clearly, these are complex and subtle matters, but with continued meditation, you will find more answers available.

Universal Wandering #2

Q: How is the decision made by certain ET souls to incarnate on Earth, while presumably others remain on their home planet, never leaving their "higher" dimension?

A: The decision-making process is not the same on all worlds and also depends on the soul's level of awareness. Spiritually speaking, the main group of Wanderers come from sixth density and had full awareness of *universal fusion*. Before incarnating they clearly knew their Oneness with All That Is, including Earth. Their transfer here was simply a matter of which souls wanted to serve the Universe in this way. Since there are risks involved (such as completely forgetting the ways of love, then getting karmically involved in prevailing human dysfunction), the decision to enter the 3D Earth system for a particular length of time is only made after due consideration.

Those souls who are ready, willing and able, and whose further evolution would best be served by the challenge of the vivid 3D illusion are those who end up here. The *RA Material* notes that Wanderers come in with a mixture of "bravery and foolhardiness," having thrown caution to the wind, like the Major Arcana Tarot card #1, *The Fool.* This may be why some ET souls feel like some kind of mistake has been made. In their rush to come to Earth in selfless service, they may not have prepared adequately for the trials they are now facing down here on the ground.

The Record of ET Service

Q: If most Wanderers on Earth don't know their purpose and are caught in human confusion, isn't their service here pretty useless? Sending ET souls to Earth seems like a great failure to me.

A: It is true most Wanderers cannot remember their purpose here. RA said that only about 10% have pierced the veil to recall their cosmic roots. And it is also true most of them are trapped in limited, ego-bound Earth conditioning, which generates alienation, self-pity, and in extreme cases, personality disorders. You could certainly say that this world salvage project has not been a smashing success; the degree of love/light offered, at least in 3D terms, is far less than had been hoped. But to call it a "great failure" seems a little excessive. From another angle, any degree of true love/light offered is important, and without a doubt, many souls on Earth have been helped.

Nevertheless, the thrust of your question is right. I'm sure that when our 3D cycle ends, a lot of time will be spent in higher-dimensional ET councils discussing how and why their service rendered fell short of expectations. Yet, it is no great mystery. There are many factors working against Wanderers' awakening as well as their effective offering. Here is the real short list:

✦ The relatively successful work of negative ET groups (primarily Orion) has controlled the thinking of generations, and before that, had significant sway on the 3D planets from which most Earth-souls derived (i.e. Mars, Maldek, etc.). With this long legacy, they have successfully embedded their elitist notions in politics, religion, business, and legal systems. In marriage, love has become identified with possession; in personal life, Self-will is shackled to selfishness. As the social matrix containing all Wanderers, it usually takes several lifetimes just to recognize some of the many distortions on Earth that are simply considered "normal" here.

✦ As a result of all such confusion, greed and materialism have run rampant for quite a long time among these souls. It is grounded in a narrow scientific world-view, fertilized by rugged individualism held in high-esteem, and watered by the spiritual apathy and disempowerment seeded by dogmatic religion. Add to this the basic ignorance of love and group-harmony that is just normal for 3D races (not yet in the density of love, 4D+), and you have a potentially devastating experience for naive ET souls. Many Wanderers stay somewhat disoriented for centuries, and you can often see this among "lovey-dovey" New Agers.

The main reason Wanderers are confused is simply built into the contract: agreeing to human genetics and the normal 3D veiled mind. In accordance with the Law of Free Will, Wanderers "become completely the creature of 3D in mind and body" (RA), agreeing to forget their origin, identity, and purpose. Once done, ET souls are pretty much on their own (karmically speaking), and so self-generated distortions from one lifetime are carried over to the next and the next, unless they are healed through love and balance. According to cosmic plan, there is no other way higher dimensional souls can come en masse to this world—and owing to their desire to serve, they agree to all such restrictions and drink the potion of forgetting. Unfortunately, given the nature of human consciousness and society, their spiritual sleep has generally continued.

Perhaps I could estimate the overall effectiveness of Wanderers on Earth (throughout the entire 3D cycle of 75,000 years) at about 30%. This means that 70% of their potential love/light has been baffled by mental dysfunction of one sort or another. Is this a great failure? Maybe yes, maybe no; as always, it depends on your perspective. To Higher Self and the elder ETs living in the Light of Unity, all is complete and whole and perfect—here, there, and everywhere. To the One Infinite Creator, whatever proceeds from operation and usage of the Law of Free Will is rich vivid catalyst, and grist for the mill of continued Divine play. No complaints here.

But for a weary Wanderer it is understandable, and I do see your point. I think you are ready to go home!

On Taking Human Form

Q: *Why do ETs need to incarnate in human bodies? Why can't they simply stay in the UFOs and do whatever they need to do up there?*

A: There is no cosmic law that tells ET souls they have to take human form. The decision is their own choice based on their personal commitment to service and the deeper needs of the situation, (the calling of humanity and Earth itself), which is felt quite clearly in the higher realms outside the solar system. However, the possibility of rendering useful service is tremendously enhanced by taking birth among us—whether or not the Wanderers recall their roots.

Some Wanderers come here to perform a particular task, such as those publicly known as inventors, statesmen and scientists, while others are simply here to radiate embodied love and light. If and when they pierce the veil of forgetting and acknowledge their greater identity and purpose, their service becomes even more effective. Such awakening involves spiritual realignment, reconnection and return to inner Self, which allows us to realize and appreciate divine love and cosmic design once again. Metaphysically, this opens a channel to the spirit which can benefit many people, as well as amplify the effectiveness of whatever service we choose to offer. To offer oneself in physical form is a much greater self-sacrifice for ET souls, and can be far more effective in a one-to-one way than had they stayed up in their UFOs.

More on the Wanderers' Veil

Q: *What is the veil of forgetting under which Star People live while on Earth?*

A: This "veil" is simply a temporary severance (in our physical 3D space/time experience) of the ET soul's normal link-up to his or her own Higher Self awareness (which was previously intact before coming to Earth). The veiling is cosmically ordained, required by laws of the solar system itself, and exists for as long as the ET chooses to incarnate on the planet. Essentially, it is in place to protect humanity's choice, which is their option to accept or reject the reality of "cosmic law" and the existence of a multi-dimensional Universe. None of the benevolent ETs, be they incarnated Wanderers or those in UFOs, wish to force themselves upon humanity.

Through deep self-reflection and meditation you can remember your forgotten identity and life-purpose, but to entirely regain all the "home-realm powers and abilities" one must dedicate one's life to selfless service, meditation, sacrifice and radical detachment from all elements of personality. This would be no different than the spiritual path of many Eastern religions and all mystery schools, beginning with the Egyptians and South Americans—whose teachers also happened to be ETs!

Psychological Explanations

Q: *Most psychologists would say that your so-called "ET souls" are simply adults who were abused or emotionally wounded as children and have now chosen this strange sense of identity to feel special. What do you think about this?*

A: I think this type of explanation is probably true for some people, and in fact, several of those I interviewed in my first book did come from dysfunctional families with some degree of trauma in childhood. However, most of them did not, and many were quite mature psychologically—what would be called high-functioning, which means they functioned quite well in normal human society. Moreover, many of them did not feel special at all, and sometimes, considering themselves ETs made their lives more difficult.

The whole question of ET identity really concerns the validity of *subjective knowing*, based ultimately on intuition and what spiritual traditions the world over call "expanded awareness." The modern field of psychology represents just one way of viewing the Self and concerns only one mode of human experience: conditioned patterns of thought, feeling, sensation, and behavior. These psychological explanations, no matter how reasonable they sound or useful in some cases, do not eliminate the possibility of the metaphysical or transcendental. Considering claims of ET identity, we must acknowledge an entirely different aspect of human experience and Self-nature at stake.

Benevolent ETs and Human Free Will

Q: *If Walk-ins and Wanderers are really from ET civilizations much older (and presumably wiser) than Earth's, then why don't they just step forward as our leaders and solve our problems?*

A: As I have said many times, benevolent ETs won't save us from ourselves. They're only here as midwives to humanity's birth as self-conscious souls. Through sharing love, wisdom, and an appreciation of Oneness, they can only support choices we make according to our own free will.

Furthermore, since most people do not really take UFO matters seriously and choose to remain indifferent to seeking direct ET assistance, those who watch over humanity *cannot* intervene directly— even if the alternative is some measure of planetary destruction (as was the case in Atlantis, which is said to have perished under its own aggression about 10,000 years ago). However, if and when a significant percentage of the population sincerely calls for aid, there can be direct contact and intervention. But this depends entirely on the conscious calling of humanity.

Wanderers and Negative ETs

Q: *If some ETs on Earth come from planets which are kind and loving, I assume that other ETs come from worlds that are warlike. Why don't you write so much about them?*

A: Indeed, some ETs do come from hostile and conquering worlds, and when they incarnate on Earth they can be called "negative Wanderers" (negative only in the sense that they reject universal love). There are far fewer of them here than benevolent Star People, but they can be found in the highest ranks of worldly power—autocratic, controlling, intensely self-serving, and quite effective—"enjoying the fruits of power," as RA would say. The reason I do not dwell much upon their ways (in contrast to other channels and researchers who speak endlessly upon the evils doings of Greys, Reptoids, Draconians, and so on) is generally because most people are not concerned with this sometimes troubling, always serious discussion. Additionally, my work is to amplify the Light, not battle its absence. In my understanding, the best way to serve is to radiate Light, not to oppose darkness. It is quite important, however, to appreciate, understand, and not shy away from really coming to terms with the workings of negativity—in the development of wisdom, it is essential for those of us who embrace Unity. But not to fear—there is ample darkness around for your study!

Negative ET Influence on Channels

Q: *The RA Material says that channels who seek positive information are "high priority targets" for the Orion group and negative ET interference.*

How can we know if a particular channel has been compromised and their information distorted?

A: Generally, individual channelers are first offered various "ego-lures," in an attempt to lead them away from the pure desire to serve others. Simply put, these telepathic suggestions from Orion ET sources amplify whatever latent desire for money, power, fame, and pride that the channels already have. The classic example is the "guru-dominator" (a role you can see in action with some popular channels in the U.S. and Japan), whose spiritual organization controls the money and personal lives of his or her followers. This represents an energy re-orientation to more self-serving ways of conduct.

For other channels, more subtle temptations can also be offered by negative ET groups: the glamour of receiving detailed information on ET plans and hierarchy, plots and cover-ups, and near-term predictions of frightful catastrophe or happy-face ET mass-landings. In this camp you will find channels whose books and lectures drown us in fear-based warnings, or baffle us in cosmic facts, figures, names, dates, and places. This kind of information sounds spiritual, but it's merely trivial.

Not surprisingly, when RA was asked about the percentage of channels in the world today who are compromised by negative ET interference, they declined to answer directly since they considered a direct answer to "infringe upon the free will or confusion of some living." Instead, RA offered the following advice to help us develop our own discernment:

"We can only ask [you] to consider the relative effect of *philosophy* and your so-called *specific information*. It is not the specificity of the information which attracts negative influences. *It is the importance placed upon it...*"[1]

So judge for yourself: if the channeled material preserves the thread of eternal philosophy then it is likely to be pure. In this case, it will support greater self-understanding, self-appreciation, a balanced way of life, and the full-bodied development of love, wisdom, and will.

---

1. Elkins, op cit., Vol. I, p. 225.

Such qualities of true Self are the foundation of *all* traditions of ageless wisdom, East and West, and are at the heart of the teachings given by RA and the other elder extraterrestrials. In contrast to negatively-influenced channeled works that offer sensational, glamorous trivia, *all pure teachings begin and end with the essential.* As RA once noted, true spiritual work shall always "begin and end in the Creator."

ET Abductions #1

Q: *If aliens are from older and wiser worlds, why do they terrify and abduct people?*

A: This question brings us into the issue of cosmic good and evil, the genuine polarities of ET life. As I hope you know by now, there definitely are aliens who seek domination, control and conquest. Meanwhile, "there are other groups, who forever have our best interests at heart. Whether we like it or not, some planets and their entire civilizations have developed themselves along the "evil line," and the Creator gives total freedom to this choice. These groups, although spurning love, still exist within the greater Infinite Love, and are also progressing along their path, developing body-mind-spirit (all the while denying, however, real love and unity). Of course, the aims of these groups have nothing "to do with the work of most ET Walk-ins and Wanderers, who only want to help.

ET Abductions #2

Q: *Is it possible to stop having abduction experiences, and how can I end these ET contacts?*

A: In my experience, there seem to be few abduction experts and therapists who offer ways to terminate unwanted contacts. Many of those who specialize in the field actually seem to consider such contact (which, as true violation, is definitely worthy of the term *abduction*) to be some sort of planetary wake-up call, some kind of wonderful opportunity for humanity—so they have no interest in trying to end them. Sometimes you will even find so-called experts arguing with experiencers who feel traumatized, trying to convince them they created their own terror through misunderstanding.

In my opinion, some of these experts are just whitewashing the unpleasant aspects entirely, the most obvious example being the now-fashionable use of the term "experiencer" instead of abductee. To me, this is just a form of twisted, politically-correct double-talk (trying to alter perceptions of reality by changing the labels), which the specialists justify by saying that the new label helps minimize a person's overwhelming fear and sense of victimization. However, the fear, trauma, and sense of helpless victimization are just what the aliens intended. To minimize them is ultimately to rob the abductee of the very catalyst for their empowerment—the motivation to terminate contact!

According to RA, if these qualities of fear, terror, and violation are present, the contact was most likely of a negative nature, offered not to help humanity, but to increase the power-base of self-serving ET groups. In the long run, their goal is no less than planetary conquest. If the contact generated terror and helplessness, doom and disorientation, then we **are** talking about abduction. Let us not mince words, please—and I can assure you I am not falling into some kind of "cosmic racism," as I was once accused of doing by a very positive channel who should know better.

Some psychologists in the abduction field are just normal clinicians documenting an unusual population, attending to the needs of their clients, hoping to increase public awareness. Others are simply curious about alien technology (i.e. implants), and seem to be playing detectives hot on the trail of a clever villain. Unfortunately, almost none of these workers have sufficient metaphysical background, so they cannot really offer much in the way of healing and protection.

Only a few leaders "in the field" seem to understand the deeper principles involved here—the universal laws of consciousness, polarity, and multi-dimensional energy. If you have had, or continue to have abductions and want to end them, you must do work in consciousness—developing greater and more centered awareness, beginning with absolute self-acceptance of all the emotions involved, to ultimately dissolve the mind of helplessness that actually attracts self-serving aliens.

The qualities of will, discernment, and compassion (especially for yourself) must all be increased. Developing true will leads to real empowerment ("You cannot do this to me"); clear discernment leads to clear knowing ("I no longer need this experience"); and compassion generates forgiveness ("I accept myself for having allowed such abuse into my life, but I do not need it any longer"). It helps to find a healer or counselor with a grounded spiritual perspective (see the list of resources in the appendix), and embark upon formal meditation practice. Using traditional Buddhist, Hindu, and Hebrew mantras can also be effective in terminating negative ET contact. I recommend you read Appendix 2, "On Counseling Abductees and Contactees." Remember, as an expression of Universal Spirit, *the core of your Being is boundless power.* Within you right now is all the power you need to overcome negative ETs. The only question is your *will-full-ness* to access it. For a complete online discussion of abduction, see my interview with researcher Deborah Lindemann at www.universal-vision.com.

ET Abductions #3

Q: *A friend of mine has been having what seem to be abductions, waking up in the morning with memories of flying and marks on her body. How can I help?*

A: When we talk about abductions, we are certainly venturing far from the self-discovery process of Walk-ins and Wanderers. Although some abductees are in fact ET souls, they have been violated, traumatized, and hurt by their experience—which is exactly why we can use the term *abduction*. When I counsel people with these experiences, the first question I usually ask is simple: do you want these contacts to continue or not? For many, such "alien relations" fill an emotional void: longing for a protector, a comforter, a powerful source of greater life-meaning. Such psychological dynamics often reveal the common link between childhood abuse and later-life abduction: damaged self-esteem opens a door for negative alien intrusion. In many cases, the person is operating from a deeply heartbroken need, and they are confusing power for love. They often have an inner void of love (not too unusual in this world), and have not developed enough self-love to fill it, so they attract alien power without love. As within, so without. Our external relations always mirror our inner self-process.

So, before terminating negative contact, a person must look to their own needs, and clearly recognize which course of action provides a path of empowerment and self-respect. After that, there must grow a conscious dedication to greater spiritual alignment. This involves some sort of serious decision to sever subconscious links with the abducting ETs, intensifying their personal call for contact and fusion with Higher Self, guides and protectors, and then learning how to honor and freely express their inner will for positive control: *"I will **not** allow this type of experience in my life."* Admittedly, it is usually difficult to terminate negative abduction contact, but it can be done. I know several people who have. In some ways, it is no different from the mystic path of overcoming inner demons (obstructions of mind). It takes will, more will, balance, and self-kindness. Furthermore, dedication, commitment, and firm resolve are essential. You must truly believe in yourself and raise your awareness to a higher level than the aliens.

Wanderers' Choice #1

Q: *Do all Wanderers come here willingly? Have you come across anyone who felt like being here was an accident or they were forced here against their will? I've never felt like I wanted to be here.*

A: I have met many people who feel like they did not want to come to Earth, but thought that for some reason, unknown to them, they ended up here. Most of these people felt severe alienation and homesickness, and some even had suicidal thoughts. If we apply a psychological interpretation, we could trace their sense of "accidental birth" to some kind of intense emotional pain experienced earlier in this life or in past lives. However, bear in mind that just because they had this kind of psychological process does not mean they cannot also be an ET soul, as mentioned in an earlier reply ("Psychological Explanations"). For the most part, however, I imagine many of the people who have a sense that their birth was some kind of mistake are probably Wanderers.

Conceivably, there could be "accidents" in inter-dimensional soul-transfer; perhaps it is possible. Yet it is hard to imagine positive Wanderers being forced to come to Earth against their will (as they almost always come from groups already unified in love), or that Higher Self might make some kind of mistake (since we can assume it knows what is needed for its own evolution). In my opinion, the idea that one had some kind of accidental human birth usually comes from a mix of personal emotional conflict, past-life karmic burdens, and pre-birth wounding that is sensed but not healed.

Finally, more than a few Wanderers have programmed for themselves (before birth) tests and life-challenges that they now feel are too much to handle. In this case, the only thing that can be called a mistake was their pre-birth assessment of their ability in physical 3D to deal with the chosen hard times. Nevertheless, I do admit the possibility that in rare instances some Wanderers have ended up on Earth by mistake. Being reasonable, we can assume many scenarios are possible.

Wanderers' Choice #2

Q: *What if an ET decides he or she has "had enough" and wants to go home? Don't I have the right to leave when I want to, before completing some kind of contract?*

A: Normally, ET souls' pre-birth agreements are not broken in the middle of the cycle, midway through a series of chosen incarnations. This sense of follow-through is just the same as with Higher Self, which normally won't "pull the plug" (withdrawing life-force) to leave the body in the middle of a lifetime of pain, sorrow, and missed opportunities. Perhaps the most important means of evolution is the right to fully experience the consequences of our choices. The aim of incarnation is not to have a good time, nor cut it short if you can't, but rather to learn the lessons of love, wisdom, balance and faith—the ultimate antidotes to despair and hopelessness.

No conscious soul denies itself opportunities for learning, nor would the Higher Self—which is why it does not just evacuate all the ET souls having a hard time down here. In my opinion, if a Wanderer feels he or she has had enough and wants to go home early, it is probably because that person is missing opportunities for personal growth here on Earth, and of course, has a lot of inner pain. There are certainly situations in which a premature exit from the body entails no karmic debt, but they happen only in rare instances to expedite soul evolution—not to relieve one's discomfort, which is, in any case, simply the consequence of the person's own spiritual imbalance.

Remember the old saying, "you create your own reality": if you are having a hard time, it's pretty much your own doing. I do not mean to be judgmental, but we are totally responsible for the quality of our consciousness, and most of our external conditions (our "life") are the direct result of our own previous choices. As RA would say, there are no accidents in evolution, although there are mistakes. Rather than hoping for rescue, it would be far more effective in the long run to discover the means of rescuing ourselves.

Wanderers' Choice #3

Q: *You said that some ETs end up in mental institutions; why don't their home planet people just come and take them back? How could they be so cruel as to just leave them there?*

A: Another question from a Wanderer looking to take an early flight! Again, the path of soul-evolution is not traveled via protection from pain and sorrow. Instead, evolution is the opportunity to develop all aspects of the divine equipment, accessed through body, mind and spirit, under the guidance of Higher Self. According to the Law of Free Will, all souls have the right to make their own choices, but for the full development of consciousness it is absolutely necessary to experience the results of our choices. No soul finds itself in a mental institution by accident; no one ends up with a miserable life by accident. In all such cases, a major portion of responsibility for the creation of those conditions has to be taken by the soul involved, having made certain choices towards those ends either before, during, or after birth in the present lifetime. This is the operation of karma and cause-and-effect, which is one of the basic foundations of soul-evolution, ET or otherwise.

If you think your homeplanet people are being cruel by not rushing to the rescue, then you may also consider this a universe of endless cruelty (an idea which is, not surprisingly, shared by more than a few Wanderers and others who feel helpless), since there is such tremendous suffering all around us. Nevertheless, the principle of what is called *karma* suggests that there are definite causes to all tangible effects, and that we constantly create our reality, both individual and collective, inner and outer, through our continuing thoughts and deeds. According to this view, it is imperative to experience events fully, since they are a perfect mirror of our soul's activity and point of evolution. As cosmic beings still on the path, Wanderers are no exception to the rule, and like everyone else, we have to learn our fair share of responsibility through life-experience, both happy and sad.

Wanderers' Reincarnation

Q: *I really feel like this is my last lifetime on Earth. Is this possible?*

A: More than possible. It is actually quite likely. Many of the Wanderers now remembering their cosmic roots have been here for many lifetimes and are finally at the end of their contract. Most of them made previous agreements to remain here for a particular length of time, so it is normal that their veil of forgetting (forgetting both identity and purpose) is finally wearing thin. But not to worry: homecoming awaits you! There will be many other benevolent ETs coming here to take your place in Earth's new civilization, so the planet will still have a lot of help available.

Sharing Your ET Ideas

Q: *In your book you detail the problems Walk-ins and Wanderers have with loved ones. I want to tell my parents about my experiences, but I'm worried they'll misunderstand. What should I do?*

A: Sharing your thoughts about your higher-dimensional origins is not easy, and it should only come after a long process of becoming familiar with the issue yourself. If you do not know your own thinking, how can you explain it to others? But after you have come to peace with what you believe is real, then it is important to share your conclusions with those who are close. However, you may never know how much they really care until you open up.

And therein lies the problem: how do you disclose such radical notions to those whose reactions you can't predict? There is, of course, no standard way to break your "secret." However, if you stay calm, sensitive to both their potential confusion and your own feelings, you can keep your balance. Just remember: go slow, do not force anything, realize that some of your loved ones simply cannot handle these ideas, and be willing to find other people who can (and they will likely become the nucleus of your next support group). You need to realize that some losses cannot be helped, and you are not responsible for other peoples' reactions. Above all, try to trust your inner resources and do not be afraid to go your own way when you have to. It's all for learning.

Wanderers' Dreams and Out-of-Body Experience #1

Q: *When I was young I used to have dreams of flying in spaceships with people who seemed to be like my family. What do you make of this?*

A: I cannot say exactly what happened in your dreams, but I interviewed many Wanderers who had this type of experience. What you are recalling in these dreams may actually represent a type of "bleed-through" memory of having been with your ET group, either before coming to Earth or in out-of-body states as a child while "asleep." As children, we are usually more open to remembering multi-dimensional experience, as we are carrying far less mental baggage. That you still remember these dreams is also important. Their content may point to particular aspects of your total self which now demand attention—developing certain skills or resolving certain issues. The meaning of these dreams is available within your own mind; the answers are waiting for you.

Wanderers' Dreams and Out-of-Body Experience #2

Q: *I have had several dreams with a group of white-robed beings that seem to be doing some kind of ceremony. Have you ever heard of this before?*

A: Although your question does not give me too much information to work from, and there are many explanations for this kind of dream, I can share some idea of what this experience is all about. In most cases, such a "dream" is not really a dream at all. It is a memory-fragment of a genuine out-of-body experience in another dimension (such as the astral plane, or for Wanderers, a higher density that may have little to do with planet Earth). While some people have reported this kind of experience taking place in their own home (such as a group of beings circling around their bed in a non-threatening way), most of the time this type of ceremonial contact occurs in dimension beyond the physical 3D world. It is a kind of formal group meditation ritual, which can have many aims.

You have to remember that once outside the body, most of us have far greater awareness of our cosmic relations. I used to call this my "night job," as opposed to my day job in physical 3D form. Not only is it true that we're spiritual beings experiencing life as a human being, but moreover, most of us have ongoing formal service obligations as part of non-physical groups that may or may not have that much to do with Earth evolution. As in the writings of 20th century Theosophy, there really are Masters (accomplished beings at, or beyond the level of Higher Self), invisible ashrams (spiritual teaching centers), and esoteric energy-rituals performed to assist interplanetary evolution. Sometimes, the images we recall from this kind of dream represent a composite-memory of many different elements, both subjective, imaginative and objective metaphysical.

In the case of Wanderers, robed beings with an air of great solemnity are often one's own family—which means that the person who has this kind of experience is an integral member of the group. This is not quite the same as the typical ET contact, which creates a feeling of being visited by strange aliens (benevolent or otherwise). For many

Star People, a ceremonial-type contact is the trigger for awakening to ET identity, or to greater remembrance of ongoing activity in other realms.

Many times, the ceremony that is being performed relates to world service—assisting planetary evolution by invoking, amplifying, and transmitting cosmic energies (what the Hindus call *prana* or universal power). This is no different from what the so-called Hierarchy of Masters and Initiates do to help the Earth. The only difference is that they are fully conscious of what's happening, while we (who consider it a dream) actually splinter our recall upon returning to the physical body. If you look deeper at the images in this kind of dream, you might discover exactly what relationship you have to these beings, and just what role you're playing in the ceremony.

ET Near-Death Experiences

Q: *What happens when ET souls have a near-death experience? Do they see people from their home planet, or do they only meet people from Earth who have previously died?*

A: Since I have not personally had an NDE (a near-death experience), I cannot really say what is standard for Wanderers who do have one, or if there is any standard experience at all. But basically, according to theory, who you meet during an NDE really depends on who is available (since some souls who could help you have already taken "re-birth), as well as which souls can best re-direct you back into body, back to your 3D form.

Like all souls on Earth, Wanderers may have many beings helping them from inner planes (the non-physical dimensions that interface physical 3D), including past-life karmic friends, teachers and angelic forces, as well as ET family. I am sure some souls from back home can re-direct wayward Wanderers who need to get back into their body from an NDE. Bear in mind, however, they may appear in non-ET forms, which would certainly be necessary for most StarBorn, since most of us have totally forgotten the way we were.

Wanderers' Home Planets #1

Q: *I feel like everything I learn on Earth is somehow transmitted to my home planet, so they experience everything I'm going through. Have you heard about this before?*

A: When we talk about the purpose of ET souls coming to Earth, a more subtle goal that is often ignored is the development of the home planet group. Since most Wanderers come from worlds or realms with complete social and interpersonal fusion, whatever is experienced by one is known to all. And while you cannot see them with your physical eyes, I assume that each Wanderer's home-planet group knows full well that he or she is here, and remain connected at a deeper level. So they struggle as you do, and learn as you learn.

One of the people I interviewed in my first book felt that she came from Sirius, and had chosen before birth the tremendous negativity and social conflicts that she experienced throughout her life here. She believed that dealing with these struggles was part of the education of her Sirian group who needed direct experience of human conditions to better serve humanity in the future. It is interesting to realize that despite the spiritual maturity of those home-planet (non-incarnated) benevolent extraterrestrials, they can be quite naive when it comes to Earthly matters. Therefore, Wanderers in 3D form also form a bridge from their home realm onto the Earth, and back from Earth towards their greater cosmic family.

Wanderers' Home Planets #2

Q: *If a Wanderer has been here since Atlantis, doesn't that mean that by the time they get back to the home planet, the people they once knew have all changed? How awful to go home and find out that everyone's gone!*

A: To deal with this kind of inter-dimensional measurement, you have to understand that time on Earth is not the same as time in "higher" or more light-filled densities. For example, 25,000 years here may be equivalent (in both subjective experience and linear time) to 25 days there, in the same way as out-of-body travelers often relate that their epic journeys took place in a mere few minutes of Earth time (check the works of Robert Monroe, for example). Most likely, of more concern in this kind of situation is the fact that since Wanderers do wander, when you return to the home group some of your friends may have already left to serve on other 3D worlds. Of course, you can always sign up for another tour of duty and go join them!

Wanderers' Home Planets #3: Implants

Q: *How do our fellow ETs ("in space") know who and where we are? Do all Wanderers have some kind of implant? Do they keep track of all of us?*

A: Contrary to some New Age channels and healers, I am sure most Wanderers do not have tracking implants; furthermore, Wanderers rarely have abduction-implant experiences. Passing along the notion that "everyone is implanted" is a fine way to grind us into a sense of helplessness, weakness and passivity—which is why, I believe, negative ETs are promoting this particular concept. Contrary to opinion, human souls on Earth are *not* fully controlled by evil ET rulers. There are forces of darkness (anti-soul, anti-love) both above and below, but the degree of their control depends solely on the degree of our being out of touch with Higher Self. Their power depends totally on our disempowerment. How much control they have over us depends on how much power we give up.

Since most Wanderers come from ET groups that are fully telepathic and mind-linked (what RA calls a "social-memory complex"), it is not hard for the total system to keep track of each member of the whole. This condition is similar to what develops from meditation practices that synchronize mind and body. Consciousness comes to pervade our entire form, and we grow aware of the Life-energy in every portion—ultimately, every cell—of the physical body.

Likewise, our home family (especially in elder races) is also aware of its wholeness, and lives in a quite expanded state of group unity. Additionally, many of us are in regular contact with home-group souls through ongoing out-of-body travel, which, however, is generally forgotten upon our return to the body, upon "awakening" in the morning. Most Wanderers are still in the loop and linked up to the home group, so tracking devices are not needed. Some ET races may make non-physical implants (i.e. "astral body beacons"), but since it is not my specialty, I am no authority here.

Wanderers and Anger

Q: *I have a real hard time dealing with anger, and I just want to run away and hide when people start to fight around me. I wish I could handle this. Do you have any suggestions?*

A: For ET souls, strife and conflict were basically absent from the home world group. Most higher-dimensional worlds are unified and harmonized, with all members cooperating for the common good, with no more petty anger and selfishness. Coming to Earth (a world of duality, confusion, and distorted egotism), Wanderers are generally unfamiliar with the forms of negativity and often try to avoid them. Some ET souls even withdraw from society, or turn misanthropic.

If you want to cultivate wisdom and will (which are qualities of the higher densities and chakras beyond the heart, which represents fourth chakra or fourth density, associated with love and compassion), then try to be with it. If you can learn how to feel and accept the energies of conflict, you can then use the light of mind to realize their origins and so develop greater wisdom. If you can bless and try to "see into" the anger storming around you, you can also develop a greater sense of center, quiet empowerment, and standing firm. Of course, it can be most difficult.

Nevertheless, fearlessness can grow alongside the wisdom of seeing clearly, and the will can be cultivated by standing still amidst the storm—which certainly doesn't stop you from taking action if need be. If we can achieve balance, then discernment can tell us if there's some way to serve the combatants, which in many cases simply means keeping cool and offering words of reconciliation. You may also need to right a wrong and take corrective action. If you can develop the needed qualities to deal with anger, then your human training has been most successful, and you will be the toast of the town with your home planet elders, even though they haven't seen strife in aeons!

Wanderers and Health

Q: *I am a Wanderer who is pretty well-adjusted to Earth life, but it seems I am always getting sick. Is this related to being a Star Person?*

A: I have met a lot of Wanderers who live with chronic ailments and illnesses that just do not go away. In fact, allergies are one of the most common traits of ET souls on Earth. When a person feels severe alienation over a long period of time, the physical body gains a kind of disorientation that impairs its normal adjustment. Just like the body of Earth, which stores and retains the energy of disharmony created by humanity over the millennia (then coughs them up in geologic upheaval), so too does our own physical body store and retain the energies associated with our troubles.

When a person feels depression, despair, and estrangement for many years, this compounds their energy center blockages, and their body shifts to accommodate these perceptions. As RA noted, "the body is a creature of the mind." When the mind has *dis-ease*, so too will the body. Living in silent sorrow, as many Wanderers do, the result for some is chronic ill health.

It is also common for ET souls to choose a distorted, unhealthy body so that the limitations of physical infirmity can be a catalyst to greater spiritual seeking and sensitivity to human sorrow. There are also some Wanderers who have not been here before (they are in their first lifetime in this solar system), and knowing that this is their one and only chance to experience Earth's 3D cycle, they program a sickly body to fully taste the limitations of 3D! Of course, from a soul perspective, having a weak body is no punishment or restriction, but rather a set of distortions that might provide an opportunity to accelerate growth, if met with sufficient wisdom and self-love. For Spirit, the greater the limitation, the greater the potential learning.

Finally, I have also met Wanderers who seem to have taken upon themselves some type of group or family karma. By voluntary agreement, they have chosen to take birth into a human family in which everyone is dealing with some kind of serious hardship (in terms of health, relationships, finance, or self-esteem). In these cases, it is likely that they chose this family to be of service, hoping to help ease the burdens of those around them by sacrificial self-constraint. The beautiful little girl whose body is twisted and deformed by childhood polio may well be a high-density soul intending to bring light into the family through her example of courage, offering her body to generate catalyst for her parents in the hopes that they will open to greater love (by their desire to care for her). Ironically, they feel sorry for her ("poor little girl") and pity her, while at the soul-level she had compassion for them (and therefore chose infirmity)! Actually this is quite common. So for Wanderers, what is normally an expression of karmic limitation (born of necessity for soul-evolution), can also be chosen as a form of service.

Wanderers' Difficulties

Q: *What do you think is the single most difficult issue for Wanderers on Earth? Everyone I know who feels like they're from elsewhere seems to be having a pretty hard time right now.*

A: In my opinion, there are two major challenges that trip up most Wanderers, although you will find countless permutations on these themes. The first challenge is posed *by the nature of third density itself* (i.e. this particular level of existence, the material/physical world), and the second is *the nature of this particular civilization*, our particular Western society. It is nearly impossible to make a smooth adjustment to life on Earth given these two factors (although these conditions are exactly why we are here in the first place!). Wanderers often take many lifetimes to resolve the conflicts and confusion they have acquired around these issues, and are most likely still in the process of healing their multiple wounds. Ironically, most ET souls are totally unaware of the inter-dimensional psycho-dynamics that lie at the root of their difficulties, as they imagine themselves "just like everyone else."

Regarding the issues of "third dimension," we should remember that it is part of the cosmic plan at this level of being that awareness is veiled. Therefore, it is entirely natural that souls in 3D forget love and their essential oneness with God and each other—this is but the required operation of the Law of Free Will in a density of spiritual choice. It would be a mistake to curse this apparent limitation of 3D. We had better get used to it, and get used to the fact that the only way to pierce the veil is through transpersonal consciousness, through meditation and inner work.

After this, the second assault comes from human society itself, notorious throughout the galaxy for its aggression, ignorance, and self-denial—boasting an incendiary mix of pride and arrogance, much lacking in compassion and self-awareness. Coming from elsewhere, Wanderers also tend to get confused over humanity's denial of spiritual reality, thinking that "everyone should already know that," but here on Earth, they don't! Nevertheless, we need not become self-critical, as even RA confided that they "cannot plumb the depths of the distortions which infect your peoples." It may take Wanderers many lifetimes to understand human society—a society which doesn't even understand itself! Whatever the affliction may be, it sure doesn't feel like home…

Wanderers' Difficulties #2

Q: *A friend of mine is quite detached from society, and while he realizes he is a Wanderer here to serve, he still avoids close contact with people. Why is this?*

A: After awakening to ET identity, some people lose all desire to be a part of this world. Actually, some kind of collapsed motivation is common, and really comes from a desire to return to more harmonious dimensions. While we have complete free will to do as we like, and no ET elders are standing around forcing us to engage in society, this kind of withdrawal is like licking our wounds in the corner.

Of course, many Wanderers feel tremendous wounding and society suffers from great disharmony, plus the more sensitive you get, the harder it can be to live in the middle of strife. Yet, this disharmony is just why we are here, and if we avoid it, aren't we also avoiding the very purpose of our life? For some people, social detachment does open the door to productive creativity or intensive self-work. But if it hardens into bitter disdain or reluctance to give a hand where a hand is needed, then it stems from emotional blockage and does need healing. Forgiving yourself and those around you is a good first step, and after that, simply ask yourself what you really need. Your degree of social engagement is, of course, totally up to you.

ET Children

Q: *I think there are many special children among us today. But whenever I've suggested to teenagers that they might be StarBorn, they don't seem too interested. Why is this?*

A: Without a doubt, there is almost zero peer-support among today's youth for being an extraterrestrial soul! It is rare enough for American teenagers (or teens anywhere) to have a mature spiritual perspective, and there are countless social influences distracting them from self-reflection. They may think the TV series *Star Trek* or *Babylon V* is cool or that *X-Files* could be real, but their interest usually stops right there. It's one thing to be entertained by unsolved mysteries and a strange universe, but quite another to consider the real source of our interest.

For teens and adults alike, the question "why am I interested in these things?" is rarely asked. Nevertheless, as that generation grows up, their basic openness and the emerging public reality of cosmic community will help them achieve greater spiritual vision. And remember, for those children who are Wanderers, this is generally their first lifetime on Earth, so they are just getting their feet wet. For more discussion, see the chapter in Section I entitled "The Children of Today."

Healing Lost Idealism

Q: *When I was young I was very idealistic and had great hopes for my life, but as I got older, I became somewhat bitter. Do you think this is common for Wanderers and what can I do about it?*

A: Personally, I have felt quite a lot of bitterness myself, and many Wanderers who are serious about helping the world and who understand the status quo/power elite (which maintains injustice, deception, and deceit) have also become quite cynical. Sometimes they are downright hostile towards the world and even humanity as a whole; at the extreme end, it can become toxic and even lead to sociopathic tendencies. Every once in a while I encounter rage and human-hatred in my sharing with Wanderers. I imagine that once upon a time, all these angry souls were sweet children, sincere helpers, idealistic servers—yet today they have become totally spun around.

This type of reversal, well understood by the English Poet William Blake (who sang of three phases of Life: *Innocence, Experience, and Higher Innocence*), is a process of getting weighed down with world-weariness. The soul begins fresh, pure, simple, appreciating life and naturally being kind. Then over the centuries through multiple lives, the soul encounters harsh society, competitive and striving, still operating under tribal law—dog eat dog, look out for number one, nice guys finish last, etc., etc. Incoming Wanderers, or any young soul for that matter, may react quite strongly to the general lack of love and compassion, the sharp sense of separation, and the mass denials taken for granted here. It is easy to become bitter, and easy to lose hope.

Starting from a mind of great innocence, human dysfunctional patterns are internalized, and are then interpreted as a sign of a damaged self, or felt as loss and insufficiency, or proof of our being unloved, unworthy, abandoned. Herein lie the seeds of future-life karmic liabilities. To make matters worse, these feelings are rarely identified by the conscious mind, and they usually remain unexpressed for fear of making things even worse with our human peers. The soul, beginning its cycle of human incarnations, thus becomes wounded, crippled, and doesn't even know it. Future lifetime programming would then be needed for healing and rebalancing the core sense of self.

How can we overcome the mantle of 3D Earth-human sorrow? Well, there is general advice applicable to all, and there is guidance specific to Wanderers. Considering what's applicable to all, we must understand that spiritual evolution is self-generated. We must pull ourselves out of despair. For all of us, native or resident-alien, the ultimate healer is always Self, which is the basic source of self-acceptance, forgiveness, understanding and strength.

Often, bitterness is the fruit of old pain compounded by isolation, and healing can come through opening up to trusted friends and loved ones. When we learn to embrace all aspects of our experience with unconditional acceptance, then we can better handle the slings and arrows of life on Earth. While the healing process begins and continues from within, it is greatly supported by friends and partners. As it proceeds, greater self-alignment and self-sufficiency grow, along with a greater ability to make peace with the world—which really means making peace with our own pain. Yes, it can be done. I know my own experience, and I know the experience of many other Wanderers.

Additionally, there is also solace in seeing the big picture—considering our previous history before coming to Earth, and our future course after leaving. Our life is far greater than all we know each day, and not only do we have cosmic family waiting in the wings, but we are also thoroughly loved, known, and accepted by countless souls in spirit. It is not necessary to live out our days here in misery, pining away and waiting for salvation. It is far better to make the most of this life, which is an opportunity for accelerated growth. Wanderers and all who are seekers should never forget the tremendous power we have within us to improve the quality of our lives, wherever we happen to be.

PART B:

HUMANITY AND THE GLOBAL PROCESS

» Chapter 13 «

New Age or Apocalypse?

Can we be so blind as to imagine that centuries of global warfare, strife and conflict have no lasting effect on the life of Earth itself?

I OFTEN THINK about the future. In fact, I probably think about it every day. I have no doubt this is a special time in history, a turning point, a time when multiple forces are converging, clashing, and coming to fruition. It is a time of great individual confusion and soul-searching, together with a growing sense of global community. Of course, sectarian divisions of all kinds are also raging, and many people feel their personal liberty under attack. As humanity senses our greater solidarity, we can also feel ourselves splitting apart at the seams. It is a time of sharpening polarity.

But this brief social review does not tell the whole story. There is also a prophetic undertone to the present time Perhaps the loudest of the prophets crying in the wilderness are the those of various New Age persuasions sharing their dreams of imminent Utopia, and the more pragmatic scientists and futurists who predict social implosion and environmental chaos. And Christian fundamentalists, warning of fast approaching *Apocalypse* and the false Messiah, are right by their side. So you might ask, what will it be? A leap into Paradise or collapse into Chaos?

As I see it, the end of this century and the beginning of the next will treat us to both: an unprecedented, rapid decay of current civilization followed by an equally stupendous rebirth, with long-term implications beyond our wildest dreams. Ultimately, I also expect wondrous things for Earth and her people, but before that happens, a profound *Dark Night of the Soul* will shake humanity to its roots. In the language of Wall Street, I think we can look forward to some major corrections on many levels—personal, collective, and metaphysical.

While alarming for some, this kind of shakedown may not be such a bad thing after all. Without going into an extended social critique, I can only say that such crisis is not accidental; given human consciousness and our history of strife, it is unavoidable. Stated simply:

Humanity on Earth is fully responsible for the misery on Earth, and the root causes of disharmony and confusion must be "worked out" in the body and soul of the planet.

Actually, these are not New Age ideas at all. They come straight from Buddhist and Hindu teachings on the Law of Karma. According to this view, all things are causally conditioned, so what happens today is due to previous causes, and present actions sow seeds for the future. If catastrophic Earth Changes devastate the planet, it will be no accident. There will be real, identifiable causes. Can we be so blind as to imagine that centuries of warfare, strife and conflict have no lasting effect on the life of Earth itself?

Current science is not equipped to calculate the subtle, cumulative effects of combative human consciousness on the environment. Our science, military, and industrial complexes will certainly deny responsibility for geological upheaval, and turn a blind eye to the long-term effects of dam building, oil drilling, strip mining, nuclear testing, deforestation, industrial emissions, chemical pollution, and so on and on. Unfortunately, not many people in positions of worldly power appreciate their responsibility for maintaining our world as a healthy, happy home. And why not? Simply because they are usually souls on the negative path of self-service, and "kindness to Earth" doesn't weigh into their considerations.

However, the real point I am making is not to assign blame, but rather to raise the issue of how we view such upheaval. In the stock markets, crash equals correction, not catastrophe, because it restores sanity to a grossly imbalanced, inflated market. A similar kind of imbalance and inflation describes our materialistic, image-obsessed, competitive human civilization very well, and our assessment of its worth is also unrealistically overvalued. This is not to deny the valuable technological advance of so many fields; without doubt, there have been many improvements over the centuries. But if we take a close look at the money-based culture which we all take for granted, which most people simply assume is "just the way it is," we see that it has come to captivate our lives. The subtle, trickle-down effects of world consumer-culture are far more destructive than most of us imagine. They are directly related to high divorce and suicide rates, mass neurosis, terrorism and ethnic unrest everywhere. It is not entirely wrong to say "money is the root of all evil."

One does not have to be a fortune-teller to know that the next 15 years will be full of upheaval. For our own peace of mind as well as Earth's destiny, it is essential to ponder the meaning of these changes, both before and during their occurrence.

In this second part of Section I, we will expand our focus to explore various dynamics essential to the present time on Earth. Taking a spiritual perspective, we will look deeper at the UFO issue and how it relates to human destiny, and draw a portrait of global society on the edge of spectacular change.

» *Chapter 14* «

SURVIVAL AND THE EARTH CHANGES

As usual, it's up to each of us to set priorities, which will ultimately depend on the quality of our thinking, the intensity of our commitment to serve, and our ability to walk in balance.

After many of my lectures, I am asked about upcoming Earth Changes. People want to know what will happen, where it will happen, and of course, what we should do about it all. While I am in no way a prophet along the lines of those who make predictions, I could be considered one in the old Greek sense of the word, in which "prophet" is defined as "one who speaks out." I certainly have my own ideas about the future, as we all do, but I prefer not to dwell much on this kind of speculation. While I do think it is important to consider what may be ahead, it is essential to put this whole matter in perspective. Regardless of what happens, our path of learning continues.

I must say, however, I was not always so calm about Earth Changes, and for me, it has been a process of getting a general outline of basic prophecies, considering my personal role and function during the tumult when and if it occurs, and then putting the predictions and my own reactions into clear perspective. This kind of balancing usually leads us to ask "What should I do?," which is the first step in starting to face our priorities.

I used to frame this issue in quite narrow terms (i.e. being selfish or selfless), which led to a dichotomy between "saving your skin or serving the world." Today, however, I don't think our personal survival decisions have to be an either/or choice, since many good-hearted people will choose a middle way—voluntary withdrawal to so-called safe spots, remaining with friends and colleagues, and continuing their work (which, for most of us, will involve some form of service). Regardless of the particular changes that do occur, such as geological and social upheaval, there will be a growth of spiritual communities of like-minded people. Actually, this gathering is already underway, and I know more than a few people who have moved from cities to remote areas. I am sure this will accelerate in the next five to ten years.

I must confess, though, that I was quite shocked when first reading *The Law of One* in the late 1980s and coming upon their response to a pointed question about "the coming planetary changes." RA answered in no uncertain terms:

> "The [Earth] changes are very, very trivial. We do not concern ourselves with the conditions which bring about harvest."[1]

Well, that is certainly easy to say if you are sitting in the safety of higher dimensions! However, RA's comment does reveal an important perspective, a view probably shared by other elder ET groups whose main purpose is to support human evolution. In their opinion, earthquakes, floods, and tornadoes are simply additional catalyst which may or may not be used to develop greater awareness, as we continue our endless journey on the path of soul-evolution, continually refining love, wisdom, and the realization of One with All That Is. RA considers Earth changes to simply be the outer conditions associated with Earth's transformation, just a by-product of millennia of human disharmony. They consider such changes somewhat inevitable on our 3D world as we move through global graduation to what they call fourth density—a dimension characterized by selfless love and compassion. To souls who live to serve and grow, global upheaval is just part of the landscape. Really, no big deal.

In 1981, when asked exactly where Earth is in its movement into the new cycle, RA spoke from the perspective of Earth itself as it struggles to accommodate new cosmic energies, while still straining beneath a dysfunctional, destructive civilization:

> "This sphere [Earth] is at this time in fourth-dimension vibration. Its material is quite confused due to the society

---

1. Elkins, op cit., Vol. I, p. 67.

memory complexes [societies] embedded in its consciousness. It has not made an easy transition to the vibrations which beckon. Therefore, it shall be fetched with some inconvenience."[2]

Interestingly, they note that Earth is already in its new vibration, which some people can even now feel through an intuitive sense of "greater light." Yet, these massive inconveniences will affect all of us—Earth, humanity, and the many spiritual beings here to assist the birth of a new world. How can we consider them just trivial? Why does RA treat them so lightly?

Well, the answer is a little subtle. From the perspective of those who shepherd Earth's transformation (which happens to be the main galactic event attracting so many extraterrestrial races), geological upheaval is like Gaia's labor pains: not ultimately necessary, but inevitable in this particular family. ET elders understand that their greatest service to humanity is not rendered by focusing on the pain (nor by giving specific predictions), but rather, by alleviating it as much as possible. This they have chosen to do through continual spiritual encouragement, and a wise emphasis on the principles of personal transformation and soul-evolution. In other words, ageless wisdom.

Earth changes are considered simply a consequence, a result of cumulative human disharmony over the ages that continues to take its toll on the body of our planet. Likewise, the severity of upheaval depends entirely on the intensity of the cause. Since the quality of human consciousness is the primary cause, so too is human consciousness the solution. Therefore, the more love and light we generate, the less intense these inconveniences will be.

And so, we come to a deeper understanding of the work of Wanderers. Their presence is intended to bring love/light which adds needed energy to Earth's transformation, lessening the severity of geological disaster. Their contribution is made, to some extent, whether or not the Starseed awakens to his or her own cosmic origin—although service is usually far more effective when they do pierce the veil

---

2. Ibid., p. 93.

of forgetting, since this increases self-understanding. Realizing one's ET identity is not ultimate, but it is an important step in the right direction. For those who have been asleep to their own cosmic roots, it represents a greater appreciation of truth, and esoterically, a potentially greater radiation of light. Of course, such light can also be offered by anyone who lives from the heart and walks in kindness and balance.

But again, from our perspective, can we reasonably tell someone who has just lost their home in an earthquake that their upheaval is merely trivial, simply the result of centuries of human psychic disharmony? This kind of response would seem to be the height of spiritual arrogance and insensitivity. How can you tell parents whose family possessions were carried off by floods that it is simply a matter of "additional catalyst for your increased polarity on the path of service to others?"

Clearly, we have to make adjustment to the realities of time and space, and to the perspective and needs of those who do not perceive the spiritual dimensions of planetary change. All upheaval generates pain, and the work of those who serve is to comfort and support those in pain. Being sensitive to sorrow, we cannot minimize others' emotional loss; in many cases, it is entirely inappropriate to share our version of the deeper metaphysics at hand, at least at that time.

I have no doubt there will be Earth changes continuing unabated for the next 10 years, until the end of the cycle around 2010–2013 A.D. I do not know exactly what changes will occur, though I tend to agree with the general predictions offered by current and ancient prophecy (you can check the books by Sun Bear, Gordon-Michael Scallion, and Delores Cannon for details). In the years ahead, we will probably need to make many tough choices, and our sensitivity to inner guidance will be essential. Without a doubt, there were lightworkers in the Biblical city of Sodom, in the chaos of towns quivering in the last throes of Atlantis, in Hiroshima, Nagasaki, and the Warsaw ghetto. We cannot assume their presence there was a mistake.

For myself, I have become much clearer about my priorities, which means doing my work till the end, wherever and whenever that may be. As always, it is up to each of us to set priorities (whether we are a Wanderer or not), which will ultimately depend on the quality of our thinking, the intensity of our commitment to serve, and our ability to walk in balance. While love counsels self-sacrifice, clear wisdom does reject untimely martyrdom. There will be countless opportunities for service, learning, and intensified personal growth in the next 10 years, and while I would not exactly say Earth changes are trivial, they are simply the physical consequence of metaphysical causes in human history. Whatever they will be will be. ***Our work remains the same***.

As all crisis brings challenge, these crises will provide a clear challenge to our values, and the best preparation we can make is internal—knowing our values and why we are living here on Earth. In the Buddha's original teaching of the Noble Eight-fold Path, "Right View" was considered a central factor: in the next decade, a balanced view of global events and the right use of catalyst will be a key to our growth.

In the next chapter we will see how the UFO-research community is meeting some of these issues, especially the question of ET presence.

» *Chapter 15* «

THE GULF BREEZE CONFERENCE

A FEW YEARS AGO, I spoke at the annual *Gulf Breeze UFO Conference,* one of the largest East Coast meetings. Normally, I'm not invited to such groups, since the main speakers are usually ex-military, hard-evidence UFO "experts" who lead the charge for government disclosure, abduction researchers and experiencers, and a potpourri of saucer videos, hypnotic regression tales, and cases of direct contact. You will almost never find ET channels at these conferences, and no discussion of Walk-ins, Wanderers, or ET family. Although cosmic matters are their bread-and-butter, these gatherings are usually quite low on serious metaphysics.

Unfortunately, most so-called UFO experts have little understanding and even less appreciation of spiritual principle, so they cannot see cosmic contact from the perspective of soul-evolution. Proceeding from a rational-materialist bias, their trail goes round and round, and the major topics discussed at UFO conferences today are about the same as they were ten years ago.

And so, if I am not invited to speak, I rarely attend such meetings. While it is interesting to hear about the latest cover-up, secret evil project, or doom-and-gloom prediction, it is not worth sitting through all the excess wondering. Frankly, it is painful for me to watch them flailing about—the confusion between positive/negative ET agendas; the childish hope that humanity will "wake up" when human leaders are forced to reveal hidden UFO data, and the near-total lack of spiritual focus. There is generally no understanding of path, meditation, and the glory of real cosmic design.

However, what is really hard for me at these conferences is the complete reversal of what the UFO/ET contact phenomenon is all about: spiritual assistance to humanity and the importance of love.

For better or worse, you will find more talk of love and compassion among your typical Sunday churchgoers than among most veteran UFO researchers.

Nevertheless, when I was asked to speak at this conference, I immediately accepted. If they wanted me, then maybe they are more open than I thought. Actually, since I had been recommended to the main organizer Vicky Lyons by Michael Lindemann, a respected UFO researcher and friend, I came in on a red carpet. As the I Ching or ancient Chinese divination book says, I was "a weak line in a strong place" (a relative unknown among big-name researchers), but surprisingly, I became the featured attraction at the conference.

Vicky Lyons appreciated my approach so much that she kept me in the spotlight, letting me give lead-off presenters both Friday and Saturday mornings, and having me moderate the speaker panel on the last night. Everything was arranged (with a little help from upstairs, I assume) to give me maximum exposure to present the spiritual purpose and value of the UFO presence on Earth. Perhaps the time was right for some deeper information on cosmic purpose.

Since mine was the first lecture on the first day, the hall was packed with nearly 500 people. And though they had to pay extra, about 350 people came to my workshop—more than I had ever had before. I was quite surprised, but as I learned later, many people appreciated my presentation, and dozens came up to thank me later in the weekend. *They really got it.*

As for the other presenters, they really *did not* get it, which was not much of a surprise. Representing the abduction issue, there were Budd Hopkins and Prof. David Jacobs, both of whom certainly have no sugary illusions about the visitors. On the contrary, they painted a dire picture of ruthless alien intent, mind-control abuse, hybrid agendas and approaching world conquest. Understandably, they consider negative ETs unstoppable, they have no idea of spiritual protection, and have naught to say about benevolent ET groups. Though both of these researchers are sincere and do care about those they are treating, because they do not have much interest in divine power or Higher Self, they have only got half the picture—the dark half. And in the shadows, as usual, nothing is clearly seen...

Also in shadows, with apparent good intent, there was Linda Moulton Howe. A well-known author and film producer, she is quite famous in the UFO-research community, and has had a regular place on *The Art Bell Show*. She did her initial work on the cattle mutilation phenomenon, and has expanded out from there. Today, she is deep in the black world of covert projects and shadowy government agents who sometimes support her work. They give her tidbits on underground bases, secret groups, high-tech weapons, and the great mighty power of ETs (who had evidence, it was claimed, of having genetically mastered our race). Sound like negative-source disinformation to you? Of course, Ms. Howe eagerly relayed these secret bits of information, and did not seem to worry about the possibility that she was being led astray by some of her contacts. She truly believes her material is essential, since it (presumably) helps us understand covert government complicity. Unfortunately, it does little to help us understand ourselves.

Her oversight came into focus, for me, as she continued the presentation. She showed us dozens of photos of recent U.K. crop circles, the latest batch which is no less than holy, and after that, proceeded to report a new abduction case in all its gory details. She then suggested that both forms of ET contact may well come from the same source! This struck me like a hammer as the summit of nondiscernment, complete blindness to vastly different forms of influence. To equate crop circles with abduction, not recognizing the enormous difference in consciousness between them (sacred cosmic geometry, on the one hand, vs. traumatic scarring soul-abuse, on the other), was simply amazing to me. I was really shocked.

That a famous UFO researcher could entertain this notion, continue to sell books and be invited to conferences all around the world, makes me want to go back to the monastery. No wonder so many people are confused, when those at the top have so little discernment. I understand why the Buddha's first thought upon realizing enlightenment was that no one would understand him if he opened his mouth. I guess appreciation for subtle spiritual truth has always been rare.

But Linda Howe, Dr. David Jacobs, and Budd Hopkins were not alone, as I found out during the speaker panel. Billed as a dialogue on alien agendas, "The Question of Good and Evil," I had hoped in my capacity as moderator to tease out "expert opinions" and provoke lively debate. On the contrary, almost none of the speakers had any conclusions, and when it came time for audience *Q & A*, not a single person even addressed the issue of polarity! They simply asked individual speakers about their own individual work. It was no group event at all.

Interestingly, a favorite speaker analogy used to support their non-position on cosmic polarity was to compare ET-human relations with our treatment of animals. It goes something like this:

> "Cows may think we're evil, but we eat them just to stay alive; we don't hate them. Arctic seals may be terrorized, but we're just tagging them to track global pollution. Beasts may call us Satanic, but they're just ignorant. It's all for their own good…"

And so goes one expert opinion on abducting ET motives.

Of course, the analogy is far off base, since there is a major difference in consciousness between humans and animals. As self-conscious souls, we are absolutely equal, in our essence, to any and all ET groups. But since many UFO researchers have little soul awareness and little interest in the metaphysics of cosmic law, the fine points of universal morality, human free will, and spiritually polarized agendas are lost on them.

Indeed, without soul awareness humans **are** just like animals, and metaphysically, this is exactly the true point of difference between these two kingdoms. In fact, it is just this distinction that negative ETs hope to blur. Indeed, RA noted point blank that true abduction is:

"...a means of terrifying the individual and causing it to feel the feelings of an advanced second-density being such as a laboratory animal..." [1]

Unfortunately, as the "UFO experts" equate the human treatment of animals with the rough handling of abductees by abusive aliens, it supports this very same negative ET agenda! In making people feel like animals, obviously, those aliens have been somewhat successful.

So while much of the audience appreciated the light I was shining, most of the speakers on-stage, frankly, could not see it (or so it seemed)—and they are supposed to be the experts. All in all, however, I considered the conference a great success and I was very pleased to have been invited. It was really nice to see that most people had a pure desire to learn, and their seeking was truly spiritual. I can only hope that this continues and grows in the UFO research community—making the union of material evidence and careful metaphysics. Only through such integration can we truly understand the uniqueness of the present time.

In the next chapter, we will revisit the somewhat sad story of the *Heaven's Gate* group, another case of grossly mistaken metaphysics.

---

1. Elkins, op cit., Vol. I, p. 224.

» *Chapter 16* «

A MISTAKEN GATE

I WAS IN TOKYO, JAPAN at another UFO Conference when the news hit about *Heaven's Gate* and their spring 1997 mass-suicide in San Diego. If you are like most people I know, initially you were shocked and confused, and maybe a bit scared, fearing an ugly aftermath in U.S. society for all of us who care about UFO/ET matters. Perhaps by now you've forgotten all this, or perhaps you're sick and tired of hearing about Heaven's Gate and their tangled teachings—yet, the whole event, and the media circus surrounding it, is too important for us to pass up. In this chapter we will focus on this particular drama, played out by some quite sincere players, special men and women who aspired to go "Beyond Human"... answering what they truly considered "The Last Call" (their terms).

Although the Japanese newspapers gave full-page coverage to the suicide and its background, I did not realize its magnitude until I returned to San Francisco. On my answering machine were impassioned calls from ABC News and writers from *Newsweek, Washington Post* and a Boise, ID newspaper, plus calls from friends and colleagues around the U.S. curious to chat about what happened. At the beginning, I had little to say, since I considered all of this just typical cult behavior, comparable to the other mass-suicide we all know—the Jonestown, Guyana deaths, and the Jim Jones group. The actions of Heaven's Gate seemed to be the result of confused psychology and blurry metaphysics. However, after reading some of their material and thinking more about it, I realize there is much more to say about this group, and about the particular gate that they chose.

Interestingly, a colleague and close friend of mine in San Francisco almost joined the group a few years ago, and he knew some of those who died. You may ask, what kind of person is he? Is he just a typical cult-follower, disempowered and desperate for meaning, confused and longing for escape? Is he personally weak and easily duped? Actually, understanding his motives is not that easy. If we take a closer look at "the friend who almost joined up," we can learn more about the magnetic pull exerted by the group, and why their suicide had such a strong effect on Wanderers and spiritually-minded people all around the world. We may also learn something about ourselves.

Like those who died in San Diego, my friend also longs for "a level above human" and realizes the limitations of human society and the physical realm. Like spiritual seekers everywhere, he values self-purification and acknowledges an apparent cosmic struggle between good and evil, darkness and light, confusion and ignorance. He has been deeply involved in metaphysics and meditation for many years, studying and pondering UFO issues and ET contact. He has read *The RA Material* quite well, and today he realizes that he is a Wanderer. He is certainly no beginner on the path, and you can even read his personal story in Section III, Chapter 2, entitled "Moments of Higher Awareness."

With all his apparent maturity in spiritual matters, how could he be lured by Heaven's Gate? Why did he nearly surrender autonomy to follow their rigid way? Of course, the answers are unique to his own life-path and personality, and derive from a deep sense of alienation and aimlessness, but there is more here than just psychology. As the group itself proclaimed, they offered a gate to freedom, and although to many it was clearly a mistaken gate, the human thirst for salvation is so strong, and the urgency of the present time on Earth so severe, that their appeal bypassed logic and the intellect. Our longing for heaven springs from the deepest levels of Self, indeed from the core of Self, its very Will-to-Be. It is no exaggeration to say that the search for freedom and a gateway to "heaven" (however defined) is a primary motivation in human life.

I cannot stress enough the power of such "liberation theology." The soul itself longs to be expressed, to shine in fullness through personality into matter. Our deeply-based need for freedom, our longing for individualized versions of Heaven, reflects no less than the soul's demand for its own Self-discovery, which is the purpose of its very existence and the cosmic plan. It is for this reason that the work of evolution is sometimes called the path of return.

So why do I say that theirs was "a mistaken gate?" The answer can be found in the shock felt by most of us upon seeing their grisly death, viewing TV images of 39 bodies neatly laid out with purple cloth atop their heads. What a waste, I thought. Simply put, suicide is not a path to heaven. Despite their creative mix of apocalyptic Christianity, body-denying asceticism and naive UFO-adoration, they missed the mark. Killing the body does not open the gates to Heaven. While many Wanderers and seekers might agree with portions of their metaphysics (such as the existence of non-physical realms and the value of personal discipline), their rigid lifestyle was simply unbalanced.

After reading some of their works, however, I do have a better picture of why they did what they did. For openers, they were basically Christians who operated out of quite ordinary Judeo-Christian beliefs. In their writings (one of which is entitled "Beyond Human: Session 1" and was posted on several internet sites) their bias is clear. They write, in part:

The Bible was the only authentic record we have of the Kingdom of God's relationship with man...

Jesus came in as an opportunity to restore man to God in a relationship that was pleasing to God...

Satan's primary effort was to give misinformation to humans.

As Christians, they are also locked into dualistic thinking: God or Man, Jesus vs. Satan, sin or salvation, Heaven vs. Earth. So their approach to liberation and enlightenment was also dualistic. If their members could only "drop all the behavior that was not common to the Kingdom of Heaven," they imagined its gates would swing wide open. They rejected desires of the flesh since they assumed, rightly, that we do not use such physical bodies in the level above human.

Of course, cosmic duality is common to many mystic traditions, and asceticism is often considered a path to salvation. But in the Eastern religious systems that, at least to me, seem most highly developed (such as Buddhism, Hindu Vedanta, and Chinese Taoism), there is a much more subtle understanding layered in. They realize that the quality of our experience is determined by our perception, and so salvation depends on your state of consciousness. Practices of body-denial may or may not, in and of themselves, effect the required change of awareness.

In these traditions, (1) the rigid line between material and spiritual worlds is considered to be an illusion; (2) our sense of suffering and separate-self is held to derive from ignorance and limited perception; and (3) the keys to Heaven are found through the self-generated transformation of consciousness. To the mystic, the path of return does *not* mean physically returning to a particular place (and certainly *not* jumping aboard some comet-veiled UFO craft!), but rather returning to a state of being which is, in reality, our true nature. Buddhists call this "state" *nirvana* (literally, "blowing out" or extinguishing the flame of craving and becoming), Hindus call it *sat-chit-ananda* ("being-consciousness-bliss"), while metaphysical folks call it "Higher Self." Whatever the name, it represents a state of conscious unity with All That Is. You cannot get a better Heaven than that!

This teaching is one of the priceless gems given by Oriental religion, still largely unappreciated in the West. It is the notion that freedom is earned by developing awareness, not by dogmas, creeds, amulets, or good deeds, ascetic or otherwise. Going further, the foundation of this teaching is an even greater jewel—an understanding that human nature is infinite, and that the Absolute Creator and the True Self are, in fact, One Being. These ideas come from millennia of personal insight gained by yogis and seekers in meditation, and can be attained in practical realization by anyone, if you take the time and make enough right effort.

While they held some very ordinary Judeo-Christian beliefs, Heaven's Gate also considered UFOs to be "spacecraft from the Kingdom of Heaven"—a notion which is far more accurate than it appears. All students of fourth density esoteric history know that human-ET contact in previous ages was placed in a religious/mythic framework, and that many ET groups from fourth density do come to Earth in spacecraft. This higher density just so happens to be "the level above human"—which, according to *The RA Material*, was indeed the home density of Jesus, the Wanderer. Right on the mark, Heaven's Gate also claimed that Jesus was an ET from this level. However, they were led astray by their naive, childish trust in all the internet postings that claimed that the comet Hale-Bopp had a hidden UFO-twin. For a bit of perspective, we should not overlook the fact that all such frenzied UFO talk is almost totally forgotten today. Beware of sensational claims!

The Heaven's Gate group believed that the craft, flying shrouded in Hale-Bopp's tail, would whisk them to the next level. In their one-dimensional Christo-cosmic view, they seemed to imagine that "since all UFOs are from the next level, then they must be available to take us back there." This notion seems unbelievably naive, and is like abandoned children longing for long-lost parents to come rescue them. It seems also to be a variation on the theme promoted by Sheldon Nidle and his Operation Victory group, who made grand predictions for benevolent ET mass landings in late 1996 (stemming from Mr. Nidle's popular book, *You are Becoming a Galactic Human*). I have heard that they continue to make such predictions, although previous ones have fallen flat and the core group has splintered. To me, this is just another example of confused psychology mixed up with blurry metaphysics.

Obviously, what happened to Heaven's Gate is not an isolated event, and I think we can expect more claims, cults, sensations, and media frenzy in the future. As Harvest approaches, the 3D cycle unwinds, and Earth Changes heat up, I will not be surprised if the collective mass psyche spins out in a multitude of directions. Yet, we will be just fine if we keep centered.

The members of Heaven's Gate, wherever they are now and many of whom were likely Wanderers, certainly deserve our sympathy and love, not scorn or contempt. They sought the eternal goal, just as all we do, the only problem being that they chose a mistaken gate. Their legacy should be a reminder to all of us about the importance of having discernment, personal balance, and essential self-trust.

In the next chapter we will take aim at their main detractors—the hungry-buzzard media, which seems to relish disaster and tragedy (just check out the latest headlines). We should have no illusions. Far from being messengers of truth, mass media is instead the prime source of both sensationalism and disinformation surrounding the UFO/ET matter—and unfortunately, they are the main force shaping public opinion.

» *Chapter 17* «

WHY ARE THEY LAUGHING?

...the real answer is that most people are not seeking truth and really don't care about a wider vision of the universe...

IN TERMS OF SHARING IDEAS about cosmic life, things were tough even before Heaven's Gate. During the promotion for my first book, I took quite a lot of hits. After about the 20th radio interview in which I was attacked, ridiculed, and considered something of a freak, a puzzling question arose in my mind. I was truly confounded, and I asked myself a simple question:

Why are they laughing?

I certainly never expected red carpet treatment, and I was fully prepared for skeptics questioning the basis of my conclusions. Talking about people who say they're from other worlds is not easy in any setting. But I didn't expect to be taken as the butt of adolescent humor ("Do they have prozac on your planet?"), direct attack ("Do you also consider yourself a moron?"), or beer-belly indifference ("Come on Jack, let's get back to the music!"). For many radio talk show interviewers, my own sense of ET origins was the main fascination, and they couldn't stop calling me "alien." Furthermore, they often forget I had written a book! Perhaps only 25% of the hosts even questioned me about my research at all, and I did over 70 interviews! In the face of such ignorance and mishandling, I have much greater appreciation for all the kind Wanderers I have met who feel severe alienation, day in and out.

After all the assault, the question still remained in my mind: *Why are they laughing?* I am quite familiar with standard psychological interpretations, which consider mockery and scorn to be fear-driven defenses against feelings and ideas that a person feels to be threatening. But this explanation didn't go deep enough, and my questioning still could not rest. The idea then struck me that humanity has always rejected and even tried to destroy those who present ideas contrary to the prevailing dogmas. Didn't they burn the early (and genius) astronomers who claimed that Earth orbits the Sun? One of the greatest pioneers of modern times, Albert Einstein, once said something to the effect that "great minds have always encountered violent opposition from mediocre minds." Should we assume that mediocre minds control the U.S. media, or is this already obvious?

I am sure most people would be satisfied with this kind of psycho-sociological interpretation, since it does make sense and does explain a lot. However, I still felt the need to take my question further, since I had an inkling there was something more going on here. I also knew that this is a kind of mental-spiritual practice—using a question, like a spearhead, to penetrate deeper and deeper levels of meaning. This process is not unlike the Zen Buddhist use of the *ko-an* (literally, a "word-head," from Chinese), which takes awareness down to the roots of mind. Deeper meaning is often covered by what appears to be merely obvious. Sometimes we can learn a lot by holding tight to our questions.

First of all, how can we explain a civilization that crucifies a soul (Jesus) who, for all intents and purposes, gave his entire life to convey a message of love, brotherhood, and justice? How can we understand an entire planet that arms itself to the teeth, then cries over global warfare and terrorism? What do we think of a society eager to spend billions of dollars on fantasy sci-fi entertainment, which then heaves blame on those who say they have made contact with cosmic life? As Jodie Foster said in the movie *Contact*, "when you talk to God it is called prayer, but when God talks to you then you're considered *crazy*." Realizing human short-sightedness and hypocrisy, we could certainly say they are quite confused. With so many mistakes being repeated, I would also say humanity does not learn much from its own experience.

Is it any surprise that benevolent ETs do not do public landings to announce themselves and offer unconditional aid? Is it any surprise the New Age community (and not just in the U.S.) is pock-marked with ego-based, unqualified leaders and gullible disempowered followers? Is it any surprise so few people truly understand the use of discernment? Without clearly understanding our values as a planetary race (beginning with the issue of good and evil, or rather, love vs. control), we will never be able to forge a unified direction for humanity. Remaining addicted to fantasy and escape, one may never find "the Real."

So *why* are they laughing? Perhaps the whole idea of non-human life actually terrifies them, since all they know is only what they have been taught in school and church, by science and mass-media. If these were my only teachers, I would be laughing at Walk-ins, Wanderers, and UFO seekers, too. It is a sorry state, indeed, to live in a society with leaders devoid of cosmic vision, devoid of spiritual sincerity. But sorry or not, most people truly do look to their political and cultural institutions for leadership—and if you think this is somewhat pitiful, you are in agreement with most Wanderers. While Earth human institutions do offer some ideas of value, their vision of universal life, however, is blurry to the point of being legally blind. In matters of spirit and eternity, we have to look elsewhere for guidance.

In my attempt to share spiritual concepts, I often encounter the corrosive influence of certain Judeo-Christian dogmas, which control many people subconsciously. First of all, these systems place the Divine far outside "the little shell of sinful man," and "He" can only be met through an "intercessor"—the hierarchy of churchmen or the congregation itself. Following such a policy, eternal salvation can only be achieved by following the rules of your local social club, a select group that holds the keys to heaven and hell. What about the power of Self? According to some of these systems, it is hubris to witness Glory Within. Not surprisingly, it is much more difficult to contact soul, to align with Higher Self while holding such disempowered, withering notions.

And what if you doubt the sanctity of such dogma? Well, the usual prescription is that "you need more Bible study." The antidote for doubt is more indoctrination. How often do you hear counsel to turn within and find your own truth? In strict fundamentalism (which I acknowledge represents only a portion of Christian faith), there is not a glimmer that Self is the greatest teacher, and that boundless freedom may come from inner work and needs no mediator. Indeed, there is no idea of Higher Self at all—and therein lies the great neglect of Judeo-Christian theology.

Some would say that fundamentalists are few, that most Christians are non-dogmatic, and that most other people are either atheists or non-believers. It may be so, but common religious concepts condition everyone in their own home culture. Even those who claim to follow so-called "objective authorities" (i.e. modern science), usually believe that death is the big drop-off, that physical 3D is the whole ball of wax. If I held such a soul-less view, I, too, would laugh at the silly people who claim to be ETs! "Why should we take it on faith? Science hasn't confirmed it!"

Again, the need for proof is fine, but why are they *laughing*, instead of just asking questions? I think the final answer, which lightworkers and spiritual seekers may find disturbing, is that most people in this society are not seeking higher truth and couldn't care less about a wider vision of the universe. Which brings us back to the difference between "normal people" and those who say they are ET souls (and all of us who seek to learn and serve): *"normal people" are not seeking!* Most people on Earth are content to live their lives according to the status quo—finding material, personal pleasures where they can, dull to the spark of aspiration that could reveal greater life-meaning. This kind of aspiration, a yearning for personal transformation, is the dividing line between those who have chosen the positive spiritual path (becoming, as RA would say, "polarized in service to others") from those who have yet to make a choice. Since most Earth people are spiritually unpolarized (not making efforts towards either virtue or vice), most of them are likely to laugh at extraterrestrial and cosmic notions.

By now, I have become accustomed to radio talk show hosts who mock, argue, and laugh. I always knew that trying to debate was useless, but now I know some people consider these ideas on par with the comedy club. So be it. All souls awaken to life's mysteries—some quickly, most slowly (at least, here on Earth!). It will always be that only those with eyes to see can know the path of Life.

Although the current mass media has generally replaced truth-telling and fact-finding with crass entertainment, some things are getting better. It is more difficult for people to scoff at all matters of the paranormal (partly as a result of so many sensationalizing TV shows), and public curiosity is ever increasing, or so it seems. For those of you who want to help the natives of this world (and not simply hang out with the other spiritual folks), it is not a bad idea to grow some thicker skin. You will certainly need it, if you want to speak the truth.

In the next chapter, we will jump from the commentary back to the action, and take a look at an important high-profile UFO sighting and its many implications.

» *Chapter 18* «

A UFO in Phoenix

I MUST CONFESS I never saw the photos, nor did I watch Dan Rather on network TV telling us all about this amazing event. My experience with the 1997 UFO sighting near Phoenix, AZ only came second-hand—from people living nearby, from others in the area "by accident," and from still others around the country who caught the TV coverage. Like most people who are concerned with spiritual growth and helping others (in my case, through meditation, teaching and study), I am usually not too interested in sensational events. But with this particular UFO sighting, I think it is important to consider some of the implications.

First of all, the public response (ranging from indifference to fear to outrage at the cover-up) was not surprising, nor was the official level of non-response. The governor of Arizona even suited up one of his assistants in alien garb to draw laughs at a news conference. The location of the sighting (right in the middle of what I and many UFO researchers consider "secret-alien-base land") was no shock, nor was the fact that it hung around (to be seen, apparently) for over an hour. Despite all this, if we analyze the whole event in relation to the long-suspected official alien-disclosure plan, this was not an insignificant event. If we are interested in getting a better sense of what is coming down the line in the next five years, we can learn a lot from this UFO in Phoenix.

Dr. Richard Boylan, a psychologist and UFO researcher, has made many predictions over the years regarding the imminent official disclosure of ET information. Unfortunately, but not surprisingly, few of these have come true. So much for timetables these days. They are nearly always wrong, which is also the case with predictions of Earth

Changes and UFO mass-landings. The vast majority of these claims, sadly, serve only to discredit the claimant.

Nevertheless, we do see geological upheaval brewing, and there do continue to be UFO sightings, isolated landings and direct contacts around the world. The moral to the story here is somewhat subtle: even a misled messenger may bear some of the truth, and the reality of an overall trend cannot be dismissed by apparent setbacks and mistaken details. Although Dr. Boylan's dates have been wrong, I do think there has been and continues to be a public conditioning program in regard to UFOs and ET life. I agree that some form of disclosure does lie ahead.

If we consent with the general theory that a deliberate UFO cover-up from the U.S. government, military and media sources is going on, we may rightly ask about this Phoenix saucer's nationwide prime-time television coverage:

Why did it happen at all?

The same network of information control that has kept decades of UFO reports from U.S. print and electronic media existed both before and after the Phoenix event. The media forces that blacked out previous sightings could have blacked out this one, but they did not. Was it simply a case of media overwhelm (over 10,000 local people were said to have seen the UFO, many of whom took video), or was there some deliberate intention behind the apparent break in media silence? Exactly how did this information find its way onto family TV viewing sets across the nation?

Following this same line of reasoning, we need to look at the function of this event in the overall plan and timeline for official UFO disclosure, if we assume that such a secret policy really exists. And from this stone we jump to the next:

*Just **who** was the pilot of this ship?*

Simply put, either it was made on Earth, or it wasn't. Putting aside for the moment those craft that are the result of secret human-based technologies, let's look at the second choice—a genuine alien visitation. In that case, at least according to the metaphysics I trust, we must then consider either a positive or negatively-oriented ET source—either of whom may appear in our skies, yet whose agendas are vastly different. In discussing the benevolent groups, RA noted that:

> "Their purposes are very simple: to allow those of your planet to become aware of infinity, which is often best expressed to the uninformed as the mysterious or unknown."[1]

You could certainly say the Phoenix UFO was "a mysterious unknown" that helped some people "become aware of infinity," but is that enough to conclude that it came from those ETs here to help humanity? Actually, this is not enough information. To really figure out which group could have been running this particular craft, and therefore what role (if any) it played in the ongoing disclosure drama, there are two other points we should consider, both of which come from *The RA Material.* I am relying on this particular source in our discussion because it supports our discernment, yet it also doesn't shy away from calling a spade a spade.

While discussing benevolent ET craft-sightings, those that come from what RA calls "the Confederation" (see Section I: "Inside the Confederation"), RA indicates that:

> "they appear in thought-form capacity for those who have eyes to see..."[2]

Even if the Phoenix ship was a thought-form or holographic image, can we really imagine that all 10,000 people who saw it "had eyes to see"—meaning that they had spiritually prepared themselves for such a revelation? I really don't think so. This is the first sign, at least to me, that it was not "the good guys" who were hovering over AZ to wake people up.

Secondly, in another volume of their teachings, RA notes that mass

---

1. Elkins, op cit., Vol. I, p. 95.
2. Ibid., p. 99.

sightings or UFO flaps are all from Orion, which is the main group behind negative ET contact (i.e. abductions, implants, mutilations, and high-tech weaponry transfers). While we may think that such high-visibility UFO "publicity" (such as the Hudson Valley, NY flap several years ago) serves to awaken the masses to the reality of UFOs and thus boost our spiritual growth, RA flatly disagrees:

> "This assumption is incorrect. The flaps cause many fears among your peoples, many speakings, understandings concerning plots, cover-ups, mutilations, killings, and other negative impressions. Even supposedly positive reports which gain public awareness speak of doom...
>
> The audience brought about by Orion-type publicity [UFO flaps] is not seeded by seniority of vibration to a great extent. The [other, non-random] audiences receiving [requested] "teaching without stimulus from publicity will be more oriented towards illumination." [3]

The point here is that although some people gain inspiration from random UFO mass-sightings, most people end up further confused. Furthermore, since the audience getting this kind of negative-ET, Orion-based UFO publicity is not comprised of people with active spiritual seeking, few of them can even use these experiences for personal growth. It is like being given an esoteric initiation when you're not particularly interested. The seeds will lie on rocky ground.

Bearing all this in mind (especially the randomness of the viewers, and their disoriented response), I think it is doubtful this was a positive ET Confederation ship hoping to awaken the local residents of Phoenix. This only leaves two other possibilities: an Orion greeting or a craft made on Earth. If it was the former (an Orion ship doing as it pleased) as I suspect it was, then such a brash display is certainly no cause for celebration. It suggests much greater boldness and a show of undisputed force on their part, and almost smacks of taunting our human so-called leadership.

---

3. Elkins, op. cit., Vol. II, p. 118–9.

If it was, on the other hand, the product of secret human technology, then it certainly fits into the continuing drama of social ET-conditioning—preparation for more disinformation to come. In fact, according to Dr. Boylan quoting Col. Phil Corso (reported in *Ufocus* magazine on page 4 of the Winter 1997 issue), the U.S. government does possess "enormous Black Triangle antigravity craft, back-engineered from extraterrestrial UFOs." Of course, this, too, could be a piece of disinformation, meant to assure conspiracy followers that such a huge ship is really "one of ours." In any case, that local city authorities had to fight state and federal authorities for investigation is irrelevant, since the locals were surely out of the loop, as they are peripheral to the plans of either source (either Orion ET or "black-agency" Earth-based groups). Both of these groups are quite adept at cover-up operations, which is the main reason why so many questions remain.

Personally, I am not sure which of these two groups was responsible for the huge craft hovering before a stunned Phoenix audience, but in either case, we are certainly seeing the progression of Earth's end-times. This third and final-act scene involves the last power bids of both groups—the negative ETs who know at some level that Earth's 3D cycle is coming to a close (and with it, their presence here), as well as those power-elite human groups who seek world domination and also hear the clock ticking. I cannot say for sure whose craft it was, and like most of us, I can only make an educated guess, based on intuition and reason. I am sure, however, that this event was no accident, that it was part of someone's overall plan, and that we have not seen the last of it.

So you may ask, how to proceed in a world gone mad? How to keep balance when everyone around us seems to be drunk while the social fabric is tearing? We have certainly seen other dramas before, such as the *Heaven's Gate* mistake, the *Hale-Bopp* implosion, Sheldon Nidle's mass-landing blowout, and many UFO-disclosure predictions gone flat. As usual, conflict and controversy surrounds the field, and it is quite easy to fall for the fantasy of the hour.

Interestingly, while most of us feel called to help out and serve in a world deeply divided, to keep from being overwhelmed by externals we have to go deep inside. As Earth hurtles towards its own bright destiny, such strange events will continue. *Our challenge is to keep clear.*

Chapter 19

THE CHILDREN OF TODAY

They too are here to serve, but their service comes fresh from an awareness of social justice and harmony, since the worlds from which they have come reflect humanities' next step...

ALONGSIDE THE CONTINUING UFO DRAMAS, there is also a quiet changing of the guard going on, a gradual replacement of those who have served long and hard on the front lines by those still fresh, still eager to lend a hand to the Great Work on Earth. Many of the people I have met in the last few years, those for whom ideas about Wanderers and cosmic evolution resonate strongly, feel that they are "soon going home." I regularly hear people say, "This is my last lifetime," (or they wish it was!) and I too feel their fatigue—like war-weary soldiers longing for R & R. Some of these people are those I call the "long-contract" folks, Wanderers who have been cycling in human incarnation for thousands of years, some since Atlantis, and they are quite ready to go home. Fortunately, I believe soon they will be going home. This may not be empty hope. Instead, I think it represents a clear inner knowing.

But nature abhors a vacuum, and no planet is left without assistance—especially Earth at its present point of development. If we believe that a New Age, a new world, a new cycle of human consciousness is dawning, then we can appreciate the urgent need for support. As a newborn doe is frail, thin, and weak in the knees, so, too, is humanity timid in its new body—a global culture based on honesty, trust, equality, and simple kindness. Coming from a long history of mistrust and strife at all social levels (ethnic, religious, economic, political, and so on), humanity is not quite comfortable in its own skin. Yet, we *must* evolve; the cycles of evolution demand it.

Our Earth humanity seems to be a case of collective denial and self-rejection, a massive fear of trusting each other. World history reveals clearly the human tendency to magnify and exaggerate differences, and today's hi-tech society (ever more interconnected) actually encourages anonymity. What is left of community with 500-channel TVs available to comfort us alone in our room?

But now, we are at the threshold of a new cycle of civilization. From mottled seeds of separatism, how can we ever bear the fruit of social unity? Clearly, a society laced with mistrust and selfishness is in for some readjustment. Many of the Wanderers who now know their identity and purpose also sense that they have done their part, and that they are really on their way out. Who will take their place? Since we are not alone in the universe, and helpers are always ready to step in, who will help humanity lay the groundwork for enlightened society, based on spiritual vision and universal principles? Well, perhaps your 10-year-old daughter and your 8-year-old son.

I have heard many tales of exceptional children from women who consider themselves Wanderers or lightworkers. Many claim to have felt a divine presence overshadowing their pregnancy, and many felt blessed and protected. Stories of precocious 5-year-olds talking about past lives, friends and family in outer space, or nightly visits to far-off worlds are quite common. I have heard of near-toddlers giving spiritual guidance to their humbled parents, and then scolding them for personal mistakes. *These are definitely not ordinary kids.*

Yet, many of the children are not starry-eyed dreamers: they are also grounded, mature, and effective in the world—and I mean *this* world! The young son of a New York writer I know had his own TV show on the Sci-Fi Network; another friend from Arizona has a teenage son who arranged, without prompting, official meetings with school officers, so they could voice concerns about his work. International UN children's conferences regularly feature children giving major presentations to the assembly. I have seen many a little angel in the audience standing enraptured at my lectures about benevolent ETs and grand cosmic design. Believe it or not (and I have met many who do), these are the souls who will establish the Kingdom of Heaven on Earth.

Mothers of these kids often glow with pride, apparently aware (at some level) that something exceptional is going on. They may feel a sacred duty to protect and care for their young ones, as if guarding them for special work to come. In fact, many of these women also expect some kind of social upheaval in the offing, and are already considering where to take the children. They sense that they are part of a larger scheme, a larger spiritual design that definitely involves their kids—and I think their perception is absolutely correct.

If you feel these ideas resonate, then you should also realize that these souls are quite conscious and aware. They are more than able to handle the normal demands of growing up, and they have tremendous spiritual resources at their disposal. Simply put, they know what they are doing and they know why they are here, and they are ready for any and all Earth Changes. When I was younger, my grandmother used to call me "a little old man cut short," which points to the same kind of maturity under pressure these kids can muster. Nevertheless, they are also young and sensitive, and like all children their age, they often struggle for acceptance from their peer group.

Of course, they need our support as much as do all children. Their hopes, dreams, and cosmic curiosity need fertile soil to take root, and their frustrations and disappointments need comfort and care. Some of them are deeply concerned with planet Earth—the biosphere, the animals, and global peace. They too are here to serve, but their service comes fresh from an awareness of social justice and harmony, since the worlds from which they have come reflect humanity's next step. Their service is natural and unforced. By their very presence they embody the kingdom of souls who will usher in peace. Their role in future society will clarify with each passing year of their lives.

I do not think we need to worry too much about their involvement in some of the more wild ways of their peers. So long as there is love, guidance, dialogue, and honest values at home, they will eventually come back to balance. Being sensitive and group-aware, they naturally assimilate group influences, often at the cost of self-integrity and their personal values. Like all youngsters, they are simply trying to find their place. Trial and error, though painful and time-consuming, is by far the most effective way to learn.

Of course, we all hope they do not get as confused as some of the older Wanderers who have been here for centuries. Luckily, they probably will not log on enough time in our present dysfunctional society to really hurt themselves too much, although teen suicide and drug abuse seems to be on the rise, which in many cases is their response to a hunger for spiritual meaning—hard to find in a global culture that knows very little.

In the same way as we can consider ET souls the vanguard of increased human-cosmic rapport, we can see these children as the leading edge of the Wanderers. As Star People among us form a bridge to increased galactic harmony and interchange, so, too, do these young ones connect us to the new world. Their loyalty and devotion to friends will one day become the bond of love and shared purpose holding together all members of world society, and it is their task to put behind us the divisive influences of war, competition, and distrust so prevalent today.

Therefore, they bring us great hope and promise, and they do need to be protected and nurtured. We can encourage their growing self-expression through open dialogue, and we can support the honing of their latent discernment by honestly sharing our values. This includes frank discussion about how we feel in society, including our alienation and frustrations. Ironically, many of these children are feeling just the same way, although they cannot articulate it.

As they serve their elders by shining a beacon-light recalling our own purity, innocence, and simplicity, we can do much for them through unconditional love, support, and dialogue. Truly, all the world will be theirs to shape and enlighten, with our inspiration. Their time is coming.

» Chapter 20 «

QUESTIONS AND ANSWERS

Earth Changes

Q: *Some of my friends talk a lot about Earth changes and predictions. I feel helpless, like I'm waiting at the edge of a cliff to get pushed off. How can I live, knowing these things are coming?*

A: Actually, I have had to struggle with this myself, and I have often felt like I am standing at a beachhead facing an oncoming tidal wave. My fears began to loosen after having several clear dreams of protection by off-planet groups. However, my concerns have dissolved only more recently by the dedication I feel to my present work. The greater your commitment to service, the less your fear of losing the body, which is just a shell anyway! Everything really does depend on perspective.

Nevertheless, it helps to prepare, and part of the preparation is working on your attitude. What is your plan, what do you need, and what are your values? As always, if we remain sensitive to the inner voice we will receive guidance, and help is always available to those who call. Seek and you shall find, both now and later. If your life is meaningful today, it will be so tomorrow. And if you're sensitive to your true path today, that can continue during Earth Changes. Keeping faith, reason, and a degree of flexibility will help to keep clear your inner channels of communication.

Alien Autopsy and the TV Shows

Q: *Do you think the* Alien Autopsy *video was real, and what do you think about all those TV shows on UFOs and sightings?*

A: I really do not know if the claimed Roswell ET autopsy footage was real, and as you might expect, I have not spent much time thinking about it. To be fair though, we can probably assume that this video is just more of the usual UFO-composite: *real information* to pacify those in the know and leak what "should be" leaked, *concocted fantasy* to catch the gullible and discredit the whole matter, and *disinformation* to confuse everyone—yet another element in the long-term gradual public conditioning that maintains some degree of information-control at a time when complete secrecy is impossible. As I've discussed before, some sort of official disclosure seems to be on its way, and the autopsy video is probably just another part of the preparation leading up to it.

ET Mass Landings

Q: *Some channels have predicted imminent mass landings of benevolent ETs, here to save humanity and all the lightworkers. Can you comment on the probability of this?*

A: Personally, I do not think the benevolent ET Confederation has any such plans at this time. Since the direct calling of humanity still seems weak, it would infringe on the majority of people who are not seeking their physical presence. As I've written many times, benevolent ETs are here to serve all of us, and to help those who are already serving to serve with more effectiveness—which is the main reason they contact sleeping Wanderers. Would a mass landing today or tomorrow serve the growth of all humanity, or would it infringe upon those who, by their own free will choice, are still unprepared? Would it be useful to remove those who are serving from those in need through some "lightworker lift-off scenario"—even during world upheaval—when the need is far greater?

There may be a time when large-scale contact and rescue operations are both warranted and permissible. I imagine such activity might be appropriate amidst catastrophic Earth changes, and only for certain groups—a scenario which many believe occurred at the end of Atlantis, as RA notes that groups were sent out to Peru, Turkey, and Tibet. Until then, however, I would be careful about specifically timed predictions, both rosy and bleak, and in all matters I would keep discernment. As always, elder ETs are really here to stimulate our self-generated spiritual growth.

Cosmic Radios and World Service

Q: *A friend of mine is trying to contact ETs by building some sort of cosmic radio. I was a little surprised, but I wonder what you think about this.*

A: Actually, the idea of building an "astral plane radio receiver" has been around a long time; even some contactees in the 1950s wanted to communicate with ETs this way. I have read references to it in the Hilarion channel, and it was also mentioned by Alice Bailey in her teachings from the Master Djwhal Khul. They all suggested that some sort of machine would be invented by the end of 20th century that would have proven the existence of life after death. Unfortunately, it seems their prediction didn't come true—although it does appear that more people today accept the notion of "spiritual life" around us. This type of techno-spiritual breakthrough seems to be part of the Plan for Earth, so I would not be surprised if something like it already exists or comes out publicly in the next few years. It is simply a matter of synchronizing the frequencies of communication.

However, I for one, am not too interested in the project—neither its construction nor its operation. Of course, I would not dissuade anyone from getting involved, since this kind of invention may certainly help the world (if it ever saw the light of day, that is). For those who hope to improve society through technology, it could be one way of helping out. Each of us has our own path.

But if your friend is simply curious and wants to get privileged information from ETs, I would want to question his motives—which is exactly the same concern I have with those involved in CSETI, a group that aims to initiate direct human-ET contact through formal protocols such as ritual, synchronized lights, and group process. The question is this:

__Why__ are you trying to make contact, and __what__ is your goal?

After years of meditation, study, and reflection on the essentials of spiritual growth (i.e. love, wisdom, balance, and will), I really wonder what can be gained from talking to ETs. You may be amazed that I say this, since I put so much trust in the RA teachings, and they are as ET as you can get. Perhaps it is because they have answered my most pressing questions, and now I have a better grasp of spiritual essentials. Is your friend who is building a cosmic radio also interested in learning the spiritual essentials from higher-dimensional friends? Are those who are going out at night with CSETI, looking to "vector in" UFOs also looking to gain metaphysical training? Frankly, I think their motives are somewhat less devoted.

As you might expect, most people interested in Buddhism and Eastern religions do not care at all about UFO matters; such topics seem irrelevant to enlightenment. They know that "gods" too are on the spiritual path, and they are also not fully enlightened. If you really want the way of enlightenment, you can't get it from those who don't have it. So we return to the question of motivations.

What is the point of initiating contact? Do you want to become the ambassador from Earth? Do you want secret high technology? Or do you seek genuine teachings for spiritual growth? Aren't there more than enough teachings available (most of which are not even being put into practice)? For those seeking to initiate ET contact or cooperate with some ET-inspired "world salvage project," a good deal of soul-searching of motives is in order.

Furthermore, calling for metaphysical contact with somewhat self-serving, materialistic intentions does open the possibility of making real contact with negative ET groups who prey upon those who are confused or ego-based. To me, this is a very real danger for those who embark upon CSETI-type procedures, as well as those who follow dubiously channeled ET requests for their cooperation in some sort of project they have been given. Of course, trying to build a cosmic radio to help humanity see the reality of higher dimensions does not entail the same kind of risk, since the motives here are pure. Nevertheless, it is always a good idea to clarify our goals.

As there are many different stages of the path, what is good for me is not necessarily good for you, and vice versa. As always, discernment comes first. Know your motives, recognize what is essential and what is merely peripheral, and be honest with yourself. At this point on my path, I prefer to follow my own way in the world, continue my practices and service, and purify my intentions without vectoring in more ETs. I also like to keep in mind this bit of ageless wisdom:

> *True Self is perfect and contains all virtues, yet real teachers can stimulate and accelerate our spiritual growth. And thus, the great value to seeking guidance is finding support for our own self-completion, helping us pass through all attachments, sorrow, and misunderstanding.*

Of course, the ETs have spiritual teachers themselves, and I can assure you that their teachers talk about universal principles and ageless wisdom, about the glory of Infinite Creator, about the true Self in fullness and emptiness, and about the path of meditation. What else is there?

Along the way, we must be honest about our intentions. I am sure there are many good reasons to seek ET communication and a machine to show all the world, and a lot of good can come from it. Yet, if we neglect to seek our true nature, get hooked on the dope of salvation-fever (similar to those of Heaven's Gate), and possibly snowball a subtle self-denial in the process, then no amount of ET teaching can save us and the path to freedom becomes a path to jail. It all depends on attitude and intention. What we do is usually not as important as how we do it. So I have my path, and you have yours. While our Source and Goal are One, the roads in between are truly countless.

THE PRINCIPLES OF
SOUL-EVOLUTION

PART A:

HEALING AND
SELF-TRANSFORMATION

Chapter 21

SELF AND GOD

"In an Infinite Creator there is only unity."[1]

As we start Section II, "The Principles of Soul-Evolution", let's begin at the beginning, and ask some central questions. For starters, *Who are you?* At an essential level, looking into the space of silence, what really is a human being? And for that matter, who or what is God? These are perhaps the central questions of our life—forever asked, never answered. Yet, if we truly seek meaning, we must keep asking, until the answers become self-evident.

Western religions tell us that Man is small and God is great, that human beings live in error while God is perfection, and apparently, so far away. A great gulf is said to separate us from the Absolute, while at the same time, most people struggle with inner conflict and self-esteem. Yet, these two are related: *our notions of Godhead determine the wholeness of our sense of self.* More precisely, the perceived gulf between humanity and God creates and sustains self-denial, since it is no less than a projection of a perceived inner schism. When we do not appreciate who we are, God seems far away, yet when the Self is fully known, we feel the power of the Absolute within us.

Of course, according to all mystic traditions, the personal experience of both separation from God and psychological self-conflict are simply issues of awareness. There is no cosmic law that binds us to an experience of duality, opposition, and estrangement from our Source.

When mystics speak of unity, or when ET Walk-ins and Wanderers tell to trust ourselves and listen to the inner voice, they are really trying to help us shift our awareness. We need to realize that everything depends on the quality of our self-understanding, since our vision of

---

1. Elkins, op. cit., Vol. I, p. 67.

ourselves largely determines our experience. Looking within, if we only see problems, confusion and failure, then life is miserable. Looking outside, if we imagine a punishing, indifferent Creator, or an Absolute that can only be accessed through strict conduct, then we end up controlling our natural process without appreciating what we already are. Massive self-denial often lurks behind these apparently spiritual notions.

Many of us striving for higher consciousness, while working on ourselves and helping others, can be intensely self-critical. We may see our faults clearly, but if that is all we see then we are deceiving ourselves. Ceaseless self-reproach is a potent glamour, as destructive to spiritual progress as pride and vanity. Many kind and caring people shackle themselves with self-criticism—ranging all the way from chronic feelings of inadequacy to severe self-hatred and long-term depression.

For the seeker of *gnosis* or direct knowledge of the Absolute, understanding Self and God goes far beyond simply appreciating our basic goodness while acknowledging imperfections. We should understand that spiritual growth goes far deeper than achieving emotional balance. That is just the beginning, not the end of the line.

One of the greatest Sufi teachers, Jelaluddin Rumi, sang of his own search:

> *I tried to find Him on the Christian cross, but He was not there; I went to the Temple of the Hindus and to the old pagodas, but I could not find a trace of Him anywhere.*

> *I searched on the mountains and in the valleys but neither in the heights nor in the depths was I able to find Him. I went to the Caaba in Mecca, but He was not there either.*

> *I questioned the scholars and philosophers, but He was beyond their understanding.*

> *I then looked into my heart and it was there where he dwelled that I saw Him; he was nowhere else to be found.*

When Rumi sings of finding God within the heart, he is really pointing towards eternal truth, cosmic fact, *reality as it is*. What he realized can also be phrased this way:

> *The Creator is within the heart,*
> *because Self and God are forever One.*

Without further qualification, can we really accept this, or must we only see ourselves through the limitations of body and mind? Our degree of non-enlightenment can be measured by the extent to which we *identify ourselves* with conditioned patterns of personality, addictions, fears, and conflicts. A quick way to gauge your degree of Self-acceptance is to just observe your feelings upon reading the passage above. If you feel doubt, apathy, denial or confusion, then those are your immediate obstacles to divine embrace. Of course, the blossoming of God in the heart is more than just an idea. It is an experience that can't really be expressed in words at all.

Going further, we can examine some other models of Self. Theosophy and ageless wisdom teach us that human beings are composed of interlaced forces and energies. Although most of us consider ourselves a personality, this is just considered the material shell that contain such forces. Alice Bailey, in *Esoteric Psychology II*, explains further:

> "The three personality types of energy are the **etheric**, which is the vehicle of vital energy; the **astral** body which is the vehicle of the feeling energy...and the **mental** which is the vehicle of the intelligent energy of will..."[2]

However, these three energies are not the entire human being. All religions teach that there is a soul or spirit which gives Life to the personality, since personality is merely a vehicle for the divine expression of soul. The driver is none other than Higher Self. And what is the alternative? We are simply a bag of biology! When I ask atheists if this is really how they define themselves, they are hard pressed to

---

2. *Esoteric Psychology*, Vol.II, p. 8. Lucis Publishing Company, New York, 1970 (first published 1942).

agree, and they usually do not answer. I feel sorry for the hard-liners who do agree. The soul itself recoils from saying, "Yes, I am a bag of meaningless molecules."

The RA Material gives a more complete definition of the human being. According to RA, we are a mind-body-spirit-beingness-totality complex guided by Higher Self (which is a mouthful, not surprising from RA!). We may think of ourselves as simply "people," a humble term indeed, but this only scratches the surface. Just as the ocean cannot be fully known by its waves, likewise, a human being is far more than what is visible. Our life on Earth is one slice of the infinite; our normal sense of identity is but a partial awareness of a greater Self. Why do I say this? Not only from over 6000 years of Oriental philosophy, but also, more importantly, from my own personal experience.

Yet the universe is an interesting place, and if we do not want to see the entirety of our being, cosmic forces won't force us to. Higher Self, guides, angels, and benevolent ETs may send us love and light, but we are totally free to reject their blessings. Humans on Earth usually choose a more distorted way of seeing themselves, identifying with only the personality (and sometimes with only the physical body!), rather than recognizing a greater Self, which must exist in Unity. When we start to talk about Self with a capital "S," we are not far from appreciating Oneness.

Neither ET Wanderers nor benevolent visitors in the skies, neither guides nor angelic helpers will force upon us a vision of unity. As I continue my travels and teachings around the world, it strikes me rather hard that humanity, as a whole, is far indeed from appreciating oneness.

What does RA mean by saying that "in an Infinite Creator there is only unity"? Opening a door to the majesty of true nature, at the very least it means the following:

✦ Human beings and absolute Godhead are essentially the same. There is no essential separation, and the idea or experience of separation is really an illusion based on limited perception.

✦ All beings—including Buddhas, Masters, people, plants, and animals, ETs good and bad, angels, suns and galaxies—are fundamentally One Being.

✦ Divinity, or what we call absolute Godhead, is the essence of all things seen and unseen. Each speck of dust is the Infinite Creator—not a part of the Divine, but the whole Divine.

✦ The two cosmic paths of unity through love, and separation through control, are a single expression of one Being. Positive and negative ET groups express One Life.

✦ Past, present, and future exist simultaneously in a timeless, eternal present, always available and accessible if we have eyes to see. Omniscience and omnipotence are our true nature.

✦ Our perceptions of spatial relativity and apparently separate places (the assumption of a real difference between "here" and "there") is an illusion. Everywhere is Here.

✦ Every thought and fantasy we create reflects a genuine, infinite reality in some dimension.

✦ The relative imperfections we see in ourselves exist completely fused in harmony with our total perfection, right now and for all times. There is **no** real spiritual path. (Hard to swallow?)

✦ We cannot die, since our true nature is the body of the infinite cosmos. Our mind is eternal and awareness is eternal. So-called change and transformation are illusory in the reality of Oneness.

✦ All we see and all we experience is none other than our true Self. There is only one Actor on the universal stage: the Infinite One, who is Godhead or Self, the Creator of All—and that's you!

✦ All thoughts and concepts describing the Absolute are inadequate (you can burn the book now).

✦ There is really nothing to worry about, except perhaps paying your bills.

Does all this sound abstract? Then try a few lifetimes of intensive meditation! Until then, perhaps we can look to the words of William Blake, who simply said that "If the doors of perception were cleansed, we would see reality as it is: infinite." Only with new eyes can we really see and know Who and What is the Supreme, and with this vision, we will truly understand Oneness, as well as our true being. All words and teachings can only point towards this reality, and at best, inspire us to "keep on keeping on" and continue our expansion to boundless awareness.

In the next chapter, we will look at the basic fuel that allows us to drive along the bridge to Infinite Being—the Will.

» Chapter 22 «

REFLECTIONS ON WILL

The stairway to Heaven, the successive initiations into broader and more encompassing awareness, are all unlocked by will.

IT SEEMS TO ME that the central pillar of human evolution is the enhancement of Will. Whether or not we develop such virtues as love, wisdom or intelligence depends wholly on the force of our will—the focus, and intensity of focus of our seeking. The further I go on my own path, the more I realize that my unfoldment pivots upon the strength and direction of my own efforts. We ourselves determine the speed and purity of our approach to enlightenment, our fusion with true Self.

Whatever we can do may be done wholly, partially, or not at all. We may act with careful attention, from mixed motives, or with confused intention. There is no question that the intensity of light invoked depends entirely on the strength of our seeking that light (by this, I mean the "light" of greater awareness). There are many levels of spiritual dedication, from reading the words of others, reflecting on the meaning of personal experience, or further, to putting good ideas into daily practice. Following what we know in our heart often requires surrender, and aligning our efforts with what we know to be right takes discipline. Personal surrender and balanced discipline are certainly not easy. They demand Will. But they also enhance the power of Will.

Of course, the development of will is a universal principle of evolution; it is not the sole possession of any one group. Regardless of how we define ourselves (as ET, native human, divine essence, or the now fashionable "I don't know"), our path is fundamentally the same—from conflict and confusion to an integrated personality and beyond, through the lessons of love, wisdom and unified awareness, on into the lap of infinity. This stairway to Heaven, these successive initiations into broader and more encompassing awareness, are all unlocked by Will.

On Earth, those with the greatest development of Will are often found along the "negative line"—serving themselves through personal ambition and control of others, seeking wealth and power with insatiable appetite. Sadly, most people admire, respect, and even emulate these icons of selfishness. Who else do we find on magazine covers but those who have achieved more or less through selfish egotism? In this neck of the cosmos, "the successful" are generally the most self-centered, but they do show us an effective deployment of Will. ET souls and those of us who have met real spiritual teachers may realize, however, that this is *not* the case everywhere. I assure you, beyond Earth, the galaxies are filled with spiritual beings of tremendous sanctity, powerful with both will and humility. Just because power is usually linked (on Earth) with love of power, doesn't mean that power itself is selfish. Actually, the selfless expression of *power in love* is far stronger.

Unfortunately, many good-hearted people see this condition on Earth, and though perhaps they cannot articulate it, they recoil from social engagement and the active enhancement of Will. Many New Age folks are head-in-the-sand about the extent of negativity on Earth. With stars in their hair, they are mired in fragility. Power has a bad reputation in this world, since it is usually applied for selfish ends. But fire can be used to comfort or destroy, to nourish or incinerate. Let's not confuse the substance with its application. Don't blame fire for its burn!

We could take this a lot further, but I would like to close with a passage from *The Law of One*. As usual, RA expresses in a most pithy way the importance of developing Will:

> "*Acceptance of self, forgiveness of self, and the direction of the will:* this is the path towards the disciplined personality. Your faculty of will is that which is powerful within you as co-Creator. *You cannot ascribe to this faculty too much importance.* Thus it must be carefully used and directed in service to others for those upon the positively oriented path."[1]

1. Elkins, op. cit., Vol. III, p.7.

If we can hold the reins of active, directed Will, and *still* live in the light of balanced love and wisdom, guess where we will end up? Right in the heart of Higher Self, our source and immediate destination. In the next chapter I will present some of the essential teachings that can help us make closer contact with this center of our being.

» Chapter 23 «

THE HIGHER SELF

There are countless teachings these days about Higher Self, yet I have a feeling very few people really understand what it is. While it's certainly true that this so-called "higher" self is with us all the time, it is generally treated as something "out there" or "up there." How can we know it as the center of our being within us? The first step, of course, is realizing that the purpose of life is to learn lessons, develop awareness, and further our healing and balance. After this, we need to put these nice ideas into practice—by discovering exactly what lessons should be learned, which aspects of self can be developed, and how we can heal and balance. Actually, this entire process of self-work is a return to Higher Self. But what exactly is this greater part of ourselves?

The path of self-understanding requires this kind of search, and demands that we face all the conflicts and confusions of our obvious self, also known as personality. According to ageless wisdom, "personality" is simply the union of three forces—physical, astral and mental. The **physical** consists of dense and subtle bodies (bio-chemical and etheric), the **astral** relates to emotional life, and the **mental** is made up of both lower and higher aspects (the analytical and intuitive). These three modes of normal human being are purified and transmuted through spiritual work.

Higher Self or Oversoul, (also called Atman or Monad), is considered the source of personality and its primary guide through its long eons of incarnation in all dimensions of time and space. This Oversoul is like the light at the end of the tunnel, the castle of our homecoming to welcome back the "Prodigal Son"—a metaphor, of course, for the manifest self (body/mind/spirit complex) as it returns to Oneness.

But what exactly *is* this Atman? Of course, it is impossible to describe it fully unless you are fully enlightened, and even then, words fail. But, some words can help us build a conceptual framework. According to my handy Glossary of Sanskrit Terms, Atman is "the divine aspect in the sevenfold constitution of man; his highest principle." Unfortunately, this definition doesn't go too far.

As you might expect, *The Law of One* gives us a lot more to chew on. In their view, the first thing we need to understand is that Higher Self is a sixth density entity in its own right, not some kind of nebulous cloudy thing. This means each Monad can be considered a soul that has achieved enlightenment through its own efforts along its path of evolution (usually in an earlier portion of the Creation or another solar system). This is the metaphysical basis for the statement that, in essence, all souls are from elsewhere, not only Wanderers. So Higher Self is an old soul.

These ideas are already quite radical, and remind me of the classic Tibetan Buddhist teaching that considers some high Lamas to be emanations of particular Buddhas and Bodhisattvas (who, in the Vedanta/ Theosophical system, would be sixth, seventh and eighth density souls). You could say that we, as a manifest body/mind/spirit, are also emanations of particular oversouls, which have passed through their own soul-evolution, so Higher Self is your own private Master!

Additionally, RA notes that Higher Self has "full understanding of the accumulation of each entity's experiences" through all lifetimes, and is therefore aware of exactly where we stand on the path. Furthermore, it is aware of all the lessons needed to achieve full Self-realization, and is like "a map in which the destination and roads are all well known." Atman knows the entire path of evolution back to Itself, and knows exactly how to get there (or rather, how to get here!).

With this in mind, we can consider Higher Self a tremendous resource for personal growth. In fact, it is both the source and central resource of our entire evolutionary path. It (our inner being) knows our full past-life history and present point of development, the complete path to unity-consciousness and every iota of energy healing and balance that we need to achieve Its own sixth density enlightenment. However, the degree to which we use this resource is totally up to us.

Like all good Star Born and Confederation ET groups, the Higher Self strictly follows the Law of Free Will. It will never command our behavior nor issue demands; it waits for the calling. Along this line, RA explains further that:

> "Higher Self can program [our 3D life-plan] only for lessons and certain predisposing limitations if it wishes…the remainder is completely the free choice of each entity, a perfect balance between the known and the unknown…"[1]

To contact this inner being, we have to open "the proper pathways through the roots of mind." In other words, we must activate what RA calls the spirit-complex or gateway, which is an energy field between higher mind and Monad, between personality and the transpersonal. In physical terms, this is the relationship between pituitary and pineal glands in the brain. The key to such bridge-building is *meditation*—not because of its moral value, but because it is the most efficient method of activating the *sixth chakra* (the forehead or brow center), which in turn activates the seventh center and develops the needed energy fields in the head. This creates access to cosmic mind and power.

What actually happens is that the energy fields associated with sixth and seventh centers begin to blend forces in the subtle, etheric channels of the head, and a "gateway" is opened. Like a stream of light inrushing and downpouring, the pure Will of Higher Self streams into body/mind/spirit (us!), and in time, our personality is wholly transformed. It may be felt as a tingling in the forehead.

Yet, meditation is not enough, and each of us has significant areas of imbalance that require healing, which is best accomplished in our primary school house: daily life experience. To address these issues, Higher Self programs each incarnation (before we take birth) for particular lessons and certain predisposing limitations, such as childhood illness, educational opportunities, family influences, or social

---

1. Elkins, op. cit., Vol. II, p. 64.

forces. The purpose of Higher Self programming is the hope that our specific 3D experience gives us catalyst for growth. In response to such catalyst, Higher Self "hopes" we are inspired to seek greater wholeness and self-integration in the various regions of our total body/mind/spirit that require healing and balance. Life experiences that seem to "come to us" of their own accord often represent forms of catalyst that have been planned by Higher Self for specific learning. There aren't really too many accidents in this journey we call life.

Therefore, if we want to contact Oversoul and progress towards greater unity (i.e. non-dual consciousness), then we have to understand and deal with the specific lessons that we intended to learn by programming our lives as we have. These are the specific issues of our present life, and are as unique as one's astrological chart (which is often a clear picture of just what the Higher Self has planned for us).

And so we need to look closely at the particular difficulties that life seems to be handing us, which of course, are just forms of catalyst (reflected by the world around us) intended to stimulate our efforts. These spurs to growth take many forms, including intimate and social relationships, worldly jobs and career, the arena of public service, and all creative pursuits. If we have conflicts in any of these arenas, we can be sure there are hidden lessons to be learned—and hidden within each lesson is the face of Higher Self.

If you really want to contact your Source, you can begin with self-reflection regarding your own life-lessons. Try asking yourself, "Why did I choose my parents, my body, and my early influences?" Looking deeper can help you unlock greater understanding about the specific spiritual lessons you have set for yourself. And by the way, this kind of inquiry is a form of meditation, and also has the power to activate sixth chakra. By doing so, you will draw closer to the essential Self and slowly unwind all conflict, struggle and paradox. This is the path of Unity.

» Chapter 24 «

Despair and Opportunity

...standing alone at the junction of hope and despair, self-trust and futility, he chose the way of opportunity...

I recently read an inspiring article in the *Yoga Journal*. As an example of self-healing, the article gave a brilliant example of human potential and uncompromising devotion to the path of higher consciousness. It told the story of a man who rose from the ashes of devastating injury to a meaningful and productive spiritual life, and it is a testament to the force of directed Will towards wholeness. In my view, there is no function within Self as central as Will; it is the key to success or failure, speed or slack on the path. This story, entitled "The Real Miracle" (*Yoga Journal*, Jan./Feb. 1997) is really about human genius, and it shines a light for all to see that *the centering of Will alone has the power to take us from despair to glory*. Here is the story.

In the early 1970s, Mitchell May suffered a devastating car crash, after which he was told that his leg would need amputation. Yet, rather than surrender to a life of limitation, he refused his doctors' advice and chose to keep the leg, even though he was told its massive infection might prove fatal. Nevertheless, by dint of great effort and the spiritual energy of Mr. Jack Gray, a master healer with whom he worked closely (a man whom I would consider an adept or white magician), Mitchell May went on to heal his leg completely. Today he, too, is an expert healer.

Of course, the happy ending did not come overnight. Along the way were years of physical pain, mental discipline, rigorous practice and purification, trial and error. But fate was also at work here. Mitchell May had what could be called "a karmic link" with his teacher (who had actually predicted they would meet), and his accident was probably no accident at all. The crisis it posed was likely planned by Higher Self as the major crossroads and growth-opportunity of his lifetime. What

I found so inspiring was the force of commitment with which he took up the cross and mastered his fate.

At the most obvious level, we can see how day by day, one small step at a time, this man overcame extreme pain and despair. He trusted himself at the deepest levels, from which emerges the power to triumph. He met head on the challenge of self-healing. Resisting defeat, he recognized opportunity where others saw tragedy. Whether or not Mitchell May knew it, this was the crossroads which likely determined all his further growth in this incarnation. It required a reversal of perception in which he could perceive his latent potential, and realize opportunity in grave crisis.

I assume this was a man who had already developed inner strength, a man who had laid the foundations of character through a lifelong process of self-trust and self-acceptance. Such foundations were needed in order to even perceive a choice and summon his will to make the requisite effort. He made a conscious decision to keep his body intact, to persevere in the healing and training with Jack Gray. Standing alone at the junction of hope and despair, self-trust and futility, he chose the way of opportunity and brought forth his will to forge the situation as best he could. Certainly, the ability to appreciate a crossroads and proceed along the "hard way" of self-possession was also born of previous choices, so numerous he surely could not count them all. It is important to realize, however, that this type of choice is not confined only to crisis. In fact, we stand at all sorts of crossroads all the time.

How often do we feel stuck, at an impasse and blocked from what we want? How often do we feel resigned to "cruel fate" under heavy clouds of doubt? It is easy to see how life throws us roadblocks, how things do not go our way. We all know what that is like. It is much harder to see the opportunities that lie latent in all such situations, the unlimited "choice-fullness" of each moment. Taking a personal blow, we can grow empowered or enraged; emotional limitations can lead us to poison our self-confidence, or instead, reinvigorate self-reliance. Truly, the glass is neither half-full nor half-empty. *It is clear.*

The Law of One books give an exercise to help us develop our range of free choice—a practice for discovering the treasure of the moment. When asked for a tool to accelerate growth towards realizing unity with all, RA gave the following:

> "*Exercise One.* This is the most nearly centered and usable within your illusion complex [the 3D world]. The moment contains love. This is the lesson/goal of this illusion or density.
>
> The exercise is to consciously see that love in awareness and understanding...
>
> The conscious statement of self to self of the desire to seek love is [a] central act of Will..."[1]

The practice is simple (though easy to forget), and it is comprised of two levels: (1) realizing what is, and (2) realizing our choice. Regarding the first, when RA says "the moment contains love," they are pointing to the essential quality which underlies all experience: the unconditional love of the Creator, the Grace which allows us to live, move, and have our being. Understanding this Presence leads eventually to liberation, because it calls forth vision and perception of what is eternal.

At the second level of the exercise, RA points to the latent freedom hidden in the moment: *the choice to realize love*—seeing, feeling and responding from unconditional acceptance and kindness to all, especially ourselves. This turn of perception is no little matter. It is a potent statement from conscious self to Total Self; an invocation that fuels the further desire for truth, an embrace of Divine Providence, an honest acceptance of and alignment with the Real. It reveals the most sincere seeking, and as such, it potentizes Will and resonates with our core at which personal will is one with universal flow. Seeking love is seeing love, and seeing the Real empowers all further seeking. In the same way that Mitchell May discovered how momentous decisions are built upon the incremental foundations of a thousand lesser daily acts, all true spiritual growth is self-reinforcing. You can trust the value of any teaching or spiritual practice by its long-term effects when

---

1. Elkins, op. cit., Vol. I, p. 113–14.

integrated into your life. The proof is in the using.

And just as conscious seeking is a choice, so too is resignation. Sorrow does not just rain down on us. Despair is generated by a freely chosen response to circumstances that challenge us at points of conflict, confusion, and weakness. Mitchell May dug deep within Self and brought forth Will. With stern resolve, he applied it deep into his pain and despair and chose opportunity, not tragedy. As RA noted, "the moment contains love"—promise, bounty, and richness. That we feel estranged from such abundance is our own doing, and whatever we have created through ignorance can certainly be refashioned through loving wisdom.

Many people interested in the spiritual side of UFO and ET life often tell me about special contacts they have had with beings of light, ET or angelic. What they usually do not realize in their awe is that these beings are always around. Their presence can be known and felt all day long. Moments of higher contact are simply moments of opening our eyes to the multi-dimensional reality that ever is. This is not to say that Masters are online 24 hours a day for your every whim (like spiritual 7-Elevens), but the loving face of true nature is ever shining. Basic wisdom and compassion do not take time off. They are always available because they are what we really are.

Yet it can be quite hard to find this in the heat of the moment. If the mind is disturbed, if emotions are roiling and thoughts are spinning like a tape loop, how can we perceive any choice at all? At this point we must turn to meditation—the formal practice of learning peace and inner silence, opening the gateway to Will and what Christians call "the beatitudes."

At the conclusion of the *Yoga Journal* article, Mitchell May remarks that "the body's infinite capacity for healing is the real miracle." Truly, this is wonderful, but it is only a miracle within a greater miracle—a single melody within a larger symphony, a symphony in which mind inclines towards spirit, and the spirit shines blessings forever. The Great Plan is the symphony, the Infinite Creator, the conductor, and all Beings, the players. To know this miracle, we need calm to bring vision, and will to make choice. At these levels of awareness, despair has long been vanquished.

In the next chapter, we will rest longer upon this axis of despair and opportunity, considering it from another angle: the "tragic" death of Diana, Princess of Wales.

» *Chapter 25* «

DIANA'S DEATH AND SERVICE

At the beginning of September 1997, I returned to San Francisco from two weeks in Japan, and just as before, I was welcomed back to the U.S. with news of more untimely death. During my last visit to Japan in March of the same year, the members of Heaven's Gate committed mass suicide in San Diego (see Section II, Chapter 4: "A Mistaken Gate"). During this visit, Princess Diana was killed in a violent car accident and Mother Theresa died of long-term illness. Seeing the pattern, a friend of mine joked that I should stay in San Francisco more often (to prevent such events!). Of course, these deaths have nothing to do with my travels, but their aftershocks were felt by many.

Not missing a step, I gave a lecture at the San Francisco *Whole Life Expo* on the day of my return. Surprisingly, nearly 50 people came, and while few of them knew my work, everyone seemed receptive and eager for a deeper message. At the end, a lady came up to the stage and asked me if I thought Princess Di was a Wanderer. After a short reflection, I said "Yes, she probably was—and Prince Charles as well!" If so, then perhaps there is more to her death than meets the eye.

From seeing her photos, Diana seemed to have a kind of radiance, and apparently she truly cared about the people around her. She certainly had a good heart, and was somewhat out of step with the complex demands of her royal role. Charles, too, seems somewhat innocent, and like fourth density ET souls, appears kindly, but not quite so quick on the ball—expressing love without a comparable degree of wisdom. On the other hand, Princess Diana may have been a somewhat older Wanderer, with a bit more wisdom than her somewhat clumsy royal ex.

That Diana may have been a Wanderer is of itself not particularly important, since there are many ET souls in the public eye (almost all of whom are probably unaware of their cosmic roots). What *is* important, however, is how it may have played a part in her "tragic" death—which means that her accident may have been *no accident* at all.

When thinking about anyone's passing over, we need to consider three options. Death may be:

1) A needed experience for karmic balance, soul learning, or simply the timely end of incarnation;

2) The result of a genuine non-planned accident, which is sometimes called planetary karma; or

3) An expression of sacrifice and world service, coming from a somewhat more evolved soul.

In my view, Lady Di did not have such heavy karmic baggage, and option #1 does not seem to fit too well. Was her death then merely accidental? If she was indeed a Wanderer, then the answer is probably no. In that case, it was certainly planned by Higher Self, with her agreement.

Like the murder of John Lennon (another likely Wanderer), the death of Diana has been the catalyst for a tremendous outpouring of love and sympathy. I know two friends who stayed up all night watching the broadcast of her funeral, which made international headlines. While Diana apparently did much good during her lifetime, she seems to be have done even more *after* her passing—helping all those who in some way identified with her purity under duress (a form of sacrifice, to be sure) to open their own hearts a little bit further. Self-offering is the way of all Wanderers and Servers, and as RA noted, "love and light go where they are needed." Perhaps at a higher level Lady Di recognized the love that was latent in the millions who watched her from afar. Perhaps she knew that the stimulus of an apparent "tragic early death" was a potent way to help bring it forth. If so, then we really should not grieve, mourn, or feel sorry for her. Rather, we can appreciate the power and beauty of her final act of service to the whole world.

In the next chapter, we are going to change gears and explore some of the basic principles of self-healing, then look at their application to daily life.

» Chapter 26 «

TO THE HEART

The heart of the discipline of personality is threefold: know yourself, accept yourself, become the Creator.[1]

As we discussed before, there has been a recent acceleration of catalyst for many people as the planet prepares for a major cycle-change in its evolution—a movement into greater love. Our individual and collective processes are also cycling faster, bringing us greater challenges. Perhaps you can affirm this in your own life. But what is the point of all this challenge? Seeing within them our lessons for growth, the fundamental learning is unconditional acceptance in the heart.

In recent times, the major catalyst to my own growth has been the work I have done to prepare a new seminar, "The Infinite Self: Healing and Balance." This workshop is a synthesis of all passages from *The Law of One* that concern the essential principles of growth: the mind/body/spirit complex, Higher Self, seven energy centers, and the path of healing. I first combed the four volumes and compiled all relevant passages, then distilled 48 pages of raw quotes down to a 16-page outline. It was a lot of work and I had been planning it a long time, but it felt absolutely necessary. Having at last completed the task, I have a real sense of accomplishment. But that is only part of the story.

After sitting so long with the teachings, then setting them down into workshop outlines, I feel steeped in the mind of Higher Self. The basic message here is summed up in the title: "The True Self is Infinite, and Our Way Proceeds through Healing and Balance." To heal others we must first heal the self. To walk in balance we must first find balance within, and between body, mind, and spirit. It sounds simple, and perhaps it is, but it surely is not easy. But it is about self-training, as RA notes:

---

1. Elkins, op. cit., Vol. III, p. 127.

"The heart of the discipline of personality is threefold: know your self, accept your self, become the Creator. [And] this third step…renders one the most humble servant of all, transparent in personality, and completely able to know and accept others."[2]

On the initiate path (a path of accelerated growth through disciplined study, meditation, and service), just achieving the first step requires radical, total and absolute self-opening. In practice, in the crucible of daily life, this leads to the second step: learning how to accept all aspects of personal experience, whatever comes up. Of course, it is easy to accept the pleasant, but hard indeed to accept what we do not like. Aggressive, demanding or so-called "negative emotions," odd ailments and illnesses, seemingly useless thoughts and distorted notions, self-defeating beliefs and obsessive patterns—all these are grist for the mill of total acceptance. To mill such energies, we must first bring them to the heart. When we open our hearts to the fullness of all personal experience (whether we like it or not), the result is unconditional love of all. Simple.

Although the first step of the training is knowing yourself, and the second is then accepting yourself, they are really not all that different. We cannot understand our patterns unless we open up to receive them, and at least minimally surrender to our personal process in the moment. But simply "being with" our anger, desires, or self-defeating beliefs is just a first step. According to RA and other esoteric traditions, all such psychological experience comes from blockages in the first three energy centers—traditionally located at the base of the spine and in the sacral and solar plexus regions. Importantly, their healing can only be effected through the heart, using the universal solvent of self-love and unconditional self-acceptance. Not easy, but again, simple.

I hear many people asking spiritual teachers the same old question: "How do I deal with my negative emotions?" First of all, realize that they are not negative at all! They are simply emotions, or rather, a certain degree of wounding, inner conflict, and self-damaged wholeness. Secondly, realize that you can only heal them fully by loving them

2. Ibid.

fully, and then, simply be with them! As with a counseling client I once advised to "celebrate your stuckness," in the process we simply allow all such feelings to be as they are, neither hating, controlling, nor denying them. In my experience, this kind of treatment is the fastest way to dissolve them. After repeated patient practice, their intensity will decrease. That is a law of metaphysics.

Such self-work is *identical* to the healing of our seven energy centers (nodal-points in the human subtle body). In this process of unblocking, balancing, and full activation, it is no less than the development of the energy powers of healing. This is because these energy points (from the potent red-ray root chakra at the base of the spine, to the transcendent mystery of violet-ray crown chakra atop the head) are both the *vehicle of personal growth*, as well as the means of healing others. In reality, the quality of our service to others depends solely on the degree of balance and activation of our energy centers—our *own* degree of healing (as in the old maxim, "Healer, heal thyself!").

But before we get into the details of world service, we should know what actually is the practice of bringing all experience to the heart. To illustrate, I will choose some examples from my own life, which also gives you a sense of the so-called accelerated catalyst many of us are now experiencing. Having first been steeped in the teachings of infinite self and the way of balance, I was, however, prepared for these onrushing energies.

For starters, bringing all experience into the heart has meant welcoming the pain, doubt, and uncertainty that arose after I gave a workshop where not a single person showed up! In another case, it meant sitting with the discouragement of feeling invisible amidst a disorganized New Age expo after being warmly invited to come, then making great efforts to attend. Actually, these disappointments turned out to be blessings in disguise. After I opened up to the pain of dashed hopes, I realized that *only the quality of one's own effort really matters*. Public response is beyond our control. Moreover, I had a somewhat ecstatic experience, while sitting in the empty lecture hall with chairs arranged all around me, as well as on the train returning home. I intuitively felt the presence of higher beings around me, and realized the lesson being shown. Whenever we open up to greater acceptance, a little more freedom comes our way.

Since I work not only in the U.S., other challenges have rushed in from abroad—more catalyst for learning, more material for heart-embrace. A few years ago, I was negotiating with several groups in Japan and the Philippines for teaching. Along this rocky road, I learned to accept my anger and frustration born of repeated language and culture misunderstandings, of being a target of gossip and back-biting from sources I had assumed friendly, of going for months without a reply to questions I considered essential, then having to change my travel plans several times over. Such challenges, with all their various blocked-energy expressions, continued for a long time.

Nevertheless, I can see how all this intense interpersonal friction has been a form of hard training, not particularly different from the many-hours-a-day Buddhist meditation retreats I attended in the past. I even started to feel some gratitude for the situations, as I realized that all the so-called trouble I experienced was wholly a product of my own blockages. *My* desires, *my* expectations, *my* hopes and fears, *my* assumptions and ideas of success and failure—all these gave birth to the quality of *my* personal experience, regardless of the actions of others involved in the situation. Outside parties are as they are, but our feelings are ours alone. I learned to take responsibility for my anger, blame, impatience, and frustration. These were totally self-generated—from *me*, to *me*, for *me*. Fully owning our personal process is the first step in learning to love the self, just as it is.

A *reversal of perspective* is also at work here—from the ordinary tendency to seek comfort and avoid the unpleasant, to a more useful habit of recognizing opportunities for self-learning and self-acceptance embedded in the pain of conflict and struggle. In this way, our goal shifts from trying to push away everything that is uncomfortable, to using pain as a opportunity to further accept all of ourselves, not only what we like. In this way, we learn to appreciate both the *space/time self* as well as the *essential self*—the apparent self with which we are all familiar (usually identified with blockage, imbalance, and limitation), as well as the deeper self or what some Buddhists call True Mind or Big Self. Deeper levels of being are revealed by our movement to love, understand, and clarify our process, which demands self-trust, faith, and basic appreciation. While these attitudes can guide us in daily life, they also happen to be the foundation for more advanced practices, begun only after the personality becomes silent, harmless, and naturally loving.

As you might expect, RA (who claims to have given initiation teachings to the early Egyptians) also addressed this adept path, which accelerates the practice of bringing all energy into the heart:

"The seeker seeks the One, and the One is to be sought by the balanced and self-accepting entity, aware of both its apparent distortions and its total perfection. Resting in this balanced awareness, the entity then opens itself to the universe, *which it is.*"[3]

This quote also reveals the essential perspective required to bring all experience to the heart: *awareness of both our apparent distortions as well as our total perfection.* If we can learn to rest in this mind of great Self-trust, full love will be our path to completion.

3. Elkins, op. cit., Vol. III, p.34.

Chapter 27

SHATTERING ARMOR I

WE ALWAYS TALK ABOUT SPIRITUAL GROWTH, but it means little unless we get down to details. To be specific, *how do we really grow?* With all sorts of conditioned patterns (our normal ways of thinking, feeling and acting), *how do we ever move into freedom?* We can talk all day about love and light, Higher Self and the Christ, but to be frank, the mechanics of personal transformation are usually quite painful. Although our true nature is already enlightened, unless you have become a Buddha since the last chapter you are *still* not manifesting your total enlightenment in the physical world. Though we all want to grow as much as possible, hoping does not do too much either.

So, why are we not enlightened right here, right now, when that is our true nature (i.e. Higher Self)? It is not because of evil aliens, nor the "vibratory prison-net" some claim they have spun around the Earth. It is not because of original sin, nor the many dysfunctions of human society (which do, of course, spin their own webs of distortion). This matter of why we are stuck is not as simple as it seems, and peering into it gives us an important angle to better understand our lives.

According to Buddhism, the cause of suffering, dissatisfaction, and even rebirth is ignorance and grasping. We can break this down into ignorance of our true nature, and grasping at false notions about self and the universe. The primary problem is that *we believe in our ideas*— about ourselves, about so-called external phenomena, about everything! We believe that our own interpretation of events is in fact the true nature of the event itself. In philosophy, this is called *reification*: "to convert an abstract concept into a thing," and to Buddhists, we perform this type of conversion whenever we make fixed ideas out of raw experience, and then make things out of ideas. This is called living in a dream, and all but the fully enlightened still live in some degree of illusion.

As expressed in the Heart Sutra, one of the most important Zen teachings, the Buddha taught that both name and form (material objects and ideas) are, in fact, empty of solid self-nature. This means that things are as they are, and not as we label them. Our definitions do have value in consensus 3D reality, but their spiritual power is limited. In other words, you must forget yourself to know yourself, and you can only "save yourself" with a radically expanded view of self. Likewise, you can only save all beings (one of the primary Buddhist vows) by realizing that they are *already* saved. Of course, these teachings all proceed from the main Buddhist doctrine of no-self, which posits that what we really are, our true nature, is beyond all dualistic conceptions whatsoever.

Are you thoroughly confused yet? Actually, I hope not, since I think there is a lot of value in such high philosophy. As I often say, *love is not enough*. Wisdom is also needed, especially if we are to drop false views or what Buddhists call "cherished notions" (our pet delusions). Even though you may feel far from enlightenment, it is good to get a sense of the road ahead.

Western metaphysics give us another angle. While they do not talk about no-self or emptiness, they basically say the same thing in a language with which we are more familiar. In these systems, the primary cause of suffering and non-enlightenment is considered self-identification with conditioned patterns of personality (i.e. physical-emotional-mental), which leads to mis-alignment with Higher Self, our core being, at one with All That Is. Any and all sense of separateness is a product of non-connection and non-integration with our core being.

As RA noted, the purpose of evolution is to eliminate all distortions to the Law of One—to clear obstructions in awareness to full realization of boundlessness. Ultimately, realizing Oneness is the same as no-self and emptiness, and the goal is to become transparent to full cosmic awareness:

Enlightenment is, of the moment,
an opening to intelligent infinity.[1]

Honestly, we cannot make this kind of supreme opening without *radical* detachment from both ideas and personal conditioning. From the view of full enlightenment, our ways of grasping include emotional patterns, consciously held thoughts, and the deeper sub-strata of beliefs about reality and the nature of self. While there is relative value to all such notions, and we do need a mental grasp of the principles of evolution, they are still labels pinned to raw experience, and we cannot realize boundlessness or unity while checking the labels. If you pause in breath meditation to see how well you're doing, stillness is immediately broken. As an old Chinese Ch'an (Zen) Master once chided:

...to talk about a thing is to miss the mark...

Taking a deep breath, you might now be asking, "OK, so what about armor-shattering?" It just so happens that the primary mode of life-catalyst designed to help us evolve, helping us clear old patterns of blockage and realize Oneness, happens to be shattering armor!

Esoteric astrologers have long understood that Uranus can have a strong decrystallizing effect, a rude awakening that shakes out old patterns. But this kind of shock to the system does not only come from starry forces. It is an integral mode of soul-contact, a common event in the life of all seekers. Not only is crisis an opportunity for growth, but the magnitude of the opportunity is often proportional to the extent of the personal devastation meted out. In other words: *the greater the crisis, the greater the gift*; the more shattering, the more potential Self-opening.

Before we end this chapter, let me give you an example:

Case Story: A mother is wracked by panicked helplessness at the possible dangers to her son and only child on his upcoming overseas travel in a volatile, poor nation. But after her panic settles down a

---

1. Elkins, op. cit., Vol. I, p.161.

bit, her husband of over 20 years has mini-stroke symptoms and ends up in the hospital for a few days. Shock upon shock; the crisis is compounded. Her old patterns of thought and feeling (denials of mortality, fears of abandonment, self-doubt, and illusions of security and non-aging) are all dredged up, and her cycles of avoidance and limitation (embedded in status quo stasis) are shattered by repeated blows.

As she struggles through a landscape of loss, the cracking ice underfoot throws her back upon her own inner resources. Ultimately, it presents an opportunity for renewed self-confidence and self-esteem, faith and trust, and a chance to more fully accept real-life limitations. As the magnitude of the crisis points to the scope of the opportunity, a crossroads is offered for her to either take a major step forward in empowerment or, instead, a regression back to fear and helplessness.

We could even say that such compounded crisis signals the advent of a new cycle of soul-evolution. Yet, as always, free will prevails. As RA would say,

> *…the purpose of incarnation in third density is*
> *to learn the ways of love…*[2]

And so, the gifts can be received or repulsed. Such life shock can be seen in countless ways, used to buttress both faith and bitterness. It all depends on attitude—how the experience is met and used, where the responsibility is laid, and the degree of latent self-appreciation brought to bear on the situation. To unlock doors to learning and growth, however, one must use the keys of self-love and self-acceptance. And from that opening can come even greater expansion, which will ultimately lead one to final release in the ocean of boundless being. Of course, however, this is a mystic achievement far beyond the work of psychological self-acceptance.

On the way to such final release, all our armor must be shattered. As in all true healing, old patterns and distorted energy fields must be

2. Elkins, op. cit., Vol. III, p.39.

interrupted for new light to enter. In the next chapter, we will explore how the same process is occurring today on the global stage, dealing rude blows to the sleeping souls of Terran humanity.

Chapter 28

SHATTERING ARMOR II

In the last chapter, I touched upon one of our most common experiences—being overwhelmed by situations, breaking down, and then having a chance to go beyond limitations. As a death and rebirth process, it takes place on many levels, and can be called "shattering armor" because old forms and personal patterns are destroyed and refashioned to make way for the new. Likewise, the death of a physical body comes when it can no longer fully anchor the light of soul. In a sense, you could say that soul has at last outgrown its shell. While this kind of "phoenix rising" happens dramatically at the individual level (as we pass through all sorts of cycles, shifts, and life losses), it also governs collective evolution, and happens to have a starring role at the present time on Earth.

As we all know, many prophets, channels and indigenous traditions have predicted severe Earth changes in the next decade, and attribute it in no small part to dysfunctional human consciousness. As Gaia is a living system, sensitive to human thought and energy over the ages, I totally agree. Yet most of these speakers also consider it a cleansing or time of purification. Sure, it looks like that and will look even more so, if and when wide chaos occurs, but this level of analysis is too simplistic. Although it concurs with common sense, the reward vs. punishment model of karma is somewhat childish. Actually, the laws of soul and planetary evolution are far more subtle than that. But to really appreciate the beauty of our collective world armor-shattering, we need to know a bit more about personal karmic process.

When we turn our attention to the Great Work of individual soul-evolution, the first thing to understand is that there definitely is a piece of work to do: the total development of the body-mind-spirit system.

While it is a joint collaboration between Higher Self and ourselves (we being its light-spark in form), the work is guided by our own free will through the choices we make each step of the way. Nevertheless, there are discrete lessons programmed into the scripts of each lifetime, and while Higher Self cannot learn for us, it has ample tools at its disposal to optimize our potential to achieve specific goals. As we can all attest, the process of shattering armor is one such tool used to help us raise the pace of soul-evolution.

Beneath the unique lessons slated for all souls in 3D form, there are primary types of energy adjustment which must be made. As the basic agendas of particular lifetimes, these include:

✦ **Rectifying imbalances:** i.e. decreasing excess and supplementing deficiencies. A simple example is adding emotional sensitivity to a soul that's already got great mental power. This could be done by taking birth in a loving, poor peasant family without educational opportunities.

✦ **Growth in particular areas:** i.e. development of particular soul-qualities. Such qualities are usually found in the basic trinity of love-wisdom-will, but also include the radical reversals and redirections that pepper pivotal lifetimes. Examples include the basic transit from material to spiritual concerns (often inspired by significant people and events), or shifting one's emphasis from partnership to self-based learning (which is strongly catalyzed by the death of a mate).

✦ **Balancing responsibilities:** A more advanced form of balancing, this is ultimately a way to refine the direction of will. A common example is the balancing of personal needs with the demands of others. This is one of the main lessons offered by marriage and family life.

✦ **Karmic returns:** Similar to the old reward-and-punishment model, this allows re-integration of personal energies previously accumulated or split off. Examples include past-life violence and current domestic abuse; great karmic merit and extreme good fortune; and chronic emotional avoidance that draws to us relationships full of drama. These are also forms of readjustment.

Regarding individual soul-evolution, the point is simple: previously imbalanced choices necessitate specific re-balancing experiences, all of which are known and aided by Higher Self, and must be met with love and acceptance by the soul in veiled 3D-incarnation for successful resolution. Karma is thus offset, and body-mind-spirit readjusted when we heal our wounds, forgive our enemies, embrace our shadow, and take responsibility for painful events. But, this can only happen *after* full-frontal direct confrontation—being wounded, meeting enemies, suffering the shadow, and absorbing trauma. While you could certainly judge all this as "punishment for past sins," nevertheless, such hardships are actually various forms of greater self-exposure, fully known by Higher Self as a *potent catalyst* likely to inspire us to make the needed adjustments in attitudes and mental-emotional biases. From the perspective of Higher Self, there is no "bad" karma.

We can surely consider these difficulties to be "times of purification and cleansing," *but events in and of themselves cannot make us grow.* They are simply the lawful result of our previous choices and our ways of thinking, feeling, and action. Evolution via incarnation proceeds through a continually self-mirroring process of life experience. Neither reward nor punishment, events and what they "bring up for us" are the basic forms of catalyst designed for self-learning, re-balancing, and spiritual polarization (i.e. the paths of virtue and vice). Shattering armor, in and of itself, does not purify. *We purify ourselves.* It is not even accurate to say that "life teaches us particular lessons," since only *we* can do the learning. Life and events are just as they are. *We* are the boss of whether or not we get anything substantive from them. Let us at least give ourselves due credit.

When we look at the world process, there are even more complex dynamics to consider. Intertwined with individual soul evolution and karma, there are also:

(1) the life-path of the planetary Logos Itself (Gaia);

(2) the lives of the animal/plant/mineral kingdoms;

(3) devic or angelic groups at all levels of evolution;

(4) interdimensional ET races related to Earth (so-called "inner civilizations"); and

(5) the group-soul life of Humanity itself, the collective Oversoul of humanity.

While we cannot go into the details of such thickly interwoven group karma, still, all these players have some degree of influence on world events, and are, in turn, influenced themselves by the global process. They are all players in the current dimensional shift on Earth.

Therefore, in the same way that Higher Self programs life experience as catalyst for personal growth, the planetary Logos offers Earth changes as an armor-shattering type of catalyst to all groups who partake of Earth life. Just as individuals respond differently to similar challenges, so, too, will each group make different use of the chaos. But in all cases, the karmic process proceeds according to universal laws of cause and effect. For humanity, geological upheaval offers a needed interruption in our chronic spiritual complacency, and may inspire some to see "the error of their ways," and choose a more balanced, heart-based lifestyle.

As with individual catalyst, some of the larger world changes are planned from above, while others are wholly the product of humanity, either directly or otherwise. Yet even those events modulated by higher levels are intimately tied to human consciousness. The more humanity acknowledges and accepts its latent dis-ease (anger, fear, greed, and ignorance), the less severe the Earth changes. As humanity takes off its own armor, there is less need for external assistance.

As always, divine counsel remains the same: *Soul, Know Thyself!* Simply put, the root purpose of the entire manifest creation is self-knowledge, and the function of all life events (whether programmed by Higher Self; chosen through wisdom or ignorance; experienced alone or in relation to others; or occurring at social, racial or planetary levels) is to mirror and inspire our efforts to move forward in evolution. In other words, to help us move from conflict to harmony.

The sequence here is easy to trace, but also most elegant. Over lifetimes, our personal and collective distortions (lack of love) exquisitely create the karmic patterns that then generate the conditions (planned by Higher Self or drawn in by ourselves) in which those very same distortions can at last be healed. Bear in mind, the karmic process of environmental mirroring for greater self-knowing need *not* be traumatic at all. In fact, on most 3D worlds it is not. But, when souls and soul groups create all sorts of mental-emotional barriers to the inner light (at both individual and social levels), then all such walls must first come crashing down before real Self-discovery can begin.

Chapter 29

Applying Fertilizer

The shattering of old armor, both personal and collective, is obviously our grist for the mill, the basic stuff of our spiritual learning. Once we know that, we then need to focus in upon our own particular way of being in daily life situations. For it is not only in meditation and in service to others that we learn the basic lessons of self-revelation. It is in the heat of the moment, as we deal with our intimates, talk with friends, deal with our jobs and sit home alone. In all such situations, weaving the loom of personal life, we experience some sort of catalyst— some sort of sensory, emotional, and/or mental process. These are our typical ways of thinking and feeling, intense or mild, pleasant or otherwise. This is the basic stuff of personality experience.

When we then add a desire for spiritual growth, we have to expand our view from not only the stuff of experience, but also to *how we relate* to the stuff of experience. As I continued my counseling in the U.S. and abroad, I saw time and again the truth of this principle: *what we think and feel* is far less important than *how we relate* to what we think and feel. In other words:

> *What we commonly call my shit, my crap, and my garbage, is, in point of fact—if we are keen enough to see it—the major catalyst we can use to fertilize our growth of love-wisdom.*

This idea first became clear after a counseling session I had with a European woman whom I had met in Japan, and who happened to be in San Francisco at the time. Despite her long background as a healer, she was quite stuck in her own process concerning her marriage. She and her spouse still lived together, but they had not had intimacy for months; and after a brief episode of infidelity on her part, the husband was still enraged. She had already acknowledged her responsibility and now wanted reconciliation, but she could not really confront the misery of her home life and the heavy grudge still nursed by her spouse. Actually, they were both stuck.

After some back and forth talk in the session, a bolus of tears and sorrow welled up in her, and—eyes red and bloodshot—she cursed her process: "I thought I'd finished all this crap years ago…"

I told her, "If you had really finished it, then it would not be coming up now. If you had really healed it, you would no longer be feeling it." In time, she agreed. And after the session, walking down the street, I saw the front page of our local weekly alternative paper, running a story entitled "Fecal Matters" (no doubt, an exposé of local corruption or the newest sexual fad in our Babylon-by-the-Bay).

It was then that I put two and two together: our old encrusted emotional issues are the very stuff of self-transformation, as they offer us head-on catalyst we can use to love ourselves more, accept ourselves more, and understand our process more than we already do. This so-called crap is the fertilizer of love-wisdom if we know it, accept it, and understand its generation—then move ahead to forgive the self and others. Seen in this light, it is damn good crap! It is worth far more than its weight in gold, because unlike gold, the inner growth from *this* fertilizer you can take with you.

For this lady and her spouse, what healing demanded was a commitment to self-acceptance: a conscious, deliberate choice to feel, accept, and be willing to experience completely their pain, weakness, sorrow, guilt, and despair. This decision is no less than the decision to love—which, as always, begins with self-love. This simple act of decision (simple, not easy!), would be the fastest and most direct way to "open" her heart chakra further, to generate more energy in the fourth or green-ray center, and accelerate a true and real reconciliation in the situation. What she considered her "old crap" is, in fact, if applied in the heart, rich fertile fertilizer for developing love and compassion. Knowing this, the only question left is whether or not she really wanted to apply this fertilizer to her own process.

After our work together and some more of her own self-reflection, she did, in fact, try to welcome her emotions a little bit more. And so she could then move on to wisdom, the fifth or blue-ray center (throat chakra). We then looked at deeper dynamics:

*"**Why** have you been unwilling to feel yourself,*
***what is** the state of your partnership,*
*and **what are** your alternatives at this point?"*

This type of inquiry requires *more* effort (hey, no one ever said healing is easy!), and *more* mental focus. We quickly plunged further: she did not want to feel because she feared a complete nervous break down; she fought against weakness, because since childhood, she always thought she had to be strong; and she was afraid to feel her emotional void, because she was avoiding the prospect of being alone again. Exploring all these issues, we peered into the beliefs which undergird her so-called negative emotions (as almost all feelings arise from beliefs). Clear your limiting beliefs, and you will eventually clear the painful emotions. But of course, you must first be willing to feel them.

As we looked from this angle, we saw the roots of her present paralysis (loving a man who hates her, and living in a tortured double-bind). Her somewhat masochistic behavior (keeping herself in the path of his rage), was actually a form of self-punishment, which fulfilled a confused desire for atonement for the act of marital infidelity. It was an example of the old *mea culpa* ("I'm to blame"): long-term guilt from chronic self-blame, which maintained her low self-esteem and was rooted in some very old self-doubt and negative self-valuing. These roots were complex, admittedly so.

Thus we came to understand the *how* and the *why* of her present condition, as well as the mixed feelings of her spouse, who had been threatening separation for months, all the while hanging onto a pity-me role of victim-cum-torturer. Simply making the conscious direction of will needed to reflect more deeply, and thus discover these facts, is also a form of catalyst that fuels the growth of wisdom and discernment. She emerged from our sessions renewed.

As we looked at her options, we decided that the best course would be to voice the insights she made, give the relationship a time frame, and consider the painful fact that the partnership was probably over. Having the *will* to face the music, as she had, is *also* a form of catalyst (consciously chosen) for the growth of wisdom, which can be seen in the power of a few pointed questions. Wouldn't she be better off with a man who really loved her? Wouldn't self-healing proceed a little faster if she was not living with a tormentor? Wouldn't she improve her self-esteem and gain some needed emotional strength by taking the risk of being alone? Isn't loneliness preferable to being coupled in a caustic union? Confronting these answers takes guts, but it also leads to the further growth of will (sixth chakra activation), as well as some clearer thinking.

If she had just followed her old way—hating the sadness, blaming herself for weakness and avoiding the massive sorrow overhanging her self-punishing home—she would not have been able to take the next step in the process. What she first called "my old shit" was really a precious resource, but again, she had to open the eyes of self-acceptance (love) to see it that way. Once accepted in the heart, she could then move into mind and seek deeper comprehension (wisdom).

Situations like this are all around us. Whenever we feel conflict there is an opportunity to realize greater self-healing through the growth of love-wisdom. Are you angry at the faults of those around you, disgusted by the greed of your ex-husband, fearful of the death of those you love, regretting your past mistakes, or fearful of striking out on your own? If so, then freedom will come only by making peace with these feelings. Accept yourself and the limitations of each situation, try to acknowledge the responsibility of all concerned without blaming anyone, then consider how and why it all came to be. A simple motto: *fully conscious feeling leads to total permanent healing.* Each conflict we face in daily life can be used this way, but only if we are willing to apply the fertilizer, not keep on cursing it.

PART B:

BUDDHISM AND MEDITATION

» *Chapter 30* «

THE MIRACLE OF EDUCATION

*The spiritual path proceeds through the stripping away of all
the inessentials in thought, word, and deed...*

As you might imagine, the practice of "using fertilizer," appreciating
the catalyst of daily life, and bringing all experience to the heart requires
a *quiet mind. We can hardly even identify our process when we are greatly
upset.* As my own path has developed over the years, the importance
of staying centered on fundamental principles has become increasingly
clear. I can see that the spiritual path requires us to strip away all the
inessentials in thought, word, and deed. We ought to realize that there
are *primary* teachings and there are *secondary* teachings (or what RA
sometimes referred to as "transient information" or spiritual trivia).
Primary, essential teachings lead us to ever deeper self-integration, and
they form the core of all mystic traditions.

I recently read one of the classics of Buddhism in translation, a
work called *The Wisdom of the Early Buddhists* by Geoffrey Parrinder,
a collection of the oldest Pali-language scriptures from the time of
Siddhartha Gautama, the man whom we call "the Buddha." The more I
read, the more I could appreciate the purity of his teachings, which are
by all means "primary" and show us a true path. As opposed to much
of what can be found today under the speckled New Age banner, these
early teachings were *path-centered.*

The men and women who became monks and nuns around the
Buddha were taught not to waste time in either needless activity nor
idle discussion. Their entire lives were spent in meditation and mind-
training. One passage in this book is particularly instructive, especially
if we relate it to the current preoccupation of many with sensational
UFO matters. This story sheds a clear light on what the Buddha
himself deemed essential, more or less in his own words:

"The Buddha told Kevaddha [a householder] that there are three sorts of miracles:

There is the *Miracle of Mysteries*, by which a man becomes invisible, passes through walls or walks on water. But an unbeliever might do this by a magical charm, and because I see the danger of such miracles I detest them.

Then there is the *Miracle of Secrets*, by reading the hearts and minds of others and telling them what they are thinking. But this also might be done by a magical charm, and I detest it.

Finally there is the *Miracle of Education* by which one hears the preaching of a Buddha, awakens to it, is disciplined in act and word and speech. One thus obtains joy and peace, realizes the Four Noble Truths [the reality of suffering, cause of suffering, end of suffering, and the way out of suffering], and the final assurance of the freedom of discipleship.

This is the Miracle of Education."[1]

If we look deeper at this *Miracle of Education*, we can see exactly what "path-centered" means: holding firm to the primary teachings of enlightenment and transformation. If that is our aim, then we have to be strong and discerning, and willing to put spiritual trivia in its place. To be sure, government schemes and UFO cover-ups, black-budget technology and ET customs are interesting, but are they essential primary teachings? Do they lead to our liberation and freedom from needless suffering? Do they help us achieve self-integration, fusion with true self, and the flowers of love and wisdom? Of course, not—and it is important to remember it.

In this light, it is obvious that much of what we call cutting-edge UFO information and amazing psychic stories is secondary, and concerns merely the first two minor miracles. Mere curiosity about alien magic (i.e. passing through walls, levitating, or scanning thoughts) does not take us too far. Perhaps we should think more about the

---

1. Parrinder, Geoffrey, The Wisdom of the Early Buddhists, p. 48. New Directions, 1977.

spiritual progress we might need to achieve these powers. Of course, to the Buddha and his students, these abilities were not considered a big deal. As all yogis know, they are simply by-products of higher consciousness—just signposts along the Way.

The real question, as always, is simple: *"Is it essential or not?"* If our interests and studies lead us to greater joy, peace, clarity, and freedom from suffering, then they are quite worthy of our time and attention. If we subject all our current studies and sources of information to this standard, we will save a lot of time. More than that, we can also be sure then that our spiritual path is straight, centered, and grounded in the Real. The entire teaching of the Buddha, and all true Masters, has but one central goal: our freedom from ignorance and suffering. And so we are told:

> "Whether wonders beyond the powers of ordinary men are performed or not, that is not the object for which I teach the Truth. The object of teaching the Truth is to destroy ignorance in the one who practices it."[2]

In the next chapter, we will take a closer look at the Buddhist path and the central practice of mindfulness: focused awareness to see things as-they-are, going beyond all illusion.

---

2. Ibid., p. 55.

» Chapter 31 «

MOMENT TO MOMENT

FOR A LONG TIME I imagined that my next book would be titled "Moment-to-Moment Living." I envisioned it as a textbook, a collection of reflections to take us back to the preciousness of the moment, which is really all we have. Since I am not sure when or if this book will be written (at least on Earth), it seems like a good idea to explore this theme in this present moment. Let's be here now!

In Buddhism, the path to greater sensitivity in the present moment is achieved through "mindfulness practice." There are many forms of this practice, and the root of them all is breath meditation, which in the local Pali of the Buddha's time (a derivative of Sanskrit) is called *ana-pana-sati*: "in-breath, out-breath awareness." It is really the foundation for all other work on the Buddhist path, and it is a powerful tool to develop concentration and one-pointedness. As those who meditate know, it is almost always difficult to stay focused on a single object (our breath or anything else), as countless distractions of thought, image, and feeling get in the way. Yet, if we cannot simply watch our breath in a quiet way, how can we expect to be clear and discerning in daily life, which is all the more complex? This is exactly the problem most people face: unable to rest and be still while alone, we are not truly present with others. This is a *big* problem, and the only solution I have found is formal meditation practice, according to some mystic tradition.

At the start, before we can sing the virtues of *wakefulness* (which is the core of Buddhism, as even the word Buddha means "one who has awakened"), we need to acknowledge the basic condition in which we find ourselves most of the time. What is the diagnosis? Unfortunately, human minds are generally speedy and distracted, unfocused and unsettled, never resting and always jumping from thought to thought.

To borrow a phrase from Buddhism, we have to acknowledge the "monkey-mind" before we can liberate it.

Another thing we will see right away is one element of the Buddha's Four Noble Truths: the fact that "all conditioned things are impermanent." Looking deeper we will also find that this perpetual restless mind is itself tied to suffering, what the Buddha called *dukkha* or dissatisfaction. With this kind of calm observation, we can see that everything in the mind naturally changes, shifts and flows, and never remains solid. It is our desire to keep things the same, leading to grasping both subtle and coarse, that is at the root of this *dukkha*. Mental grasping is perhaps the most profound and pervasive quality of the non-enlightened mind. It is the root tendency that leads to our commonly accepted sense of separated self. As such, it is also the root of all ignorance.

While the ordinary mind jumps from thought to thought, from memory to fantasy to feeling, at a pre-conscious or pre-cognitive level we are left with only *the bitter aftertaste of loss*, the inevitable slipping away of all we cannot hold and preserve. Though it may be unpleasant, the first step towards learning how to "be here now" requires us to steep ourselves in the curdled milk of mental turmoil—not to be masochistic, but to get familiar with the way things normally are. Like it or not, this tumult loud or soft is where we usually live. If we think it is otherwise, it is probably because we are not looking hard enough at the raw quality of moment-to-moment experience. If you do not believe me, try an hour of sitting with your breath! At advanced stages of meditation, we can observe even more subtle levels of dissatisfaction. So it is said: "only a Buddha is truly happy."

Of course, this may seem pessimistic, but from meditation experience I have learned that ordinary mind indeed knows no rest. But more than that, the harder I look in mind for something to hold on to, the more everything recedes. Ultimately, all that we try to grasp slips away, which is another basic truth expressed by the Buddha, and leads us to appreciate the value of non-attachment. In particular, it is taught that the way to freedom from suffering, impermanence, and monkey-mind is through non-grasping, learning to rest in spacious mind, and ultimately realizing the illusory nature of the mental process itself. But again, such advice means little or nothing unless we have the *stability of mind to listen and receive, the willingness and desire to understand* exactly *how* to quell our confused mental process, and reverse the age-old patterns of ceaseless grasping. Here again, we see the necessity of formal meditation. Bear in mind, this is an extremely subtle process, as we can only use the grasping mind to teach the grasping mind how to be comfortable with no more grasping!

But fortunately, we can develop stability and concentration through careful awareness in daily life. Only then can the subtle splendors all around us be revealed. Moment-to-moment living means taking one step at a time, one situation at a time, flowing from relation to relation, engagement to engagement, from present focus to next present focus. The irony here is that ordinary life already expresses just this flow. Whether we are clear or not, we do travel the path of life from moment to moment. While we can certainly influence our road and some of the scenery around us (a process we can learn in weekend seminars on "manifesting abundance"), it seems more important to direct our efforts to knowing the one who is taking this grand journey. *Who* is it that manifests anything?

The kind of self-work I mean—leading to a deepened appreciation of the moment, a sense of greater potential and creative response—is based upon both *self-reflection* and *whole-hearted engagement*. Zen Buddhism expresses this kind of engagement in the most simple terms: *"When you drink tea, drink tea!"* It does not mean we have to kill our thinking (which is actually impossible), but rather, jump wholly into experience. When we give ourselves to the moment without reserve, we can experience a vibrancy and contact-intensity that, in its purest form, is full enlightenment.

To give oneself to the moment is to forget the self, and to forget the self is to drop habitual grasping through thought, checking, and emotion. In this way, we actually free ourselves from an illusory stream of mental activity, and begin to "see through" our normal patterns of self-definition, all of which proceed from the very understandable assumption that "my psychological process is real and solid." In Buddhism, the only philosophy I know of that "swallows its own tail," the ordinary sense of self or ego is considered a totally empty notion, the first and primary delusion that keeps us in *dukkha*. Their view is that only the formless, essentially bright mind-source is "Real."

Furthermore, RA says the same thing: they consider most everything a "distortion" of The Law of One. For them, only Oneness is real. Everything else is a measure of mis-perception... Again, unless you enter deep meditation, it's hard to understand this insight.

The second part of *mindfulness*, which complements whole-hearted "external" engagement, is self-reflection and sensitivity to what arises internally each moment. Although strict Buddhists might consider this a fallback to fantasy, since it involves a form-bound focus on my feelings, my process, and my needs (keeping alive the notion of an apparently real ego), it is still a useful approach to greater understanding. Although this kind of practice assumes that the various elements of psychological experience are solid (i.e. "I and my feelings are real"), and would probably be considered a delusion by some of the diehard Zen masters, who teach non-duality by shouts and screams, nevertheless, it is like removing poison with poison, using dualistic mind to gain freedom from itself.

Despite these limitations, this approach helps us understand and identify our personal process in the moment, which is a good first step that can generate more kindness and self-compassion. Such self-reflection can open the heart, develop reflexive self-acceptance, and ultimately help us dissolve attachment to these very same thoughts, feelings and beliefs. Though we may still believe in ego and a sense of separate self (which just means we are not yet Buddhas!), the energy of love that comes from really being willing to feel ourselves fully, has a tremendous transformative effect.

Centuries ago, the wry Chinese Buddhists said: "If you meet the Buddha in the road, kill him right away." Today, applied to our more humble self-healing, we could also say "when you greet turmoil, confusion, and pain, love them fully." When we meet the so-called "ego" with unconditional acceptance, it actually dissolves, since it is just a mirage anyway. It is a product of having believed in our normal 3D senses for many lifetimes, of assuming that our ordinary perceptions of duality and subject-object splitting are real. Again, from the perspective of Oneness or The Law of One (so-called *emptiness*), there is no solid "me and my feelings." *There is only the flow of the great infinite nameless.* This is no different from the Tao as described by Lao Tzu (author of the Chinese Taoist classic, *Tao Te Ching* ("the Way and its Power")). It is the great mystery that can only be entered beyond all conceptual thought. Living this reality is living full enlightenment.

For those of us who are Wanderers, this perspective helps us acknowledge that the apparent duality we live amidst in 3D is just an illusion, which may ameliorate some of the discomfort of this alien environment (and you thought *you* were the alien!). It can also help us develop a more focused, disciplined sensitivity to bring our power back inside. *If you want to be free of the all the pain of 3D duality, then pay closer attention to your own mind.* We cannot be at ease in a world full of strife and conflict when our inner world is just the same. We cannot achieve balance if we do not have silence of mind, and we cannot do too much real service when we are stuck in our own personal process. Of course, you do not have to be from elsewhere to make use of the teachings of whole-hearted engagement and thorough self-reflection. ET or otherwise, we all live in the now.

As RA once noted, "the moment contains love," which means that cosmic Love is the basis for our freely chosen experience, and the potential for loving action is ever present. In fact, when we are really clear and present, free-floating love and basic goodness can be felt as the matrix of each moment. True human nature, what RA calls "the mystery-clad being," has its source in the freedom to choose and grow as we please. Whether we appreciate this or not, is *also* our choice.

What is precious in the moment can only be seen with eyes of light, perception truly free of attachment to thought, feeling, and belief. Our ordinary ways of grasping, keeping us from simple presence, are born of a subtle sense of separation—attachment not really to a solid ego, but to the apparently solid idea of what we call ego. In my experience, it is only through deeper meditation, calm, and insight that we can come to see how subtle and far-reaching is our sense of separation from All That Is. The sense of separation is no different from the sense of ego, and this basic existential split is the root of all suffering and illusion, according to Buddhists.

All mystic traditions speak of Unity, identifying Higher Self as true Self, and teach that true Self is one with Infinite Godhead, the supreme mystery of Being. As the basis of so many religions, we have all heard these ideas before, but hearing is not enough. In practice, the path of living Unity is lived *moment-to-moment*. Each moment is like a crossroads in which we can be clear or confused, present or absent, wavering or firm. In this very moment we forge our fate, and as usual, it all depends on our fortitude, awareness, and will-to-be. Over 1000 years ago, the great Chinese Ch'an teacher Lin Chi, founder of the Rinzai School of Zen Buddhism, said the same thing:

> "Students today can't get anywhere: what ails you? Lack of faith in yourself is what ails you. If you lack faith in yourself, you'll keep tumbling along, bewilderedly following after all kind of circumstances, and never be yourself."[1]

> "There is only the "man of the Way," listening to my discourse, dependent upon nothing—he it is who is the mother of all buddhas...

> Make yourself master everywhere, and wherever you stand is the true place."[2]

It all comes back to us, and we all come back to Now.

---

1. *The Recorded Sayings of Ch'an Master Lin-chi*, p. 7. Institute for Zen Studies, Kyoto, Japan, 1975.
2. Ibid., p. 14, 17.

» Chapter 32 «

IN THE LONG RUN

IN BUDDHISM, MEDITATION PRACTICE is sometimes compared to mountain climbing:

*At first, the **Ascent**—hard, grueling, and painful as we struggle and strive;*

*Then, the **Plateau**—long, flat and boring, demanding patience and perseverance; and finally,*

*The **Descent**—quick and easy, gaining momentum as we cheerfully expect Return.*

In the beginning of practice, we fight with crazy mind, bogged down in muddy doubts and self-pity, and we do not even know if we are meditating. After the struggle, which may take years, we settle down and for the first time can truly enjoy some peace and quiet—*a silent mind*.

This is the great middle, like a plateau, during which time the practice matures and refines into our own unique expression. Here we gain character and skill, learning advanced navigation in spirit on the still seas of mind. Finally, at the last stage we start to hurtle towards our Source, towards forever, dissolving apparently endless fixed notions and patterns of feeling into a boundless condition that defies all description, ultimately laced with bliss. At this point, as RA would say, "the looking backwards is finished." Descending the mountain of self-mastery, we leave behind the ages of our dreamscape of evolution, the ancient illusory sense of separation and needing-work-to-do.

For myself, as I suspect for most self-aware Wanderers, life on Earth today is like the middle phase of meditation: we are here for the long run, and the 3D journey is far from over. And like the plateau stage in meditation, dealing with day-to-day life in 3D demands patience and perseverance. Every day we must get out of bed, brush our teeth, wash and dry and clothe our body, then go on to meet the many tasks we have chosen. If you sometimes feel fatigued, know that you are not alone. I know lots of Wanderers and spiritually-minded folks who are ready to get on the bus back Home. Weariness is common. Of course, this is also well known to non-ET servers and seekers.

Nevertheless, the countless little doings required by life on Earth are the matrix of our maturity as souls. It is like personal counseling once the stormy seas of emotional crisis are past. *Only then* can Self-revelation really begin. In the first phase of meditation, a time of struggling with the wild mind, we have no idea what spirit really is. It is only after we have cleared and risen above the fog that we can begin to see the path we're already treading. Spiritual maturity really depends on *altitude*.

And after we have gained some altitude, the next challenge is staying with it. Again, this is the long run, the efforts required *post-crisis* to make it work—the slow growth of character, attitude, and purpose. In meditation, it means long-sitting in silence with a tamed mind. For Wanderers, it means long-term adjustment to 3D life in a confused, materialistic society. And for all who serve and lend a hand, it means the slow refinement of skill in knowing how, when, why and who to serve. In the long run, we as souls gain durability, patience, and fortitude.

As for my own recent experience, having flown over 80,000 miles in 1997 for teaching and counseling, I was relieved to have the next few years for more self-reflection and inner travels. During this time, I've taken a long hard look at the issue of *quality vs. quantity*: the relation between effort expended and harvest achieved. I have come to realize that there is little value in running around to serve, or to promoting my work to those still unsure of their needs. Since only Self awakens Self, to run around urgently seeking the chance to teach is definitely an unbalanced approach.

If we can take each step slow and easy—whether we are in the ascent, on the plateau, or nearing descent—then we can remain sensitive enough to make the various inner changes demanded by the time, and thus preserve our harmony with those around us. The balanced way in meditation takes us from silence and non-doing to active engagement in service, and then back again. Like the ebb and flow of a great ocean, following our path in harmony with self and others brings grace and respect for the cycles of change. In the long run, the only thing we can really depend on is *spiritual balance*.

The next chapter continues our discussion of meditation.

Chapter 33

THE ROYAL ROAD

In a way, it is simply a practice of showing up: can you be present and alert for the entire period of meditation?

I HATE TO APPEAR FANATIC, but I really believe meditation can be a gateway to all our dreams come true—to complete freedom from conflict, to all the virtues we imagine. I think there is nothing impossible given enough meditation, including all sorts of miraculous powers, as well as union with All There Is. In my own limited experience I consider it a clear path to the infinite—and the irony is, this gate is ever before us, yet almost none of us venture in. We can talk all day and night about guides, angels, ET groups, and Masters X, Y and Z, but it remains but childish awe if we do not support it with a practice path for our own transformation. Many good students and devotees consider their Guru or ET contact to be a perfect being, yet they balk at the idea that the Highest Master is within. It is easy to admire others, but far harder to take your own transmutation well in hand. As RA once said, very few souls are willing to "progress through all the distortion leavings" (the painful, shattered and cherished illusions) on the true initiate-path. I too don't throw myself into my practice 100% (which would probably mean no "indulgent-time" and many hours in meditation a day), so I am not really pointing any fingers.

On my travels I have heard many people complaining about Earth, about feeling stuck and oppressed, about the miserable state of human society (a sentiment I often echo, to be sure!). Yet, my patience wears thin when I remember that powerful tools to our freedom are always at hand, always at our disposal. If we spent half the time meditating that we now spend feeling bad about ourselves or complaining about the world, we would already be clear and easy. As the Chinese Buddhist teacher Lin-chi (whose passages graced the close of "Moment to Moment") remarked:

"The true student of the Way does not look to the faults of the world; he eagerly desires to seek true insight. If he attains true insight in its perfect clarity, then, indeed, that is all."[1]

So simple it seems simplistic, the meditation I practice is at the core of Buddhist tradition, and begins with the *training of concentration*. In metaphysical terms, I consider it a pure exercise of Will since "the only thing which moves" is naked awareness, which is none other than the true Self who wields it. It is also a *practice of personality detachment*: remaining focused steady upon a single object (in this case, the breath), learning stability of concentration, then letting go of all else.

Of course, here is where the real challenge comes in. The "all else" that needs to be dropped is basically 99% of ordinary mind-experience, including all the apparently real sensations, feelings, thoughts, memories and moods we normally get hung up on. In meditation, if the mosquito bites, so be it; if memories of past thrills arise, just let them; if ideas of projects left undone come into mind, take care of them later. When we hold to the anchor point of concentration long enough, believe it or not, eventually the monkey-mind will stop jumping around. In the words of an ancient Buddhist text, "*The mind learns to incline towards Nirvana*," or spaciousness, freedom, non-attachment and non-grasping. But this new habit can only be developed through consistent practice. Not surprisingly, it usually takes years for the monkey-mind to appreciate its own demise.

In terms of the technique of this breath practice, the meditator holds awareness steady at the nosetip, remaining aware of the air passing into and out of the nose. In a way, it is a true practice of simply showing up, being present and alert for the entire period of meditation. "It is analogous to those Wanderers who serve the planet by their very "presence, beaming love and light as beacons planted in the body of Earth. And like Wanderers and everyone else who cares about helping the world, the practice is not particularly glamorous. In fact, it can truly

---

1. The Recorded Sayings of Ch'an Master Lin-chi, p. 14.

be called anti-glamorous, since this form of meditation severs pride, egotism, and all forms of controlling intent. It is definitely not a feel-good practice, although in the end, you will feel quite good indeed.

In my experience, meditation practice has brought gravity, clarity, and a degree of immovability to "my" character. Very little now shocks me (although a man with advanced gangrene on the filthy streets of Hangzhou, China did turn my stomach), and not too much now takes me by surprise. Not that I am all-knowing, perfectly balanced, or replete with virtue, but rather, my perspective on self, others, and life itself has grown tremendously since the beginning of meditation practice. I can appreciate a greater sense of spaciousness with less knee-jerk reflexes. I can rest in a more clear sense of center, ballast and balance, and intuit the nature of the path ahead much better. In my seminars, I often paraphrase one of the Buddha's more important sayings:

> "Karma [i.e. conditioned, fixed patterns of response] for an ordinary person is like a teaspoon of salt in a cup of water, while karma for the enlightened is like a teaspoon of salt in the ocean…"

In this analogy, the measure of salt (representing our baggage from the past) is just the same for both the ordinary and enlightened, but the *container of mind* that each experiences is far different. Karma dissolves without a trace in the far vaster consciousness of an enlightened being; the influence of ancient patterns and obstructions is simply no longer felt. Of course, *we ourselves are the master* who determines the breadth of our awareness, and thus the strength of our karma.

To be fair, Buddhist concentration is not the only kind of meditation, and many New Age teachers today offer various techniques of visualization. RA also made this distinction, and described two main categories of formal meditation:

(1) "***Passive meditation***, involving the clearing of the mind, the emptying of the mental jumble which is characteristic of mind complex activity among your peoples, is efficacious for those whose goal is to achieve an *inner silence* as a base from which to listen to the Creator... and

(2) The type of meditation which may be called **visualization**... [which is] the tool of the adept [which allows] polarizing in consciousness without doing external action, [and] has as its goal *the conscious raising of the planetary vibration."* [2]

Although different, both forms share a common goal: *the focusing of attention*, which RA calls "the one technique for this growing or nurturing of will and faith." [3] With firm will and some degree of faith in the process, we can access our true nature, the center of being from which all blessings proceed. For those who practice meditation in balance, these nice ideas are not merely wishful thinking at all. They are the inevitable results of effort and perseverance.

As with all metaphysics, the line is drawn by personal experience. You cannot know sweet unless you taste the sugar. The intellectual formulation of higher truths counts for little without practice. Reading lots of books may fill the mind with neat ideas and reveal a vision of freedom to strive for, but if the ideas are not applied in daily life they will only increase "the mental jumble." The path of spiritual growth is a process of increasing simplicity, returning to essentials, and resting in the Real. As it is done, we clear the mind-ground of emotional conflict and mental distress, so greater love, wisdom and Will can shine in a more spacious mind-sky. Eventually, we find pure awareness without a solid bounded self—in other words, Oneness. With time and continuing balance, the royal road of meditation will *always* yield a harvest of rich spiritual bounty.

---

2. Elkins, op. cit., Vol. II, p. 126–7.
3. Ibid., p. 98.

» Chapter 34 «

COOLING DOWN...

ALL OUR HEATED STRUGGLES must someday end. Our spiritual learning, our self-reflection, our efforts at self-improvement—all must one day bear the fruit of peaceful mind, gentle heart, and the ability to be at ease amidst all the hot-head frictions of everyday life. Meditation means nothing if not taken off the cushion into the heart-space of moment-to-moment situations and relationships. When we talk about healing, it means little if we cannot stop in the moment to catch the flushed passions, which left unchecked, destroy the fragile bonds of kindness which we seek to build in all our relations.

Cooling down means stilling the running-round mind, cutting through the chronic ceaseless spinning of thoughts and opinions, judgments against self and other. Even checking ourselves must one day fall away to cease, dissolving in a more quiet space where even self-control is unneeded. This does happen given enough stillness, and only that at a deep enough level of mind.

In some sense, the practice here is letting go—letting go of the need for controlling inner process, letting go of the need to exert our will on others in any way. Obvious domination and manipulation are just the most coarse expressions of this tentacle-spreading way of life; there are far more subtle expressions, of course. Even the need to help people by giving them advice we *think* they need is a form of hot-head control. Though paved with good intentions, nevertheless, it is just another way to hook into situations with a fixed agenda. Indeed, we often usually bring ourselves to a situation with some sort of floating agenda, which is exactly why we can't be cool and at ease in the moment.

But this kind of free expression of "cool-mind" is not necessarily "cool-in-heart" as well. Actually, we are not really warm at all in sensitivity, and literally, conductivity, when we are mentally jammed in a round dance whirligig of thought. True love is no less than perfect receptivity, and it is blocked the very moment we have calculation in mind, the idea that something at all should, or must, or needs to be done—or said, or conveyed, or whatever. In real mental stillness (not comatose, dead mind dullness), in real peaceful quiet and non-agenda-based mind-being—only there can we find the real fullness of genuine service-to-others. Love is shallow without wisdom, and wisdom icy without love. But the true meeting place of self-and-other union takes place only in the sanctified space of stillness. It is the only starting-place where real love as perfect acceptance, and real wisdom as perfect knowing vision, can be unfurled in their true intertwined state. As a unified expression, this love-wisdom coupling is a fine and refined way of being in service. It is also a development of character that we can truly deem mature.

In the silent way alone, what do I find to do? Actually, I do not know! The height of the silent way is total completion akin to *samadhi* in meditation—calm abiding, being at ease, acceptance of the ways of all things (no longer termed good, bad, or indifferent). In such a state, we can see time passing, yet we sense that such "passage" is also an illusion. Sure, the body ages, the sun sets and rises again, the stomach growls and fatigue comes in its own time. But here, even the way of labeling is not considered a problem, though it may well feel like a tired habit! Perhaps the only desire left when all others pass away is simply the cool, heartfelt hope to help others move out of their own confusion and back to their own perfect being.

In a Creation of unending unity, with nobody but the Creator here there and everywhere, it is ironic in the extreme (to the point of tears, actually) that Its very own sparks of Light get muddled. Muddled by their own conscious ways of knowing and perceiving, though at core, the still center of Being ever Is, even for the most despairing hell-mind souls in the depths of agony (where we have all been at times). As Earth provides "an adequate Heaven and a more than adequate Hell" (RA), we can find many who live in one of these burning pits or icy cells of astral-glamour mind. While the way of cooling down is also a means of serving others, such letting go surrender is also a good piece of advice for gaining release from painful torment.

But surrender is not will-less, nor is it capitulation to our own worst fate. The essence of surrender is simply the release of fevered intention, be it low-grade or raging. Actually, this kind of "drop-down" is not some kind of special trick or positive-thinking technique, nor is it a way of fooling ourselves out of habitual problem-making. The real quiet way of mind comes when there is a deep-level realization that mentally-willed action is simply *not* necessary, and that its ceasing is totally free of risk. When the Buddha was approached on the road by the highwayman-robber Devadatta (who later became an enlightened *arhat*), accosted and told to stop, he simply kept walking, and replied "I have stopped." It is that simple. Do you get it? Are you stopped?

The utterly cool way is not cold and detached. It is not frozen in the tundra of emotional denial, nor is it a stranger to feeling. It is simply *big feeling*, a feeling-based knowing, knowing that so many ordinary things are not worth inner struggle, and thus they need not generate roiling emotion, nor whirling thought, nor even pensive reflection on the proper or best next move. In the real cooling down there is **no** next move. It has already been made. Cooling down is the **last** move. Not separate from stillness, in its expanded state there is no willing-I, and it is no different from the Buddhist way of *sunyata*: emptiness, no-self nature, no separate figuring or grasping or clinging onto. Only *here* is found peace, and only *here* is found the greater Will to serve: the Will of pure being that knows and senses beyond all mental knowing that everything is already complete and whole and perfect. In this state of Being (actually, beyond all conditioned states), there is no longer even a drive to become cool, quiet, or to put ourselves at ease. We just are.

» Chapter 36 «

JOY IN MIND

WHENEVER I FIND MYSELF ready, willing, and able, I try to increase my time spent in meditation. For myself and all of us, the intensified practice triggers all sorts of inner movement, as the process of facing mind-as-it-is not only reveals our normal contortions, but also creates a growing field of stillness. It is not that the ordinary ways of getting stuck just drop and fall away—it couldn't be that easy!—but rather, we become less swayed by their ceaseless grasping.

Where once we felt our thoughts buzzing like bees in a basket, we later come to see them with detachment, from the sensed safety of distance and a more spacious awareness. Distress does not just disappear, but from deeper meditation we come to look upon it in a new way, with more equipoise and calm, more likely to accept than cut and run.

However, distortions are not the *only* form of mind-life observed as we plumb the depths in meditation. Sometimes, and far more pleasingly, we open the gates of joy, as I recently experienced. As I sat there in my room, following the breath without too much mind-chatter, I suddenly felt a kind of unbuttoning in my heart region. Immediately, a little stream of joy suffused the body, and I felt a swoon of happiness. I have had many experiences of bliss in meditation before—the kind of thing where you do not even want to breathe or else you will lose the delicate feeling, but this was different.

It was not exactly the bliss that wipes away all thought, that magic yoga-drug for which all meditators long (which are achieved in the *jhanas* or absorptions—from Buddhist Sanskrit). It was not quite so "tranced-out." In this case, my perception of external events remained intact. My consciousness stayed in the body, in the room where I sat. Because I avoided entering trance, the normal bridge to plain 3D awareness was preserved, although the energy state was not common at all. Through this connection to ordinary mind, I was able receive an important insight.

Apparently, simultaneous with the feeling of upwelling joy from the heart, I realized that the external conditions of my life were totally irrelevant, immaterial, and unrelated to this state. I felt a subtle dissolving of the normal idea that happiness comes from a proper arrangement of one's life. Of course, "rearranging our affairs" is useful, and can certainly help bring relative happiness. We all proceed instinctively on the assumption that getting your life in order is "good." But whatever the value of self-fulfilling activities in the physical world, in that moment of meditation I realized that *external conditions have nothing to do with inner joy*. One could live in the Chinese Gulag, as many Tibetan Buddhists sadly do, yet still experience transcendent bliss. Of course, I am not justifying oppression.

In this second section of *Universal Vision*, I have focused on the basic principles of self-healing and the balance of love-wisdom: *know yourself, then accept yourself.* This approach focuses on consciousness and our psychology, and has little to do with moving energy or direct work on the chakras. It is much more Western Buddhist than Eastern Hindu: it's plain, dull, and not particularly exciting, but it works. However, this recent meditation event was an energy movement pure and simple—unblocking energy at the level of the heart chakra, with a subsequent release and ascent of previously trapped forces. You could say it was a form of greater Self-opening (which is a far more Hindu interpretation than Buddhist, since good Buddhists are more likely to talk of no-self!). But it was also an important insight into the true nature of 3D-experience: the axis of "joy and despair" basically depends on consciousness. This insight, for me, was itself a form of healing.

But whatever the label, this experience showed me once again the primacy of one's inner state. Self-radiant joy really has naught to do with social life, and the continual manipulation of external conditions is not a path to inner joy. Joy is wholly *a fragrance of heart-mind being*, and if that is what you are looking for, you probably will not experience it for long without meditation practice.

Chapter 37

STANDING ALONE

Divine Will in Love is the centered vibration of Higher Self at our core, and the task of refining the base metals of personality into the radiant gold of spirit requires the conscious empowerment of Will.

As I HAVE MENTIONED BEFORE, meditation and the spiritual path are like mountaineering: first you go up, then things are flat, then you go down. But we can also look at the spiritual path in another way. The higher you go, the smaller the crowd! While I do not think it is true universally, since so-called higher realms are filled with light-beings, it does appear to be so on Earth. The more effort we put into self-cultivation, the more time we spend in meditation, study, service, and reflection, the more we do tend to split off from the main body of society (which, to be honest, really has little interest in the disciplines of personality and the development of consciousness). Though spiritual dedication generates more compassion, desire to serve, and a sense of unity, it generally separates us (at least in awareness) from our peers. To boldly turn towards spirit, at least here in 3D, usually requires us to turn away from the world—at least for certain periods—and learn to stand alone.

Again, it is important to differentiate Earth from the higher realms, where we find countless civilizations embracing spirituality, fully aware of universal path and design, hosting active temples of learning, prayer, and meditation well integrated into the daily life of the whole society. We do have that to look forward to, and our society is definitely moving in that direction. In the greater cosmos, there are numberless worlds dedicated to sending love and light to distant orbs (including our little planet Earth), where all souls are devoted to service, seeking greater unity with Life. In these civilizations, one need not stand alone.

In fact, their social harmony is so intense that it exerts a metaphysical force that unifies individual awareness into a greater collective Mind. Their group actually becomes one Being, a condition described by RA in *The Law of One* as a "social-memory complex"—unified knowing between all members of the group.

According to many channeled sources as well as RA, most of the Wanderers on Earth are from just this type of society. No wonder we feel such alienation down here. The experience of individual and collective separateness is intense and very real in third dimension. Being naturally sensitive and open, Wanderers often feel great pain within self-centered modern society. Beyond that, ET souls must also contend with the "interdimensional dislocation" of having lost the greater freedom and awareness native to higher realms. Some of the Wanderers who have been here for centuries have developed a hard shell, often leading to bitterness. Many more of them have simply checked out from social engagement entirely, choosing to live more or less isolated. Whether or not you consider yourself an ET soul, you too may feel alienated from the common ways of the world. But in the world or out of it, we still must learn to stand alone.

Despite, or perhaps *because* of global disharmony, the 3D schoolhouse Earth is an excellent training ground, not only for Wanderers, but for all spiritual seekers who want to accelerate soul-evolution. If you are familiar with the rigors of traditional Eastern paths such as Zen Buddhism and Hindu Pranayama, you can appreciate the value of hard training and balanced discipline as catalyst for enlightenment. Seeking love and light and seeking to share that love and light in an environment of conflict and suffering can be a huge stimulus to awakening.

As an example of this, I once lived in a Japanese Rinzai Zen Buddhist monastery in upstate New York, an austere and forbidding place called "Dai Bosatsu Zendo," which translates as "the Great Bodhisattva's Zen training temple." There, the teacher (or *Roshi*, in Japanese) made liberal use of the famous wooden Zen stick, called *keisaku.* Far from being an instrument of torture, the Roshi explained that "only the swift horses get a beating," and such a treat was reserved only for those students whose practice was already strong, to further strengthen and intensify their work. We in the West, especially those familiar with New Age weekend workshops, are not accustomed to the real intensity of hard training in Oriental schools. The true adept-path is a very serious matter, and when meditation practice connects to cosmic power and high-voltage energy rushes into the 3D body, it can literally be a matter of life or death—which I know from personal experience. Of my two closest friends and co-students there, one went temporarily insane and the other killed himself.

Of course, we do not have to embark upon such a steep path to grow. Simply living in normal society can be a great catalyst to spiritual maturity. But it is neither easy nor simple. We can see all around us the results of not being able to get along in society. The mental institutions of all nations are full of those who could not cope, adapt, or stay centered within. In most cases, those souls were unable to clear their own personal process and deal with the outer challenges facing them. Though we are intensely social beings, learning how to stand alone is a central, core learning.

For myself, as I suspect for all of us, life's course has involved gain and loss, grasping on and letting go. On the path of meditation, I have learned some of the skills of detachment from the body-mind system, and I have come to appreciate the basic impermanence and insubstantiality of thoughts and feelings. Realizing the illusory quality of one's own psychological process is the first step to really knowing emptiness, or sunyata. Understanding the basic emptiness of thoughts and feelings does not mean denial, rejection or judgment. It simply allows us to center ourselves in more spacious awareness, which could be called a quality of spirit. From that vantage point, we are naturally less reactive to the passing play of mind. This can be called "standing alone" at the level of awareness—watching the shadows and clouds, and not grasping on. In Theosophy, it is called "holding the mind steady in the light"—quiet mind, being at ease in the light of soul.

A second aspect of standing alone is much more literal. On my own path of growth, like so many other seekers around the world, I have had to detach myself from society in many ways. As I set priorities, some activities and acquaintances fell by the wayside. Some relationships had to end abruptly, while others took their place. Making a commitment to self-development, then gradually intensifying that commitment over time, always involves reshuffling the social deck. Since inner change radiates and magnetizes new contacts, as we grow, so too must our social circle. Since spiritual growth requires increasing inner contact, those who need other than what we offer will naturally drift away. Some phases of inner work demand outer withdrawal.

And yet, while I have experienced much loss in social, material, and psychological terms, the vacuum has been filled from a deeper place. As in the saying, "you can only receive with empty hands," there has been a corresponding influx of energy, meaning, purpose, and fulfillment over the years. Disillusionment led to a shattering of illusions; detachment served to sever old bondage; and the loneliness of being alone opened up to an experience of greater wholeness and self-centering. The more you seek, the more you receive. The more you offer in service and spiritual balance, the more comes to you and through you. These ideas may seem trite, but they are also facts of life.

Friends, co-workers, and true spiritual family will continue to come our way, possibly more than we ever imagined. Yet, while the community of heart may strengthen and its foundations grow more stable, there is *still* an abiding need for solitary work. Nothing is more transformative than communion between self and Self, between conscious mind and our superconscious total being. *Turning inward is the essence of all seeking, and leads straight to Will.*

As this inward turning finds its source, we will find also the sacred within. Divine Will in Love is the centered vibration of higher self at our core, and the task of refining the base metals of personality into the radiant gold of spirit requires conscious empowerment of Will in balance. As all esoteric schools tell us, the forces of will and endurance are developed through meditation, concentration, and focused service.

Once developed, we also need Will to safely stand alone.

I recently met a woman who attends the school where I conducted the research for my first book—the California Institute of Integral Studies in San Francisco. Studying indigenous cultures, she also began to uncover her own distant roots, and a lot of Starseed information about cosmic family soon came her way. While the school is somewhat broad-minded (how many places will accept a dissertation on ETs?), nevertheless, she still felt isolated, and moreover, her intellectual mind told her she must be crazy! Unless she could separate fact from fantasy, inner truth from outer fear, she was unable to remain in such an environment. Clearly, there are stages to the process of self-understanding and the development of Will. One of the first stages, which we can observe from this example, is learning how to trust one's deeper knowing. Self-trust is the foundation for all inner growth, and it is also a prerequisite for standing alone.

Yet, there is no need to worry. You could not ask for a better training camp than the planet you are living on right now! On Earth, it is not too easy to be clear, not too easy to be strong. It is not even easy to trust yourself, since you can always find a dissenting voice either in your mind or out in society, which suggests you have made a mistake or that an opposite view is better. For a planet that is not yet "in the light," where there is an apparent wall between the obvious and the eternal, dealing with incessant duality and opposition is just the way things are. Here, uncertainty is the norm, and as RA said, "understanding is not of your density." Only through persistent and dedicated effort can we become clear enough to rise above the towers of social opinion, most of which happens to be confused. This kind of intellectual/intuitive self-reliance represents a more *mental* aspect of standing alone.

If you are a Wanderer, remember you did not sign up for an easy job, nor did you come here on vacation. If you don't think you are a Wanderer, then you do not have to worry about the cosmic details, but your path is *still* based on cosmic essentials—which include balance in self-acceptance, loving wisdom in service, and unity in fusion with true Self. For all of us, the only guaranteed security that we can depend on and can take with us is found within. This notion is not pessimistic, and it is not a call to isolation. It just seems to be a fact of life here on Earth.

Furthermore, the more sensitive you grow on the path of initiation, the more you will probably feel the prevailing confusion and distress around you—the common lot of 3D humanity. Even RA was stymied by the complexity of human civilization, admitting that even they "cannot plumb the depths of the distortions which infect your peoples."[1] As our hearts open and our eyes clear to see and feel more of the Real, widespread human distress becomes ever more apparent, sometimes painfully so.

In my experience, the only escape is transformation, which is not really an escape at all, but rather *transmutation*: the development of new eyes in a new body with a new sense of self (and eventually, no fixed sense of self at all!). Like the tall sun-bleached lighthouse high off the rocky Maine coast, standing alone at ease can be a beacon to those now tossed by storms of global change. ET Wanderer or otherwise, we are all points of fiery light expressing the One Infinite Light, and compassion, strength, and brilliance is our destiny. Even in solitude, we are not alone.

In the next chapter, we will merge our study of Buddhism with a return to the development of body-mind-spirit. This time, we explore enlightenment from the perspective of a famous German author and his protégé: *Siddhartha*, otherwise called the Buddha.

---

1. Elkins, op. cit., Vol. I, p. 76.

Chapter 38

THINK, FAST, WAIT

In *Siddhartha*, the classic novel by Herman Hesse, the wizened Siddhartha Gautama (who through his own efforts became the Indian Buddha, founder of all Buddhist schools) is asked point-blank just what he can do, now that he is "enlightened." In later Buddhist literature, in particular the records of Chinese and Japanese Zen, several masters were also asked about their attainment. In those later times, in the relatively straight forward cultures of China and Japan, the teachers often replied in most ordinary ways: "Now I can drink tea and eat rice... Now I can chop wood and carry water...," or something like that. But in *Siddhartha*—which is actually a German-Indic crossbreed, a fictional account of what life might have been like in ancient India— the Buddha explains his enlightenment a bit differently. While his answer is actually Herman Hesse's version of what he thinks about enlightenment, it still bears repeating. It seems that old Mr. Hesse was relatively enlightened himself.

For some reason, I have never forgotten this passage from the book (and I hope I have got it right!), even though I last read it in high school about 20 years ago. For some reason it recently came back to me, and I think it is appropriate to consider now that we are nearing the end of our study of Buddhism and the principles of spiritual growth. It is a fine description of the goal.

In *Siddhartha*, when the Buddha is asked what he can do now that he is free, he simply replies:

I can think, I can fast, and I can wait.

It is a simple answer, but not as simple as it seems. Nor is it too easy to attain! How many of us can think clearly, logically, and accurately? How often can we even think through a problem to a useful solution?

And for that matter, how well can we wait, and how patient are we for the things we want? Like oceans and seas, the depth of this achievement is not seen by a quick glance at the surface.

Upon closer inspection, the Buddha's reply is actually quite esoteric. In previous chapters, we have looked at some of the principles of transformation, or in other words, the ways and means of healing, balance, and enlightenment. Central to that discussion is knowing and working with the body-mind-spirit system, which is the manifest self and the elements of our personal identity in everyday life. There is no achievement if we neglect to deal with personal stuff, that which arises for us, and usually for us *alone*, moment-by-moment.

Siddhartha's achievement, as conveyed by the perceptive Herman Hesse, is one way of describing the completed work on body, mind, and spirit—the perfection of the human soul. This perfection is, indeed, the state of "Buddha": full awakening to our own true nature (the Sanskrit root *budh-* means "to awaken or perceive"). This perception of the Real can only come with full purification, and thereby full control of the body-mind-spirit system. However, this is not the control achieved through self-domination (a mistaken path taken by many, many spiritual seekers!), but rather, the control that comes through full self-mastery. In this condition, there is no longer any obstruction to the pure use of Will. There is no longer any friction in personality, nor conflict within or between mind and body, nor a speck of non-knowing of the source of what we are. Full perception of our true being is full awakening, and can only grow after all forms of ignorance and self-deception have ended. Inner friction, personal conflicts and spiritual non-knowing are just various forms of confused self-awareness.

Let's consider each of the Buddha's three achievements one by one. To be able to really *think* is no less than complete mastery of Mind: full and free use of reason, analysis, and thought. Of course, there are also supernatural powers of mind that perhaps Mr. Hesse did not know of. And at superhuman levels of being, something as bulky as a thought-form is actually not much needed. When RA refers to the Council of Saturn (considered to be the administrative center of our solar system, staffed by beings who we can fairly consider to be cosmic Buddhas), they remark that choices are made by the immediate perfect blending of their consciousness, and only "when a need for thought is present" do they resort to thinking at all! I am sure that the historical Buddha also did not need to think too much. Living in Unity, the answers are immediately available. As the culmination of the evolutionary Law of Seeking (as Jesus said, "Seek and ye shall find"), eventually, there is no gap between such call and response. At this stage of the Path, one seeks *beyond* seeking.

Nevertheless (returning to the experience of mere mortals), there is no doubt that intellect is one of the most powerful tools in the human anatomy. Only through discernment, reflection and analysis can we figure out that there is a spiritual path at all. Once we know we are on the Way, we must depend on reason to navigate the course. The real Buddha (not Hesse's creation) once said that his teachings are like a raft to help us get to the other side of the ocean of birth and death, to the achievement of *nirvana* or enlightenment. Likewise, RA said that in working on body-mind-spirit, *the work on Mind is primary*. It is the element of Self most generally, and also most greatly distorted at this time. We should never underestimate the value of reason and clear thinking—powers often held in low esteem by current naive New Age teachers and channels. And though Mind itself is but a raft, you had better develop a strong mind or it may sink you! Anyway, since the development of mind is actually the growth of wisdom, it primarily occurs in fifth density worlds and is usually just *begun* on 3D orbs such as ours. No need to hurry on the cosmic path…

The second achievement of Hesse's Buddha, *"I can fast,"* is no less than full mastery of Body. To be able to physically fast, abstaining from solid (or even liquid) food, represents a degree of freedom from dependence on the material world, the four elements, and the "lower" kingdoms. Almost all mystic religions and native traditions include ritual fasting as one of their practices. And while it can be taken to extremes (such as in one sect of "sky-clad" or naked Indian Jains who starved to death after taking vows of harmlessness), fasting is an important training for both body and mind. While historical Buddhism does not include fasting practices, the monks of Buddha's time ate only before noon, and many (even today) eat only once a day. This does not mean we should blindly follow their example, since times have changed and the modern lifestyle is different, but still, dissolving attachment to physical desires is an essential part of the path—on Earth, that is! Again, in higher dimensions things are much different, since both the bodies we use, as well as the basic awareness of Self and Path are much more refined.

Finally, Hesse's Buddha said he could *wait*. While this ability is the actual summation of many lesser powers and self-purifications, the power to wait is basically the achievement of Spirit, what is otherwise called contact with Higher Self. It is also the development and activation of the sixth chakra (the so-called third-eye or brow chakra), which confers the powers of faith, forgiveness, peace, and realization of unity. As in silent formless meditation, at the sixth center we open the spirit-shuttle gateway to the seventh or crown center (in RA's description)—and at last sense the perfumed scent of Higher Self. In this activation, we realize that "all is complete and whole and perfect" (*The Law of One*), and thus we can wait, since everything is just fine as it is. In this realization, we have a true return to Source: surrender to *Tao* (the nameless Way of all Life), fusion with true Self (inner peace and intrinsic contentment, not tied to 3D conditions), and a quiet opening to all life, all beings, all things. The Buddha can wait because he has no more desire for anything other than what is always here. This ultimately confers universal presence.

In Siddhartha's great achievement of the ability to think, fast, and wait, we can see the practical results of massive spiritual exertion. As we continue our own slow work of greater self-knowing and more self-acceptance, we too move in this direction. The more we use our mind to think, our body to fast, and our spirit to wait, the more enlightened we become. Despite the cycles of birth-and-death, and despite the approaching Earth harvest and closing 3D theatre, our work with body-mind-spirit continues on.

In the next chapter, we will join some of major strands of thought outlined in previous sections. At last, we will soften our focus on the details of personal transformation, and increase our altitude once again, returning to the big picture. Having explored so many aspects of the collective and the individual, we are now ready to return to the cosmic.

» Chapter 39 «

TIME AND FOREVER

As we approach the end of our look at Buddhism and spiritual path, it is fitting to consider the greatest paradox of all: *our time-bound lives set in the context of eternity.* As you may have noticed, the second half of this book has treated two major topics: **(1)** the cosmic plan and spiritual path, and **(2)** the practical ways of self-healing and balance. While the first topic presents the basic metaphysics of Creation and its Design, and the latter shares the "how to's" of personal growth, the greater context behind all this is easy to miss, as it is exceedingly subtle and usually forgotten.

What is the greater context? In the Buddhist tradition, it is sometimes presented through the filter of *relative vs. absolute view.* This dichotomy is no less than time and forever, or to be more specific, the irony of having to work on ourselves while our ever-present true nature is absolutely perfect and needs no work at all. In discussing the metaphysics of Self, RA points to this same "paradox" (which is, however, no paradox to them at all, nor to enlightened beings or Higher Self). As an element of their more advanced teachings, the practice is only effective *after* one has already learned the basics of how to know, accept, and love our own personal patterns:

> "The seeker seeks the One, and the One is to be sought by the balanced and self-accepting entity, aware of both its apparent distortions and its total perfection. Resting in this balanced awareness, the entity then opens itself to the universe which it is."[1]

This kind of self-reflection is best achieved through the various practices of formless, non-doing type meditation—like watching the breath in typical Buddhist fashion (as we have discussed in previous chapters). But formal practice or not, RA's statement points to the

---

1. Elkins, op. cit., Vol. III, p.14.

fundamental reality of Self, the dichotomy between relative and absolute. This is the "heart and blood of the relationship between time and forever, or in other words, the obvious passage of our daily lives in physical form set in the matrix of eternity, the Infinite Being We always Are.

Again, if you have not tasted the bliss of *being-free-of-becoming*, or glimpsed the vast expanse of *seeing-free-of-grasping*, you will not really know what I am talking about. But if you do have an inkling what I mean, it is quite useful to unpack some of what is going on here. This will also be a nice summation of some of the important ideas already presented.

We start with a rather advanced consideration of cosmic metaphysics, or in other words, what in the world is life all about! Let's begin at the beginning. The ordinary, common folks we call ourselves (Tom, Dick, Harry, and Jane) are really embodied expressions of Higher Self, Who is Itself a Being of sixth density, fully aware of Oneness with All. To use non-technical terms, your Source is total perfection, and you are never separate from that Source. You are Higher Self, and Higher Self is really you. But (and here is the catch), in time and space (which includes third, fourth, fifth, and early sixth dimensions, plus all the ETs likely to show up on the 500-channel TV) we are not able to live our true identity. As we all know, we live but a fraction of our whole potential. However, it is quite understandable. *Our whole potential is infinity!*

Now let's ask the really big question. Why does Higher Self (which is itself an expression of the Boundless Creator, infinite energy and awareness) need to take form at all? Why does it need to incarnate in a fleshy body, or a even in a light-body? Why is there this long hard path of evolution in the first place? What is the point of forgetting what you are, only to work throughout the aeons to simply regain what was never lost in the first place? What's the point of all this travail?

As the primary paradox, Eastern mystics have tried to explain the unexplainable. Hindus call it *lila* ("play, dance") and some Buddhists call it *tathata* ("suchness, as-it-isness," both from Sanskrit). In the final analysis, the Mind of God is inscrutable. Creation exists just because… just because it is a good thing that it does. But why? I can only imagine that some kind of Greater Glory comes from infinite experience, though it really does not *have to be* at all.

Where does all the high philosophy take us? Well, it depends on how much you can really take it in—how much you really know You Are God. This is not a call to spiritual inflation, nor pride and ego. Remember, there are countless souls farther along the "path" than you or I. Knowing God goes far deeper than intellect (which is quite shallow anyway). The knowing I am talking about is manifest in a confidence that feels no need to hurry (since time is endless, and after this life comes another and yet another, going from home to Home). It manifests in self-trust that does not mind playing or wasting time, being indulgent or being strict (since all desires must be tasted fully somehow, to fully be transmuted). It is manifest in a broad self-kindness willing to accept and forgive (putting a stop to inner struggle and self-punishment). It manifests as faith, peace, and true inner rest.

What you choose to do with your life on Earth is your own business. The Higher Self, ever at ease, pulls no strings and holds no grudges. In its own dual-attention (*in* towards matter and *out* towards spirit), Higher Self does all It can to arrange the basic conditions we may use to grow. It also waits for the calling, just like the patient elder ETs who observe the Law of Free Will and serve only beings who seek their aid. All such old souls know the path and the greater cosmic plan. They know their God-nature and live at One. And lest we forget, they are *not* far away.

Which is just the point. Time and forever are not a paradox at all. To say that we live "time-bound lives set in the context of eternity" is a nice spiritual phrase, but it is actually just a concept. As a label pinned to experience, this type of thinking is just another illusion to be shattered along the way. Time and forever are *not* two separate things. Right before your very eyes lives a mystery far greater than words or thought can capture. It cannot be fully met by logic or reason, nor by trance or psychedelia. True infinity is not only seen through telescopes on starry, starry nights. Living vivid enlightenment, awareness of infinity, is not separate from form and the so-called 3D illusion.

As we roll into the next decade and Harvest (i.e. global ascension into fourth-density life), I think the fusion of time and forever will become more and more obvious. Many have said, and many are now feeling the *thinning of the veil* between matter and spirit—the physical and non-physical in close approach. As Earth fills its etheric grid with more and more fourth density energy (the forces of love and a gateway to higher life), we'll see increasing signs of magic, mystery, and the sacred all around us.

While U.S. politics go from bad to worse (if you think recent scandals were bad, just wait!) and world conflicts simmer, those of us with open eyes and hearts may enjoy the best years of our lives. By that, I mean the best years of our total series of Earth lives! As the last go-around for almost all Wanderers, I think we may well go out with a bang. For while global power-games intensify, we really can start to live Heaven on Earth right here and now, even before the dawn of fourth density (in about 2012 A.D.). Heaven, joy, and the worlds of light have never been closer than they are today.

As always, it all depends on us and how we use the resources available. Before he died, the Buddha reminded his circle that life is unstable and no one knows the time of death: so we ought to be diligent in meditation. Not too tight, not too loose, neither tense nor slack—this is the way to keep our seeking fresh. It is also good advice to help us stay balanced, as we journey through the last years of a messy cycle of Earth human life. There will be challenges galore, but as always, it is just grist for the mills of Love, Wisdom, and Will. *What else are we here for?*

Though I am not yet ready to go the way of the Buddha, I do have some words of wisdom in closing. Above all else, take full responsibility for your life and your daily state of mind. *They are wholly your creation.* Do not forget that *you alone* determine the speed of your spiritual unfoldment. And finally, know that the very friction of human life is a rare opportunity, not always available.

MEDITATION SONG

The basis of suffering is the dream of personality;

The dream of personality is believing in the display of an apparently separate mind;

Believing in the display of separate mind is attachment to thought and emotion;

Attachment to thought and emotion is the inability to forget the display of Self.

True meditation begins when the meditator forgets the one meditating;

Forgetting the one in meditation begins with one-pointedness;

With one-pointedness, concentration becomes stable;

In stable concentration, the mind dissolves false boundary and identification;

Dissolving false boundary and identification opens true illumination;

With true illumination, insight comes naturally.

Insight is the mother of universal truth;

Universal truth establishes personality balance beyond flux;

Flux and movement are seen as the Way when concentration empties into insight;

When concentration reveals insight, the Self begins to shine and live in mind.

The Self is totality, but only self-forgetting leads to self-remembrance;

One must renounce all seeking to remember;

Only the ardent seeker seeks beyond seeking;

Just the Self inspires Itself to renounce illusion.

There has always and only been *the One*, yet it creates through conscious forgetting;

The manifest Creation is the One in self-imposed apparent sleep;

Awakening is the One returning to One under veils of Creation;

Creation is the One for those who See.

The Great Work is the path of Creator pretending to forget;

Creation is the One playing games of shadow and light;

True play begins after attachment to dualistic thought;

The Original Thought is the vibration of ever-perfection, forever complete.

—San Francisco / July 7, 1996

» Chapter 40 «

QUESTIONS AND ANSWERS

Enlightenment

Q: *Could you define the word "enlightenment"? Everybody talks about it, but no one defines it.*

A: Like the words "love" and "spiritual," this is another lofty term that has been watered down by overuse, and frankly, sloppy use. Etymologically, it simply means "a state of having light within," which indicates a condition of brightness, glowing, shining. Of course, it points to a spiritual achievement, but I have heard the term used to mean everything from a basic recognition of soul, to perfect Self-realization and union with God. To get a better idea of the spiritual path, it is a good exercise to clarify the goal, and essentially, *enlightenment is our goal.*

Why all the confusion? I do not think it is any great mystery: spiritual teachers, like everyone else, are at all different levels of soul-maturity. Likewise, their teachings are often aimed at different goals. An ET Walk-in who claims to channel the Pleiadians may bring a message of world peace; for him or her, enlightenment means taking care of the Earth. Another teacher offers sacred geometry and Merkabah meditation; for them, the goal is to awaken the light-body (whatever that means!). The specific use of the word 'enlightenment' usually depends on what that particular speaker considers important.

In more traditional approaches, a Hindu Guru will point us towards God Consciousness; a Tibetan Buddhist seeks to uncover luminous mind and total spacious awareness devoid of ego. Accordingly, each has a somewhat different idea of enlightenment. Yet, their differences can be reconciled.

To make that reconciliation, the first thing to note is that the ultimate goal of soul-evolution can be described in a multitude of ways, and there are also specific levels of attainment (which are also described in numerous ways!). Specifically, different traditions use different paradigms with more or less conceptual rigidity. Some mystics call the Absolute a plenum (fullness), while others call it a void (emptiness). And so, God can be described as greater than great and smaller than small. At the summit of soul-evolution, a peak beyond conception, we have developed an awareness that has unified all apparent opposites. The Creator is both immanent and transcendent (in all, and beyond all). So too, enlightenment—both obvious and subtle, it is the realization of total unity.

Furthermore, each teacher in every tradition, regardless of their language-system, is *also* at a different level of being—as RA would say, with more or less "distortion to the Law of One." Each teacher is a soul with their own unique development of body/mind/spirit, with more or less purification of their personality and self-based desires, expressing some particular degree of fusion with Higher Self. Again, there are grades of self-realization, achievement, and enlightenment.

Personally, I prefer to reserve the term enlightenment for the apex of evolution—the fullest development of energy and consciousness, total seven-chakra completion, the final release from all need for incarnation in all seven dimensions of our system—a state of Buddha, Avatara. All prior achievements have their value and use, of course, but let's not minimize the goal. In such a completed state,

a) the limitless light of God pours cosmic energy through us, (Hebrew Kabbalah);

b) body-mind-spirit joins intelligent infinity, (RA);

c) we live in *sat-chit-ananda*, (Hindu Sanskrit: "being-consciousness-bliss"); and

d) there is only *nirvana* (Buddhist: "extinction of the flame of grasping at conditioned becoming").

Thus, full enlightenment is the end of evolution as we know it. In metaphysical terms, it is fusion with the Solar Logos and the beginning of the path back to what is called the Central Spiritual Sun, or Galactic Logos (the source of our sun). Clearly, it's no small matter.

Walking the path, greeting countless distortions and catalyst, it is quite helpful to remember where we are going. Yet, in truth, there is nowhere to go. Enlightenment is full being here now.

Dharma and Karma

Q: *What is the difference between dharma and karma? I don't exactly know what they mean.*

A: Both terms come from the Indian Sanskrit, and both of them are used by Hindus and Buddhists in a variety of ways. Some people joke that "my karma ran over my dharma" (meaning they have been overwhelmed by their "stuff"), and in some ways, the pun stems from a real antithesis between these two forces and how they interact on the personal path of evolution.

As far as I am aware, dharma was originally used in a somewhat governmental-legislative sense, and referred to "that which is decreed" (presumably, by the old Indian royalty). Thus it also means the Law, Truth, or Way. This meaning is similar to the Chinese word Tao which is the basis for the Taoist school and the famous text by the sage Lao Tzu, the *Tao Te Ching* ("The Way and Its Power"). In this usage, Tao refers to the mysterious primal principle of the universe: the effortless way things are, the way the Universe continues in its natural flow. Westerners might call it the Mind of God.

As is common in old cultures, the ancients derived their inspiration from a close observation of nature and inner recognition of universal principles. Beginning with a clear vision of the way things are, they progressed to the understanding that human beings do best when living in conformity with the principles of Life. Not surprisingly, dharma and Tao can also be used in a strictly ethical sense.

For Hindus, dharma refers to that which is virtuous: justice, harmony and righteousness. For Buddhists, it is one of "three jewels" at the very core of the tradition: Buddha, Dharma, and Sangha (or community). In this case, Dharma means scriptures and all basic teachings, from the historical Buddha down to all the enlightened teachers who followed the way he set forth.

When applied to the individual, dharma also means duty, obligation, and responsibility. Hindu teachers often counsel their students to "do your dharma," advising them to fulfill their obligations, whatever they may be. According to this view, the proper fulfillment of one's duties is one form of ethical, virtuous behavior—which also involves acceptance of one's individual karma, or required life-experiences. And so "dharma-as-virtue" later became "dharma-as-deed." Fulfilling our fate, or establishing harmony between the practical and the ideal is considered the way of virtue.

Metaphysically, it is also sound policy. Since all life-circumstances represent specific forms of catalyst for our own individual evolution (offering us self-tailored conditions in which specific learnings may be achieved), fulfilling our true obligations *does* move us along the spiritual path. It is a matter of knowing, accepting, and meeting our essential needs for continued self-growth.

When we then look at karma, we are talking about the inertial, causal-weight of our previous imbalanced actions at all levels of body-mind-spirit. In Buddhism, the root cause of karma is considered to be ignorance, stemming from our belief in the apparently solid sense of self and ego. This leads us to grasping, craving, and thirsting for self-defined experience—seeking the pleasant, rejecting what is not. From such basic tendencies, we lead ourselves into all sorts of confusion, or as RA would say, distortions to the Law of One. Any action devoid of love, or done without full appreciation of the all-sacred unity of each moment's experience, creates some sort of karma, heavy or light.

Most karma is generated by energy blockages in the first three chakras (at the levels of body, emotions, intellect, and social interaction), and their healing is effected by the fourth center, the heart. Bringing unconditional acceptance, love and compassion to our own experience helps clear personal karma, and leads us to greater appreciation of real unity, which is achieved by contact with Higher Self or awakening of the sixth center, the brow-center or "third-eye."

If by doing your dharma you are following the true laws of your own Being (which just happen to be synonymous with the laws of the universe), then karma will slowly exhaust. While karma represents our personal distortions that are grist for the mill, learning to follow our dharma is the milling process itself. And shifting the balance from the former to the latter, from karmic bondage to dharmic freedom, is no less than progress to infinity.

About the Chakras

Q: *Can you explain the chakras, or subtle energy points, in a simple way?*

A: The word *chakra* comes from the Indian Sanskrit, in which it simply means "wheel." In relation to metaphysics or ageless wisdom, the chakras can be considered nodal energy-points in the human subtle anatomy, and they are important for understanding self-growth and healing, the spiritual path and cosmic plan. While there are many different presentations of the centers, I prefer a seven-center model which correlates to a seven-ray color spectrum, such as you would find when white light is passed through a prism. The seven light-rays also correlate to a 7-density model of cosmic evolution.

The first step to understanding the centers is to realize that the human being is an energy system or body-mind-spirit complex, guided through evolution by Higher Self, also called Christ-Consciousness or Oversoul. We are a composite of different types of energy, and our quality of consciousness reflects the quality of the energies that we access. We can operate from an infinite array of forces, which accounts for the variation in people and which also provides our catalyst for further learning. Regarding the chakras, the path of spiritual growth requires us to unblock, balance, fully activate, and then utilize these energies according to higher will and purpose.

Direct work on the chakras is done primarily through work in consciousness, which is also called "working on yourself." Importantly, this means that we can work on the centers *without* doing special breathing and visualization exercises, often associated with Hindu kundalini yoga schools. When the ancient Greeks admonished us to "Know Thyself," they understood that since Self is an open system with free access to Divine energy, knowing ourselves as we truly are leads to conscious re-union with the Absolute. In their teachings, RA also summarized the path this way:

Know yourself, accept yourself, become the Creator. [1]

While most mystic systems divide the chakras into higher and lower (such as the three centers below, and the four centers above the physical diaphragm), it is important to realize that *all* seven are essential to full enlightenment and need to be developed in balance. Of course, achieving physical, emotional, mental, and spiritual balance is much harder than it sounds. It is usually the work of eons.

The three centers below the diaphragm pertain to our normal sense of personality: physical vigor and anchoring at the *root chakra*; emotional life and ordinary self-consciousness at the *navel center*; and power relations with individuals and groups at the *solar plexus*. As is often stressed in the teachings of Theosophy, this trio is the common point of development for most human souls, and it is the starting point for 3D life on Earth—normal personality identification. Our global transformation and the function of the impending New Age is simply an opportunity for souls to move more fully into the next chakra, the fourth or heart center which expresses loving kindness.

Therefore, most "spiritual" people on Earth are interested in learning how to heal themselves, and most teachers offer the wisdom of self-acceptance, love and peace. Taking care of ourselves in this way, we actually clear and unblock the first three centers, allowing more energy to pass into and through the fourth center, all going to the heart, *the key to universal service.*

For most souls, heart development is the platform from which

---

1. Elkins, op. cit., Vol. III, p. 181.

all further growth proceeds. At the fifth center (the level of throat chakra), we perfect pure wisdom, clarity, and the ability to hear, speak and know truth. From such activation, our opportunities for service increase dramatically. At the sixth center, the so-called third eye, we learn to embody a sense of Being in non-duality, peace and forgiveness, will and still presence. Here we contact Higher Self directly, and as you may know, formal meditation is the best way to activate this chakra. Finally, at the seventh or crown center we come to realize our ever-present perfection in full flower, which is, however, accessed through Higher Self (from the sixth center). This bridging (sixth to seventh chakras) represents a metaphysical gateway from unity to forever, accessing in-streaming infinite mind and energy, bringing the soul omniscience and omnipotence.

Interestingly, most Buddhist schools do not deal with the chakras whatsoever, even though their goal is also full enlightenment. This is because all seven centers can be developed through meditation, virtue, and disciplined self-understanding—a path of greater awareness and the disciplined use of Will. However, the seven centers are a very useful map that reveals the cosmic blueprint for the return of light to Light.

Meditation

Q: *What is the best form of meditation?*

A: On my travels around the world I have met many people who say they are doing some kind of meditation. However, when I ask them to explain exactly what they are doing, I usually find that almost no one has a disciplined practice with a clearly defined technique. Most people are using meditation for relaxation or journeying for information. In Buddhist and Hindu yogic traditions, meditation is a formal practice of concentration, one-pointedness, and insight into the nature of mind, self, and reality. In the long run it does lead to relaxation, but it goes a lot further than that. Essentially, it is a path to liberation from rebirth, ignorance, and all personal suffering.

Frankly, there is no one best technique, and there are countless practices from all world traditions that are suitable for different personality types. There are moving forms such as Tai Chi or Sufi Dancing, seated forms such as Zazen or Raja yoga, and meditations on breath, sound, imagery, the Guru, or some kind of ritual. It is best to seek the guidance of a genuine teacher from a tradition with which you feel some affinity. The bottom line is this: *it must be a practice that leads to greater peace, clarity, self-understanding and compassion*; it should help you develop a greater sense of will, strength, confidence, self-integration, and willingness to be of service to others. If so, then your practice is right on track.

Meditation Side-Effects

Q: *Could you explain the possible dangerous side effects of excessive meditation? Could you explain how someone who meditates can become as messed up as one man I know, who is a full-blown alcoholic who continually gets arrested?*

A: I have seen more than a few Buddhist teachers, primarily in the Zen school but also Tibetans, Hindu and American leaders, who seem to show quite serious personality imbalances. Assuming that they have all spent many years in meditation, it is obvious that meditation does *not* guarantee perfection. For those who heap praise on the virtues of meditation (including myself), this is a sobering thought. One may have magic powers and tremendous teaching ability, but for some, "their life does not equal their work." They may even help others a lot, yet *still* have deep emotional blockages (usually related to the first three chakras or energy centers, as explained above).

Christians who praise the grace of divine redemption have an old saying: "the greater the sinner, the greater the saint," which is certainly true. But, there is also a more esoteric principle at work here—*the power of Will.* Great sinners and great saints *both* have a well-developed will, and in spiritual science, Will is considered the *primary active force* of Higher Self or sixth chakra. For better or worse, the Will is beyond polarity, and so it may be used with or without love (I recommend you reflect on that statement!). For those on the positive path, such as great saints, their will empowers love, but for those on the negative path, such as some ETs and so-called black magicians, the Will empowers control. When the Will is accessed through meditation by those who seek to heal, but are themselves still wounded and emotionally blocked, it may inadvertently wound both self and other.

This neutrality of Will means that even those who "do evil" have access to universal power. It is the same Will that can be used to become a great saint. *All greatness depends on Will.* In reverse, a great teacher may also fall quite far, which indicates a mistaken or non-loving use of Will. As the Will strengthens, it becomes more difficult to guard oneself against such mistaken use. This is usually the root of all such teacher-scandals, and it simply means that meditation is not enough.

Meditation primarily develops the sixth chakra, and can then open a gateway to even greater power. As this energy floods into the personality, it affects all other centers. When there is still significant blockage in the first three chakras (at the base of the spine, the sacral/navel and solar plexus centers), all patterns of thought, feeling, and behavior associated with those centers are energized. Some adepts become even *more* distorted after intensive meditation, and I had a close friend who temporarily became psychotic after intensive practice in the Japanese Zen tradition. Another friend and Zen-colleague ended up killing himself. Primarily for this reason, all mystic traditions stress the importance of virtue and self-purification *before* allowing their students to jump into deeper meditation. Otherwise, what we call "unresolved personality issues" can become monstrous problems, far greater than they had been, with tremendous potential for harming everyone in the vicinity. This is probably what happened to the man you refer to in your question.

Meditation is *not* a substitute for careful self-reflection and awareness of your own personality patterns, which need to be expressed (if not in action, then at least in thought, to yourself), and then integrated in all our relations. While I believe the higher centers cannot be fully developed *without* meditation, the lower or personality centers (having to do with body, emotions, and mental force) cannot be totally healed using *only* meditation. As always, balance and moderation in all things is essential before we delve into serious practice. True meditation is a full-fledged opening to infinite cosmic power, and unless we keep harmlessness and true balance, the fire will surely burn us.

Emotional Resistance

Q: *Sometimes when I really need to do something for my growth, I feel tremendous resistance. What can I do about it?*

A: Resistance is something we all experience at various points in life, at various stages of the spiritual path. It comes in all varieties, such as strong paralyzing fear, a vague sense of apathy, or chronic distractedness that scatters intention to the wind. Although I might concur with the recommendation of one American Guru to his resistant student—"just hit it with a stick," using a rather crude approach—one approach does *not* fit all temperaments, and the matter is much more complex if we take the time to look into it.

The first thing to consider, of course, is exactly what it is we are avoiding. In some cases, we resist things that we are, in fact, *forcing* ourselves to do. If someone asked you if you really, in your heart of hearts, want to do what you are avoiding, you might discover you are not really sure you want to do it at all. You only *think* you should. Often, we think ourselves into such a bind by comparing our conduct to that of other people. "He meditates, so I should too… She has her own business, so why don't I?… They go to workshops, why not me?" This kind of thinking tends to override our own desires (which may indeed be less spiritually-inclined, such as staying home to watch TV), and sets up a good/bad psychic struggle. Feeling resistance to forcing ourselves to do what we really don't want (at the emotional level) is no surprise.

But what about the benefits that we presume will come from forcing ourselves to do the good things that others are doing? Some value may come of it, but I can assure you that you will face the same resistance time and again, until you give equal time to the "less elevated" desires being overlooked. It is important to realize that sometimes these apparently less growth-full activities (i.e. rest, recreation, indulgence, or diversion) are just what is needed. They may provide balance as we strive in other arenas, free up mental space for deeper integration, play out old fantasies to later be cleared, or make some time for self-communion. *There are often subtle unseen needs standing behind these less holy pursuits.*

What seems a road to weakness may, in fact, be the plains of ease. And in other cases, we simply need time off. If we scratch the surface, we may discover deeper issues at work here.

For Wanderers and lightworkers, resistance to spiritually uplifting activities often comes from world-weariness and fatigue. We may have a sense that enough is enough, "I'm tired of making more effort!" Of course, this can also proceed into a downward spiral of total futility and painful longing to get it all over with (i.e. "let me go home!"). I have met people all over the world with such a view, and many of them are rooting for a quick and thorough Pole Shift!

This type of analysis strikes an important chord. By not forcing ourselves to do what we think we should do, we allow hidden desires to rise into awareness. Following a line of least resistance, we may find virgin ground—the realm of what we *really* want, which may, however, be disconcerting to admit. How do you live on Earth after you acknowledge your main desire is to get the heck out of here? How do you continue the ascending path of meditation, service, and inner work (which definitely demands discipline) after realizing you are not really sure if your heart is in it? How do you maintain diligent self-reflection when you are tired of gazing into dusty mirrors? Certainly, there are no easy answers, and each of us must find our own version of the pathless path of effortless effort. As the Buddha once said, "neither tense nor slack."

The main point here is that *resistance often covers hidden desires and deeper self-conditions*, and taking a sledgehammer approach dulls the fine edge of thorough self-recognition. We do well to recall that the Path is eternal and demands no hurry at all, though there are certainly deadlines in particular lifetimes. In the end, only what is Real remains. Over time, all our "lesser desires" (i.e. sleep, sex, addiction, distraction, indulgence, and self-pity) will surely be transformed to "higher desires" (for evolution, service, constant learning, and enlightenment). Embracing our resistance and listening hard may not be fashionable, but it *is essential* for whole-self revelation.

On Depression and Dejection

Q: *I sometimes feel real depressed about life. Not just my own, but also the way things are in the world around me. Do you have any advice?*

A: Dejection, discouragement, and disappointment are some of the most common experiences of ET Wanderers and those with an open heart. Being sensitive to our own process, trying to work on ourselves day-by-day, it is absolutely certain we will feel the conditions of the people around us. Since Earth is a most troubled planet, it is inevitable that periodically those troubles will overwhelm us. As RA said, Wanderers can also be called "Brothers and Sisters of Sorrow" (coming to Earth in response to human sorrow), and once we are here, there is no way to avoid that pain if we keep our hearts open. *Open hearts are open to everything.*

However, there is a difference between dejection and depression. If you feel like life is hopeless, the world is doomed, your existence is worthless, and the Universe is punishing and fickle, then you have landed in a deeper pit than mere discouragement. There is an important distinction here. While feelings of discouragement are usually a temporary result of emotional overwhelm associated with specific events and conditions (such as typical burn-out), the state of depression is longer-lasting, and really comes from a generalized despair that grows from deeper distorted beliefs about ourselves, the world, and the universe. To be honest, discouragement is just part of the landscape. All souls who are sensitive, open, and caring go through such twilight zones on Earth. In a world of sorrow, conflict and ignorance, periodic disappointment is normal and should be expected. Hey, there is good cause for it!

Dropping into a pit of depression, however, is not inevitable. If you feel this kind of sullen gloom, then you really should try to discover how it grew, then figure out what you need. Of course, each person's despair is unique, and proceeds from a combination of individual life-conditions, personal childhood and past-life experiences. As RA said, "know yourself, then accept yourself," which is a healing prescription to first know your history, feelings, conditioned beliefs and patterns, then accept all these elements with love and self-tenderness (going beyond anger). If you feel hopelessness, doom, impotence or self-hatred, then you might need professional counseling help. *Depression is usually the hardened product of years of non-loved dejection*, and usually requires sustained self-work to fully heal.

As for periodic discouragement, the treatment is simple and more direct: take time for yourself, for rest, play, and self-nourishment. Work with any guilt that arises over saying "No" to more self-sacrifice, and be willing to sit with the pain of feeling unloved, unappreciated, or unsuccessful. Remember that all these feelings are normal, and furthermore, do not ignore the very real cycles of rest and activity. The fastest way to a goal is at your own pace, using both the brakes and your accelerator.

Beyond all this advice, there are also deeper issues at work. Peering into the cavern of your own beliefs, do you find that you really expect to save the world? Do you think you can eliminate all the evil, selfishness, and ignorance around you? The basic question is simple: *what are your expectations of your own life*—both your service and your personal growth? With unrealistic expectations, we will always be discouraged. It is the common "never-enough" syndrome. With an unplugged leak in the vessel of self-esteem, you will never be able to fill the cup of balanced self-appreciation. At the base of much long-term dejection live the shadows of self-doubt and old self-criticism.

So when is "enough" enough? You cannot save the world, and neither can I. Only Self can save the Self. We can only help. And in closing, here is an idea to consider: the purpose of our 3D life is *not* the creation of utopian society. It is the offering of choice-amidst-confusion, allowing only those souls who strive, the chance to grow into greater love and light. Humanity will be as it will be, but amidst the swirl, some souls *are* growing. All we can do is offer them useful catalyst, in our own balanced way.

Sharing Your Spiritual Beliefs

Q: Some of my friends are curious about spirituality but they seem more interested in arguing about what's real, than really understanding my experiences. How should I deal with them?

A: This kind of half-in/half-out approach is common when people feel an intuitive pull to a more spiritual perspective, while still holding a rational-materialist world-view. They yearn for the nectar of heart-knowing, yet they are still locked down by trust in intellectual logic. The most we can do is to sincerely, thoroughly, and reasonably present our experiences and beliefs, and let our friends work out their own concerns through dialogue over time.

If you see them longing to accept what you already realize as universal truths, though they are *still* fighting themselves, you can certainly tell them so. In the long run, the calling of soul always wins out, but that does not mean some people will not enter the pearly gates kicking and screaming. The most we can do is answer their questions, understand their process, and be patient. This kind of non-interfering, caring but not forcing, is good training for us too.

Dreams and Out-of-Body Experiences

Q: *How can I know the difference between dreams and real out-of-body experiences (OBEs)?*

A: Active discernment and sensitivity to the *quality* of your experience is needed here. You can train yourself to learn to sense the difference in feeling between waking up from dreams, as opposed to returning to your physical body from nighttime travel. A dream-feeling is often more diffuse, like fantasy or imagination, and far more self-circumscribed because it is truly subjective. To me, dreams feel like a movie in the head. On the other hand, a remembered OBE is usually fresh, vivid, and dynamic, mainly because it represents an objective interaction taking place at another level of being, simply recalled (usually in fragments) much later. Without a doubt, some practice is needed to refine this discernment, and using a dream journal to record your experiences can help.

The Doors of Perception

Q: *You use a quote from the poet William Blake: "If the doors of perception were cleansed, everything would appear to us as it is, infinite." In your opinion, what does this mean?*

A: It is widely assumed among those who study mystery schools that Blake was an adept, an initiate who understood the greater mysteries to some extent. In this statement, the *relationship between perception and experience* is key—the fact that *experience is determined by the quality of our awareness*. What is seen depends on the viewer. The old phrase, "for those with eyes to see," means that higher knowledge is self-selecting. You will not find it if you are not ready. And of course, the doors of perception that we normally use are not too clear.

But more than just making a comment on the normal limits of human perception, Blake is really telling it like it is: *the true nature of all things is totality and infinity*. You may ask, how can this be when all I see are separate forms, feelings, thoughts, and so on? The world in front of me certainly does not *look* infinite!

Yet, that is just the point. According to mystery teachings and the experience of deep meditation, assuming that the world in front of us is "all there is" is itself an illusion, because it is only the product of our six senses, a narrowed sample of total potential knowing. Like Plato's statement that the physical world is a shadow of the world of true form, Blake says that human beings have far greater senses that can enable us to perceive far greater reality, if those senses are but awakened. As a mystic insight that is wholly subjective, current science cannot prove the existence of such higher senses. According to seers, what we assume to be "the real world" is but a single slice or frequency of an infinite reality, which can only be known through utter mental silence in a transpersonal, transcendental state of being—a universal vision, in which there is no sense of separate self or personality. By the way, clinical psychiatry would likely call it psychosis!

Everyone who believes that they have had telepathic contact, out-of-body experience, past-life recall, or a host of other paranormal events has had a *glimpse* of such higher perception. But isolated glimpses do not give us too much, and only through formal and regular meditation practice can we gather up these scattered gems, and proceed along a path to pass through all veils forever. But do not worry, you will know when your higher centers are becoming more activated: you will be able to more fully appreciate boundlessness, infinity, and the tangible sense of being at one with life.

Sexuality and the Spiritual Path

Q: *The* RA Material *said that their own ET race evolved on Venus, and that they used sexuality as a spiritual practice. Can you explain more?*

A: In Hindu and Buddhist traditions, there is a branch of teachings called tantra ("rite" or "ritual," from Sanskrit), dealing with ceremonial magic, practice, and energy-direction. One element of this is sexual yoga: exercises, meditations, and ritual involving two partners in physical union. The idea is that higher consciousness can be achieved through sanctified sexuality, that is, conscious sexual embrace that aims to blend mind/body/spirit of each partner in divine worship and blissful union. We all know the power of orgasm upon awareness; it is no less than a taste of ecstasy.

RA indicated that enormous energy transfers can occur during sexual union: love at the heart, wisdom at the throat, unity/forgiveness and will at the third eye, and mystery/infinity at the crown. They said that when two souls are both on the path of service to others, then all the gates to infinite intelligence (God-consciousness) can be opened by such practice. True tantric yoga is based on caring, respect and unconditional love; specific ritual movements are secondary. Happily, I think we will soon see a return to such practices, when Earth society becomes more balanced after Harvest. In fourth density society, sexuality will at last return to the bosom of true, non-controlling, soul-directed love.

SECTION III

A COLLECTION OF PERSONAL STORIES

» *Chapter 41* «

LETTERS FROM THE ET JOURNAL

IN THE FOLLOWING PAGES you will find some of the letters and stories that have appeared in *The ET Journal* over the past few years. Coming from subscribers across the U.S. and several other lands, these selections reveal a range and depth of paranormal experience, and the most intimate personal process of coming to grips with cosmic identity, life-purpose, and spiritual awakening.

My Story / Seattle, WA

I just finished *From Elsewhere* and feel compelled to write. One reason is that I recognized all sorts of pieces of my life in the book, but never put them together to form "my story"…

In 1981, through co-workers, I became a part of a metaphysical group, led by a channeling teacher, that met weekly. One night, I was told that I was a Walk-in. My immediate reaction, which seems strange now, was to cringe with a feeling of being exposed. But it made sense in that this previous "person" had spiraled down in a marriage of continual domestic violence, drugs and alcohol. It seems it was a gradual change, but the first change was a disinterest in and cessation of using drugs. The alcohol took a few more years to stop, but I also took the big, all-consuming plunge into metaphysics, ETs, and so on…

I quickly put the whole Walk-in thing aside, because I seemed to fall into an ego trap, feeling very special. This is no longer a concern, but it seems your book has come to me at a great time of need. It feels like it is vital to accept and embrace this aspect of my identity to understand the feelings that still create difficulties for me.

There have been two family experiences that stand out, after having read your book. The first is that I know all the family stories, but only the ones that are often repeated to company and relatives, told over and over at gatherings. It is as if these are the only memories which were passed on in the Walk-in transfer. My mother often says "Remember when...?" this or that happened, and I have no recollection of what she's talking about. It feels uncomfortable, when she says, "You don't remember that?" and I can only say "Vaguely..."

When I went back to Ohio for my parents' 40th anniversary party, an aunt, just out of the blue, said "So where do you fit in, in this family? You don't seem to fit." This was not to be pursued, since my mother was so offended (?) that she jumped up and said "Of course he fits!"

I have also had many dreams and one "epoch" dream. Some were dreams of being on spaceships. One was like going to the dentist, but I knew I was on a spaceship and felt very comfortable getting in the chair. It was like a check-up. Another dream was in the library of a teacher (on a ship), who had a window or screen though which you could see space and stars, and I could walk through it into whatever he wanted to show and teach. I've had dreams of zooming through space, and once I was on a planet where the ground was translucent indigo (a non-earthly color), and the sky was translucent orange. It was not "home" but I'd been there before.

My "epoch" dream (I call it this because upon awakening I felt as though it was of Biblical proportions in my life), was in 1983. In it, I was in a flat terrain with a very large, old tree nearby. I see all the birds fly away in the same direction. Then, there is incredible stillness, and suddenly there are tremendous winds—I knew these were "winds of change" in the dream. I took refuge in a gully while the winds blew over the land. When they ceased, I got up. A man in sheepskin and I led a group of people to a large building, where there were ETs in human form. It was decided to have a Christmas pageant that night, so we all sang "Silent Night"—like the birthing of the Christ within.

The next morning, we all got in little boats, propelled through channels of turquoise water. The strange sensation was that the water went uphill, and at the top there were two very tall aliens who had us get out. There were two to a boat, and if you were on the left you got out and went left; I was on the right and so I got out to the right. This right-and-left seemed to be going in different directions to do different things, like moving on…

I feel like I've been drifting for the last three years. These years have been a great opportunity (meaning deep painful learning!) to learn to be "alone" and deal with all the issues everyone on the planet has to work through. Sometimes, this feels like the dregs of the previous soul, including depression compounded by familiar feelings of not fitting in. Ultimately, I agree that in the bigger picture it doesn't matter if you're a Wanderer or Walk-in. We're all here together, NOW! Reading your book gave me a sense of relief and understanding. By accepting and integrating that aspect of myself, I can stop wondering if I'm weird and move ahead in the job that needs to be done.

A Near-Death Experience / Washington State

My near-death experience was in 1965 when I know I died and came back, but only after I was shown that it was important that I return, though I really didn't want to come back here. In my mid-teens I worked on a ranch during the summer in Colorado just west of Steamboat Springs. This place was 2,000 acres of pure beauty. I worked for an elderly man, and I loved every minute of it.

It all happened on one sunny day. I don't recall if it was morning or afternoon. My step-sister and I were heading toward a large pasture at the back portion of this ranch. She was riding her own horse and I was on a stallion I'd been training. We were looking for some underweight cows when my sister spotted them in the distance, and we decided to race to the other end of the pasture, which was a bad decision. I had just gotten up speed, when my horse stepped into a gopher hole. I saw his front go down, and the only thing that came to mind was "please GOD don't let his legs break." As I saw the ground racing up toward me, I just blanked out, lost all consciousness and awareness, and everything just went black.

The next thing I knew, I saw myself on my back floating in a gray cloudy tunnel moving toward a white light. Then I was lying on my back in a half-sitting position and was looking at who I knew to be GOD Himself. He was sitting on a white throne clothed in white robes and a brilliant pure white, but not blinding, light was in front of his face. As I lay there, I could sense and feel three beings behind me working on the back of my head, and when I tried to turn around to see them, one of them said, "Lie still. Don't turn around, you cannot see us. You are not supposed to know what we look like." So I did as they asked, and the atmosphere there was one of indescribable joyous love, peace, and contentment, and everything made perfect sense.

I wanted to stay, and so I begged the Creator to let me stay and He was going to. In no time, the three beings were finished and gone. As I lay there, He showed me the Earth, seeing it as from an orbit but much farther away. I said, "What of the Earth, what is going to happen to it?" He said, "That is why you have to go back," and I said "OK" and I was back in my body on the ground.

As I came to more fully, I saw the pickup coming to a stop and the man I was working for running over to me. He looked surprised to see me awake and asked if I was all right, as I was getting to my feet. I asked him how the horse was, since I was so afraid he had broken a leg, but he was just fine. Then I said that I was fine, and that it was just a slight headache and a little dizziness. There was no blood or any bruising anywhere on me, just some dust.

He helped me into the truck and drove to the far end of the range pasture to a spring. There we got out and I helped myself to a large drink of cold water. As we were returning back to the ranch house, he kept watching me for any signs of passing out, but all I could do was think about where I had been and longing to return to that place of loving, peace and contentment.

But all turned out fine, and upon arriving back at the barn I immediately checked out the horse to convince myself that all was right, then I got back on and rode after the cows once again, not having a second thought about the fact that I died not more than an hour before. It all seemed so normal to me, so matter of fact.

A few days later, I found out from my step-sister exactly what did happen. She said that the horse went down knee-deep in a hole, I flipped over his head, and the horse rolled on top of me pushing the saddle horn into the back of my head. The horse jumped up, barely missing walking on top of my head and body, when my sister arrived at my side. She said my head looked caved in and she almost fainted, and then she rode back to the barn to get help. This whole experience left me totally inspired with love, faith, and trust in our Infinite Creator and now I have no fear of dying—I guess, because I now know what's there. I can't wait to go back…

Faith in Goodness/Norway

…I cannot help seeing ALL as light. There really is no evil, because all is within God, and He is light. We only perceive evil as a reflection of our own earthly minds (and our own darker sides). If we look behind a so-called evil being, disincarnate or incarnate, there is a divine being. A friend told me the other day, irritably, "All you see is love and light; you are blind! Just look around you, open your eyes and see all the horrible things happening," (which she said to me after giving me a regression, and stupidly, I trusted her, which got me hurt).

I told her that I get my portion of evil through the TV and the newspaper, and it's all around me where I live. I live in the poorest and most polluted part of Oslo, Norway. 50% of the people living around me are drug addicts, alcoholics, glue-sniffers, and worse—also a lot of very old, poor people. I do not focus on it (that's all); I just try to transform all this sadness by being always as close to being love as I can.

In my book, I say: ONLY THROUGH THE EYES OF LOVE DO WE SEE WHAT IS REAL—ALL ELSE IS AN ILLUSION. The ultimate goal, to me, would be to look at everyone with the eyes that Christ looked at "his neighbor." He saw no fault in anyone because he did not recognize it. He had none himself.

I think we are all extraterrestrials on Earth. When Earth was first populated, we all came from somewhere outside. Only now, in time and space, is there a rush of evolved souls coming in from higher dimensions (planets) to help propel Earth to a higher state of consciousness, and ultimately lift Earth into a higher dimension. I think the most important task is to work with our inner selves (and egos), and to LIVE all those beautiful thoughts we gain on our path. What do all those new, loving thoughts help if they are locked inside us? What good does it do if we turn our back on, or step over a beggar or needy person in the streets, without at least sending a blessing to this person?

I have sailed through some pretty tough times, and have come out of it all still believing in people and in the world...

Trouble with Gravity/Florida

I recently purchased your book and was so thrilled to find such validation in what I had believed to be my own "strange" reality for so long. I am a Wanderer and I have known this, though not always consciously, all my earthly life. From the time I was a small child, I was the black sheep of the family and always a loner. I rarely felt comfortable with humans, even hiding from company that came to visit. I gravitated to animals and felt closely bonded to nature. School was difficult. I remember being very young, perhaps second grade, and thinking "I can't believe how immature and stupid these beings are!" Teachers always commented on how quiet and well-behaved I was. I had a high IQ, but felt that school in the traditional sense was a waste of time for me. I felt there were more important things for me to be doing.

Besides having difficulties adjusting to people and school, I had problems adapting to my environmental limitations. For example, when I was two, I rode my tricycle down two flights of stairs, convinced I should just "glide" along the air and land safely. I didn't. I ended up with a fractured skull and a lot of bruises. But I was determined not to give up. Something was not right. So when I was about four, I leaped off a staircase landing in our house and again found out this Earth has its physical restrictions. I decided the Earth's gravity was too strong for me, and even today I sometimes find myself feeling "pulled down" with a dragging sensation. I also used to say the sky was the wrong color… it should be a lavender-like purple. Most folks just thought I was weird.

I was usually quiet and shy and opened up to only a few people. But part of me was expressed through my creativity, including a cartoon character I developed…called "Squak." Squak was from another planet and was not male or female, but rather an "it." I also wrote science fiction…

A Life on Mars / New Hampshire

I recently finished reading your first book and found it to be very interesting. The personal stories were both fascinating and oftentimes far out, especially those of the Walk-ins. My story is not as dramatic, and fits the profile of a Wanderer.

From a very early age, I was aware of and fascinated by the stars, outer space and science fiction. I remember being only three or four years old and watching "Lost in Space." I also did have one weird experience, or at least I have a memory trace of it: when I was six or so, after looking up at the moon I felt that for a second I was actually ON the moon. I had this strange sense of bilocation, or having my awareness far removed from my body. It didn't last long, but it left an impression.

As a child, I definitely felt different from the "normal" children, and I had a very vivid imagination. I usually chose space themes for my drawings in art class. I definitely had a feeling that people here make life a lot more difficult than it should be. I was horrified by the Vietnam War, and by many other realities of the adult world. I wondered if I would ever fit in.

As an older child and teenager, I read a lot of science fiction (and still do), and picked up astronomy as a hobby. I loved to speculate about other worlds, and became very scientifically-minded, especially in high school and early college, and I tended to favor speculation and science fiction with a basis in scientific fact. This changed a bit after a few mind-expanding experiences in college and my encounter with Buddhism.

In 1986, I encountered a possible alien artifact on a magazine cover that set the stage for my gradual awakening as a sleeping Wanderer: *The Face on Mars...* From that day forward, I've devoted a lot of time and energy into learning as much as I could about Cydonia (the area of Mars with these structures). I started corresponding with one of the researchers, and after this, I opened up a little more and told him of a very vivid, almost lucid dream I had in 1976, when the Viking spacecraft was just getting to Mars. In the dream, I was living on Mars, and some sort of unseen threat was lurking just beyond the horizon, threatening the existence of the fragile colony we had started there.

The researcher said my dream contained elements of both my present life and a distant past life on Mars as one of the Alteans about 200–300,000 years ago. He even told me my past life name and that I had an integral part to play in events at the end of the Altean stay on Mars. I was supposedly in the Altean Navy and piloted one of their flying discs (as a kid and teenager, I often fantasized about having my own flying saucer!).

I take all of this as interesting information, and I certainly don't let it get to my head! I don't have any clear memories of this past life. However, *some* of the story does seem intuitively right on, and would certainly explain my complete fascination with Cydonia. In my heart of hearts, I'm sure these objects are artificial, and I have a strong intuition that several of my past lives were as an alien.

An Adult in a Child's Body / Los Angeles

Since I was little, I always felt totally different from my other three siblings. In fact, I can even see it from photos when we were younger. They always seem to form a separate unit from me. I was often convinced I was adopted, and often they did not like me and envied me for making such and such remarks, as if I was an adult and for understanding my parents in an adult way. I also remember that I did not talk at all until I was about three to four years old. My mother thought I was deaf, etc. I remember very clearly, though, that I was thinking in adult words/ways inside my head but was too scared to talk like that.

Once I finally got to hang out with small kids of my age and observe them, I was able to figure out how to act as a child. It was then that I got the courage to start talking. My mother was shocked and totally surprised, because not only was I talking like a much older child (word-wise), but I also started talking and talking and did not have to learn any first words. I often felt like an adult locked inside a child's body, because I would understand so many things about my parents and other adults, the wars, the peace, the world, etc. already at that age. And I would correct and support my parents often by giving them advice and getting angry at them like a teacher, when they were behaving like kids and affecting their relationship negatively. That all was when I was between four and fourteen years old. They would always look at me as the adult of the entire family, who in some way was taking care of them and the other siblings.

There was a very special thing that happened to me when I was little. I used to keep the window of my room open almost all day and night, except in the winter since Rome (Italy) is cold at that time as well. I would constantly talk to God and to beings that only I could visualize. I was very worried about the world and its future and was at five years old already furious at all these political parties, fights and problems. I hated wars and quarrels because it seemed so idiotic to me and a total waste. I was amazed at how people, even those in my family, were often unable to leave each other alone and would get upset about things I would never be upset about, or which I would rather just forget for the sake of peace and getting something done.

Around those early years (I think I was five or six years old), one night I had a very intense dream. Actually, it did not feel like a dream. It felt like a real experience somewhere else. I remember a very nice yellow-orange-red light and a very caring warmth around me and in me. I found myself suddenly surrounded by tons and tons of beings, angelic beings and people from all over the world, and someone way up there filled with light who was talking to me while laughing heartily at the same time. I remember realizing or at least feeling that this must be God or at least the one that takes care of me and always listens to me and at times talks to me. He was so pleased in seeing me and talked in tongues.

The whole scene went on for a while and what surprised me was that the entire world and other worlds were watching and laughing as well in a very genuine way. I was so happy there and never wanted to leave. I was trying to convince him to keep me there, because the world was such a dark, unhappy place anyway. I was told that "No," I had to go back and take care of this world and that the peace I had envisioned and desired so much was possible and that it needed me.

To my great surprise, I felt like he literally took me or some gentle force took me and lifted me back down onto my bed and it suddenly got very dark, even though it was the morning with plenty of light— the weather was gorgeous and the sun was shining. In spite of the daylight, the world still felt dark and depressing when I came back from this experience. I kept begging him not to leave me here, because I was terribly lonely and afraid in this world (plus I always felt like a total stranger in my own family), but I heard that I had to do something here first, which made me very sad and made me start crying for a while. It all looked so grey and dark here in comparison to what I had just seen and felt.

I remember while I was looking up from my bed and making sure I was really back at home, how much I kept wishing it was not true. I felt so terribly lonely that day, and for years I would automatically start crying when remembering this event, because I missed him and the whole place so much. Today, and especially lately, I have come to the conclusion that this experience might have been a pre-announcement of what is coming and my having to play a certain role in it…

Back to Basics / Massachusetts

In my life there appears to be a pattern of my being unable or unwilling to develop either spiritually in religious community, or develop spiritually by following prescribed religious practices. It appears that I proceed best along my spiritual path when stumbling along alone, with just the least bit of help from fellow-pilgrims…

Much of my previously-developed and hard-earned faith has dropped away, leaving me with simple affirmations: I affirm life; I affirm living; I affirm the fragment of God that is within me and in us all; I affirm the grace of God that continues to spring up. I believe that matter changes form, from solid to invisible, to solid, to invisible, i.e. "birth…death," but that there really is no death in a final sense. I believe in the original One that encompasses all time, all matter, all space, all creatures, all universes, the One that pre-existed everything, and will remain One after all manifestation has become unmanifest again.

Being Sensitive / Arizona

First of all, let me say I know I'm a Wanderer. Reading your book confirmed what I'd always suspected. As a child I really did believe I was from another planet. I felt like I was lost here, and that I had three brothers here who I was also lost from, and that our parents lived far away on another planet. Where I got that idea, I have no clue, because I wasn't yet watching *Star Trek* and shows about outer space…

By the time I was about ten, I had made up names for my "missing" brothers, parents, and my home planet. At night, I would make up stories in my mind about being with my brothers and parents. I never told anyone about these secret stories or my secret beliefs. But in school, I'd draw pictures of spaceships and planets on my desk, and in my notebooks I drew pictures of my missing brothers and parents. I think I lived more in my daydream world than I did in reality.

I've never felt like I wanted to be here. If I have been here since Atlantis (incarnating every now and then), then it's no wonder that I'm sick to death of being here and just want to go home! Perhaps, back then, I came to Earth willingly, but I get the distinct feeling that this incarnation was somehow forced on me.

In the past 15 years I've considered suicide many times (I'm 35 now) and would have done it except I was afraid of what would happen to my sweet little pets if I was to leave them. Reading *From Elsewhere* answered my questions about why I've always felt so alienated and out-of-place, but it didn't make me feel like I had a new interest in being here. Perhaps, I do have some kind of "mission," but I think it's too late for me now, because life has hurt me so horribly that I believe my soul or spirit is damaged beyond repair. My physical mind seems to be working okay, but something in my soul feels very, very messed up, almost as if my soul is starting to go slightly insane.

You see, I'm a very sensitive person and also quite psychic, and every little act of cruelty that I see done to a living thing makes me hurt terribly. This is not something I've developed, but rather the way I've always been—and I've tried so hard to stop being so sensitive: but nothing works…"

The End of Seattle / Washington State

When my husband and I were driving to his doctor in Seattle one sunny day, I was watching the sights and scenery pass by when suddenly I heard a voice say, "This is what's coming." Suddenly, I was seeing total and complete devastation of the entire city of Seattle and some of the surrounding area. I felt as though I were in two different space/times watching a movie and moving through it at the same time, and seeing flashes of the present, but I wanted to see this incredible sight. I was very frightened and had to grip my jeans leg as I watched in horror.

I saw buildings toppled like trees upon one another, while others were broken off half way up. Cars and trucks toppled, crushed, and piled in heaps. Streets were blocked with debris and bridges collapsed on roadways, which seemed strange to see as we passed right through it as though it weren't there. I knew it was only a vision, but still it was incredible. I saw the huge bridge spans that used to be Interstate 5 collapsed into Lake Union, along with all the other ones. Not one remained standing. It was unnerving to pass over these fallen bridges and looking down and not seeing anything but a wrecked bridge in the water below. I looked at my husband and wanted to tell him about all of this, but he is having some major medical problems, and I didn't want to lay anything as unreal as what I was seeing on him...

Every time after that, when we went to Seattle for three weeks, I kept seeing the exact same thing all over again—moving through the same movie again. It took some doing to see it for what it was—a vision and nothing more. But, as if that weren't enough, at home at night as I lay in bed or even was doing something around the house, I started wondering if Seattle was the only city to be destroyed. I had to ask. Well, I saw Tacoma destroyed along with Portland, San Francisco, and Los Angeles. As if that weren't all, as we were traveling to Spokane a few days later, I was watching the rolling grain fields and then suddenly these miles of rolling hills started undulating as waves in the ocean.

I asked myself and whoever else was elsewhere watching me, "why?" The response I received was, "You must know," which didn't tell me much, but I accepted it. One thing I noticed when I was seeing all this devastation was that I saw no people. Days later, when I asked "why," the reply was, "It is not for us to know who survives and who does not; that is left only to the Creator." I was relieved because I don't want to know.

A Vision of the Future / Iowa

In my last hypnosis session, I asked that I be progressed to see what the future might bring. I went to the year 2016 and I was 60 years old. I was standing on a grassy plane and I could see for miles. There seemed to be fields of glowing energy surrounding me and the Earth, and somehow I knew that this was the auras of the peoples of the world, and that they were vibrating in sync with the planet, somehow nourishing it. It was a beautiful sight to behold. Then I was standing in a huge white mansion with a ceiling that was multiple stories high. Everything was white and there seemed to be a wonderful white light encircling me. I knew this was my house and marveled at how beautiful it was.

Later, I left my house and went on a path up a nearby mountain. At the top, I could see for miles and I was surrounded by the vivid green of the life on our planet Earth. I scrambled to the top of a huge granite rock and sat down to meditate, which I did daily. As my mind cleared, I started to feel my body vibrating faster and faster and I found myself in another dimension. I faced this white energy in the shape of a pyramid and suddenly beams of light shot out from the top and the bottom of the pyramid and hit me in the stomach and forehead. Somehow, I knew this was a process of renewal of energy in me, to build up my strength for my work.

After this meditation was done, I looked into the sky and saw a grid of energy that encircled the Earth. This grid was a communication network of a unified field of love that is in sync with the planet and its people. Every person contributes a piece of this energy to the grid, as I do. I now realize that this grid is in the process of construction right now and more and more people are contributing to its completion. When I relax my mind, I can sense the increase of energies and I can feel the force of my uppermost chakra reaching into space to help create the field of love and unity.

» *Chapter 42* «

TALES OF ET AWAKENING

Coming to Remember / Indiana

When I was four years old, my father asked me what was the first thing I remembered. I told him I remembered being born. When he had me explain, his chin hit the floor, although at the time I didn't understand why. I thought everyone had this memory. It is as ingrained in me as my own fingerprints. It is always clear, solid, and never changing. It is so imprinted on me that my entire life is based on it.

My pre-birth memory begins in space. I was a part of everything and everything was a part of me. There was no sound, not even deafening silence. It was the most peaceful, simplistic, all-knowing feeling... I really can't think of any words to describe it. I could see all around me, from a "center-point" if you will, except for directly above where there was a "gray/silver cloud," as I called it as a child. Below me was this beautiful blue planet, brilliant against the inky blackness of space.

Then I began to come together. It was as if trillions of tiny bubbles from the far reaches of space were emerging toward my center being. As if a portion of every planet, every star, every tangible piece of space represented an individual cell in my body. They grew closer and closer until my body was formed and I was floating on my back, looking up into this silver cloud, with the planet below me and to my left. I remember floating there, pressing my arms against my thighs, uncomfortable with the fact that I could no longer see around me. I remember telling myself it was all right, this was simply another form of being. Then I began to float down toward the planet. I did not feel overjoyed, however. I felt more like this was my duty, or I chose to do this. Because of this memory I firmly believe we are all connected and are all a part of God. I have never feared death because of this memory.

My next memory was when I first heard my "guardian angel." He always speaks to me in my right ear and loud enough to startle me and cause me to turn and look for the voice. When I was two, he warned me that if I didn't put my puppy down I was going to fall down the stairs. I can still vividly remember turning and looking for that voice. I didn't listen though, and ended up at the bottom of the stairs. Throughout my life, this voice has warned me of impending danger, of which I have learned to pay attention or suffer the consequences. From that time forward, I have always been aware there were others watching me.

I put my little elementary school friends in a tizzy, sitting out on a neighbor's hill on a starlit night, telling them about life on other planets. I would also greatly upset my grandparents when I insisted that the Bible didn't mean anything to me. I simply knew it wasn't the "whole" truth.

About nine years ago, I began becoming aware of "things" happening in this world and that something very major was coming. But what has shaken me most happened about six years ago, while I was at the shop...

It was a quiet afternoon and I was in my office slumped over my desk when suddenly a tiny, white beam of light from somewhere out in space extended toward me and entered the very top of my head and shot me straight up in my chair. In that instant, I was back in space, just after coming together under the silver cloud, but this time I heard my own voice from within say, "Take a closer look." My eyes zoomed in on this silver thing above me only to discover that it wasn't a cloud at all! It was silver-looking all right, but it was metal, was vibrating, and it was round! It was quite clearly a ship. It was in that instant also that I remembered so many of the painful memories I "swallowed" and that the intelligence on the other side of that beam was sorry, but I had "run out of time."

Suddenly, this wonderful memory I had always deemed a private gift from God had a whole new meaning. I immediately put all the events together and found myself feeling even more alone, and I really had not thought that possible. I have always felt I had some mission in life, but this put things in a totally different light...

Some of the people interviewed in *From Elsewhere* seemed to be able to stay somewhat disconnected from others. Honestly, I see no difference between me, my cat, the cricket on the front porch or the tree in my back yard. I feel connected so much to everything that I can't read the paper or watch the news anymore. I could quite literally spend 24 hours a day crying and worrying over people I'll never know, and yet, I don't seem to be able to callous myself from those feelings. It's almost "how the world goes is how I go." But at the same time, I can become so unbelievably angry with people. How is it possible to love something and despise it so much at the same time?

Moments of Higher Awareness / California

AGES 3–5: Heard voices of beings that were in various forms, and who spoke to me or conversed with each other in simple languages. I recall being able to understand most of what was said, but generally being unable to reply. These experiences were mostly in the form of dreams but occasionally occurred while alone and awake.

AGE 6: Sighted a large orange face or head at my bedroom window during dawn. It was not in clear focus, and felt evil, causing the feeling of terror, and quickly disappeared. The most vivid dream of my life occurred in which ten to twelve mature forms, all human or human-equivalent, stood around the bed in which I slept alone, chanting and turning the bed in slow revolutions. They were not unfriendly or evil, however as I became more aware of their presence they seemed to take on the appearance of familiar monsters—Frankenstein, Wolfman, the Mummy, Dracula. I froze underneath the sheets in terror, then forced myself to look. I saw nothing except darkness, and leaped out of bed toward the light switch. Continuing into the hall, I turned on every light in the house, frantic and sobbing. My mother arose and told me I was behaving ridiculously, that it was a nightmare. I hid underneath my bed the rest of that night, unable to sleep.

AGE 8: Fascination with space travel, wanted to be an astronaut. Studied basic astronomy, read about UFOs. My interest waned due to slow technological advances.

AGE 11: At night, I had dreams of traveling out of my body, sometimes every night, sometimes only once a week. They were dreams in which my senses were most acute, floating out of the house at night on Lake Avenue in Pasadena, California. I would look down on the all-night drive-through Dairy store next door, then travel in a face-down position along telephone wires. I could see cars traveling on the streets, people walking and talking, and lights of the city in the distance. I would travel by willing my body in any direction; however, usually it took a path along the power lines and transmission wires. I rose to great heights over the city several times, but when the ground details began to lose distinctness, I would become fearful and fall, ending in a sudden jolt in bed. This would cause me to wake up. Other times I would simply awake in the morning and recall the entire incident as a vivid dream. This went on for about six months.

AGES 14–16: I desired to know more than I could learn from school and the world around me. I studied my mother's books on astrology and reincarnation. I took a class called "Comparative Religions" in high school. I located books in the public and college libraries that contained occult material and asked questions of anyone I was acquainted with whom I considered intelligent. I attended Christian Church at the suggestion of my best friend's parents and studied Bible scripture with enthusiasm. I read dozens of books on out-of-body journeys, Tarot, mysticism, reincarnation, psychic phenomena, parapsychology.

AGE 15: I experienced my only conscious out-of-body journey while meditating in a sitting position on a bed during the day. I arose and floated upward, head first through the ceiling. When my head cleared the top of the roof, I was startled by the intensity and clarity of the sun, trees, birds, and motion of cars and people in the neighborhood. This caused anxiety, and I fell back into the room and became aware of my body with a sudden jerk. I was still sitting and retained this memory as a clear and vivid experience that was sharply focused and unlike any dream other than those that occurred during my eleventh year.

AGE 16: I was meditating, and had developed the ability to enter the third or "empty" space at will. I was energizing my mind and body with light-visualization techniques and mantras. I became aware of three transparent heads in my concentration point, and that there were concentrated sources of white light within their heads corresponding to the glandular organs of the brain/neck (pineal, hypothalamus, thymus). I heard the words "To become square, square yourself," in a resonant monotone, more clearly than I have ever heard words that were spoken. This was the only experience I considered to be psychic clairaudience and clairvoyance since my experiences at ages three to five.

AGES 17–37: This 20-year period transpired with no memorable experiences of higher awareness and no attempts to achieve them. I believe this resulted from a conscious decision at age 16 to pursue worldly success at all cost, and "succeed or die trying" became my personal goal. I nearly accomplished both…

A Trail of Clues / The Midwest

One of my first memories stems from when I was about three years old. I was asleep in my second-floor bedroom, when I suddenly awakened just before dawn. I ran over to the window, opened it and climbed out onto the overhanging roof (my parents would have flipped if they had seen me do this!) just in time to see a flash of light streak through the sky. To this day, I still marvel at how I "knew" it was there.

Still on the subject of my childhood, I remember taking the set of chairs from our kitchen and turning them upside down on the floor (so the chrome bars which usually sat on the floor were pointing towards the ceiling) and sitting on the backrest of one of them, holding onto the floor rest, pretending to fly my space ship!

I used to look at my parents from time to time, and at other people too, and wonder "Who are these people, anyway?" And with the experiences I have described above, and more, no doubt they probably wondered who I was!

I had strange dreams since my childhood. I saw myself dressed in a white robe, carrying a golden key in my pocket. I saw myself carrying a huge book with a cover of gold and white. I saw myself in classrooms and some of the Teachers have not appeared to be human. I knew that somewhere I had another Home, with another family, and that I have a brother (although in this life I am an only child). I felt alienated from the things that children and teenagers were doing around me, and I often felt that I wanted to go Home... wherever that Home was.

Once I grew up, however, I made an honest attempt at fitting in. I was married, had three children, worked jobs, got divorced. I was a single mom for eight years prior to meeting and marrying the husband who just passed away. Even the circumstances of our meeting were strange:

In 1989, I was still a single mother working as a nurse in a hospital. I walked to the bus stop early each morning to get to work. On one morning, I was on my way to the bus stop, when I noticed what seemed to be an extra light over one of the stores near where I caught the bus. Part of me said, "The manager must have put up a spot light," while another part of me said, "That's no spotlight and you know it!" As I crossed the parking lot in front of the stores, going to where the bus stopped, I watched as a smoky mist began to surround this "light." When the mist cleared, the light had disappeared and all I could see was the outline of five rings in the sky. Suddenly, they turned bright red and sped off. I was left feeling, "Hey, wait! You forgot me!"

There were usually at least half a dozen other people who waited for the bus each morning. But on THAT morning, no one was there. There was no one else who I could have grabbed and asked, "Did you see that too?"

As I thought about it, I had been dreaming about UFOs for about two weeks before this incident. I hadn't thought too much of it, because

I was not (and am not) a UFO buff.

About three months later, I met my husband and by the end of that year we relocated to the town where I live today. We became very active in metaphysical groups (some of which were good, some not; but then again, you have to kiss a lot of frogs before you find the prince!). Which brings me to another memory:

In spring of 1990, my husband and I bought a used car from someone we had met in one of the metaphysical groups. When I visited the woman who sold the car, she showed me a flyer for an event called "The Pleiadian Activation" to be held six months later. Though I promptly forgot it, one morning, a week before the event, it popped into my mind; so I scraped together the money and went.

At the Activation, the facilitator worked with our energy, going from person to person in the circle. When it was my turn, when she finished with my energy, she hugged me and said, "Welcome home, baby. You're not alone anymore. I love you. You're so beautiful…"

The next day, the facilitator held one more class, and mentioned that she had been just as surprised at the message she channeled the night before as I was, and she had no idea where the words came from or who said them. But it had been a message intended for me… Through the years, those words remained with me, and have been key to my waking up again. I now know that I come from the Pleiadian system, and have been on Earth for a long time.

Why Am I Here? / California

I've known I was from some other place in the universe for as long as I can remember. As a young child, I recall feeling that I must have been adopted. I dreamed that somehow I was inadvertently misplaced, and that my real family was searching for me from some far-away spot. Perhaps I was lost in a time warp, I thought, and they didn't know where to look for me or had given up the search. I was different, and profoundly alone living in a family of five on a planet covered with people. I wondered what was my purpose, and how would I find it?

When I was around three or four years old, I began receiving visits from a group of two-foot tall, androgynous beings. They entered my room through the window, and sat cross-legged on the floor up against the wall. They never approached me or harmed me in any way. Sometimes, a few would look around my room at my books and things, but usually they just sat and talked with me. I don't recall the subjects of the conversations, but I know I felt completely at ease and that they were teaching me. Perhaps they gave me now-forgotten clues to my Earth mission. I didn't see them again after my family moved to a new house when I was six years old, and my new room didn't have an outside window.

Very soon thereafter, I became absolutely fascinated with stargazing, and quickly learned many constellations and how to identify the planets. Actually, my interest in astronomy probably manifested much sooner as my mother told me that my first word was not "Mommy" or "Daddy," but "Moon." I joined the Astronomy Club at school and loved to go out in open fields at night waiting to see meteors and UFOs. I don't remember seeing any UFOs, but I often prayed that one would come get me and whisk me home.

My mother joined a meditation group when I was about ten. Within a couple of years, she realized that I was "different" and very mature for my age, and I was asked to join the group that met weekly for meditation and metaphysical/theosophical study. I hoped meditation would unlock the secret to my destiny. At age 13, I was given a psychic reading in which I was told about four of my previous lives on Earth. The first one described my life as a teacher during the early days of Atlantis, and in the most recent one I was a physician and researcher in the last century. The concept of reincarnation, and these experiences in particular, seemed so familiar. The evolutionary path of learning and growth through numerous lifetimes made logical sense to me, and felt "right" somehow.

Over the next several years, I was taught how to meditate individually and with the group in various ways. Some members of the group regularly performed healings and engaged in channeling of information from entities from the other side of the veil. The teachings felt much more like remembering familiar truths than new learning.

I spent my 20s and early 30s as a workaholic, married to a workaholic, while continuing my education. I read some metaphysical material during this period, but for the most part I did not regularly pursue real spiritual growth. My spouse did not understand all this strange stuff, and was not terribly supportive of my continued study. As a result, I chose to keep myself busy elsewhere by working long hours and collecting degrees in environmental science and public policy. This hiatus was actually wonderful, because I learned how to be more content living on planet Earth, and how to work within the system.

I received another spiritual wake-up call when I was 33. I began reading material regarding Earth, energy changes, and the new millennium. I felt a pull toward my metaphysical roots, and began feeling a renewed sense of contact with my spirit guides and those on the other side. Unfortunately, within a few months, I found myself in the midst of a divorce. After a brief, dark period, I emerged to find that I was intact, and better able to begin growing again. Ultimately, this experience was a fabulous catalyst. I've met so many friends that I wouldn't have been open to in the old mindset. I've rediscovered myself as a Wanderer, not of Earth, but here to learn, teach and help others. This seems to be a time to seek out other Wanderers to form groups for support, and amplify our efforts to assist humans in love during this time of tremendous change.

I'm sure that the process of discovering my true self and recognizing it in others will bring me ever closer to the goal of meaningful service to others, as they freely pursue their own paths of self-discovery.

SECTION IV

APPENDICES

An Epilogue

First of all, let me thank you for choosing to live on Earth. Sharing this slice of time and space, I certainly know the trials and tribulations you have gone through, because I have experienced them too. More than you can imagine, you have made a great sacrifice to be here now, whether you call yourself a Wanderer or not, and in less time than you imagine, you will be back home among your kindred souls in the greater realms of light. This is not a prediction. It is just the next phase of the cycle.

Secondly, let me thank you for reading this book, and for opening your mind to consider the quality of light I am bringing. Because of your seeking, I am here, and therefore I have this opportunity to set in words some of the light I have come to know. Making use of our body-mind-spirit, we can enjoy various qualities or frequencies of light, all of which are basically modulations of the One Light, the Limitless Light or what is called *Ain Soph* in the Hebrew Kabbalah. All That Is expresses the One Infinite Creator, which is none other than you, too, and the more you know it, the more you will see that even the body-mind-spirit complex which we use is not three, but rather one—*the* One.

As I have written many times in many ways, *you* hold the key to your destiny, no one else. So be careful: any source which leaves you with the impression that unbalanced alien groups or negative ETs can truly control you is most likely distorted by those very same deluded ET groups, who deny the existence of the omnipotent loving Higher Self and their very own essence. No matter what negative schemes and agendas come down the line in the next decade or so before our third-density Earth Harvest, *you yourself are the master of your fate.* If you work hard and truly direct your will into developing love and balance, you will make the most of this opportunity on Earth and open to even greater contact with true Self. We can make great effort, or we can make little effort. And of course, no one is perfect (at least in time and space!).

Having read this book, I hope you are left with a sense that *care in self-reflection* is most important, that each moment we live can be approached in a spirit of love and appreciation, that all aspects of personal experience can be accepted without blame or judgment, and that all essential resources for our transformation lie within ourselves, all the time. The best teaching helps us return to ourselves, and the finest light that any teacher offers will simply echo the quiet being of your own inner light, the still presence of core self. *What you need, you already have; what you seek, you already are.*

Know too, that you are not alone, and rather than latching on to the words of channels and invisible ET helpers, you can quiet and clear your own mind in greater self-acceptance and then be aware of their, or rather, *our* presence around you—which it is, all the time. Far better to activate your own higher senses than to play around with the words of someone else. If you seek benevolent ET contact, "be still and know that I am here."

In Buddhism, there is a distinction between "living Zen" and "dead Zen." The former is here, now, potent, beyond all thought—and the latter is just that old finger pointing to the moon, rehashing old spiritual notions, disconnected to the silent, potent present. As RA says, "the moment contains love," but we really cannot *feel* this and *know* this unless the mind is *still*. And when it is still, we naturally feel this calm, and naturally we feel alive.

We all follow a path to the present, seeking the limitless light ever alive in the moment. Along such a pathless-path, all the results of previous choices and mind-body-spirit distortions come up for consideration, and the speed of our healing and integration depends wholly on how we meet ourselves in the moment. As I have written before, the essential qualities of inner healing are self-acceptance, self-appreciation, balanced love and wisdom, and ultimately forgiveness and trust, no matter what we are going through. We meet ourselves each moment each day—and with the intensity and density of current Earth catalyst, we have a huge opportunity to fine-tune love, and so unfold even more of what we are.

Of course, the next 15 years will see a lot of change (which is actually an understatement!). Despite any and all outer upheaval, the real question centers on how well we use the outer changes for balanced inner growth. It is said that the true yogi or seeker of the Divine will not flinch, even when the mountain before him comes crashing down. Without being dramatic, I think we will see a lot of mountains come crashing down before the Harvest of 2010–2013 A.D., and though most of us will flinch, these "inconveniences" will certainly offer some hard training in the fine arts of peace and self-reliance. All the three major virtues will be tested—*love, wisdom, and will*—and so you might ask the following questions over and over again:

Can I accept what is happening before me?

Do I understand what is happening before me?

Can I really stand in my own power?

Of course, we always can, and more and more, I think we will be able to prove it for ourselves.

Please know that you are loved and you are not alone—which is a reflection far more useful than following strange lights in the sky and tired government cover-ups. Just remember that your spiritual family is all around you doing what they can to help you, and help you help others. Thus we return to universal service, which is not only the province of Walk-ins and Wanderers, but of *all* souls who follow the path of truth in love. The moment-to-moment choice to be still, listen and help, care and receive is most empowering, and it holds the promise of tremendous self-purification to clear the channels through which we receive higher-dimensional light. As always, choice in the moment is ours.

We all thank you, and we all work as One. Truly believe in yourself, and truly know that all you seek is already who you are. The path is now.

» *Appendix 2* «

ON COUNSELING ABDUCTEES AND CONTACTEES

An Introduction

In this short appendix, I will present some of the basic treatment considerations I have found helpful in working with UFO abductees and contactees. Although these two groups are quite different, there are common dynamics that require particular clinical approaches. First of all, these two terms are currently used in a variety of ways, and they need to be defined clearly. Essentially, they can be defined on the basis of the *quality of the interaction* and *the intentions of the initiating agent*.

Those for whom I am using the term *abductee* are people who have experienced emotional trauma and violation, and feel that their contact was of a harmful nature. On the other hand, those for whom the more neutral term *contactee* seems to apply have experienced inspiration and joy from their contact, and often feel a buoyant spiritual transformation. If we acknowledge that indeed there are both benevolent and non-benevolent ET groups (those we can call positive and negative), then using different terms for contact with the two different groups makes good sense.

Frankly, I disagree with the opinions of many of my colleagues in the field. I disagree with researchers who say "we cannot understand ET motivations," with clinicians who consider a contact-experience of fear and trauma to be merely the product of human ignorance, and I also disagree with leading UFO experts who believe that *all* ET races are either loving or evil. If you have read the first two sections of this book, you already know my perspective on ET groups and their intentions. In particular, look at the chapters in Section I entitled "Inside the Confederation" and "ETs and the Law of Free Will." It should be remembered, the notion of genuine cosmic polarity (what we could call "good and evil," or left-hand and right-hand paths) is fully supported by all mystic traditions, including Buddhism, Hinduism, Judaism, Christianity, Islam, and Gnosticism.

Also remember, the belief systems held by therapists, healers, or counselors will inevitably influence all aspects of treatment and therapeutic rapport, and so we need to acknowledge and understand our own personal, metaphysical assumptions before beginning the work. Our beliefs may obstruct and neutralize, or instead, invigorate and support the efficiency of the self-healing process. Nevertheless, regardless of these intellectual parameters, there are key concepts which guide all therapeutic intervention, and successful healing does not depend on intellectual agreement between therapist and client. True healing results from the provision of care, emotional support, cognitive clarification, and a strengthening of the client's personal will, self-acceptance, and spiritual centering. True healing occurs in a loving therapeutic relationship.

Before presenting these treatment considerations, I must also make one essential caveat regarding the healer's definition of his or her role and purpose in this work. Borrowing from modern medicine, many therapists consider it their duty to "fix and correct" those with whom they work, an often irresistible tendency with experiencers of anomalous trauma." However, this mechanistic, objectifying attitude is perhaps nowhere more potentially destructive than with contactees and abductees. With all due humility, let me issue a command: *If you feel it to be your professional obligation to return clients back to a conventional view of reality, you really should not be working in this field.* Intellectual debate over the supposed reality or objectivity of anomalous experiences can intensify the perceived or felt abuse (especially with abductees), and can actually destroy the healing process. The clinical setting is *not* the proper place for debate or argument over metaphysical theory. However, as I said before, our conceptual assumptions must be clarified before we embark upon the work with others.

The essential treatment dynamics I will present can be classified according to their primary level of influence. It hardly needs mentioning that the individual experience of ET-contact affects every aspect of personal life, from the most subjective self-understanding to the most universal questioning of one's place in the cosmos. Therefore, all levels of human experience must be honored in the work. Some key considerations, although not an exhaustive list, follow below:

The Physical Level

✦ Many clients, especially abductees, will present physical ailments associated with their experience. Unless requested, their "objective reality" should not be challenged. Whether their origin is psychosomatic or a result of genuine inter-dimensional contact, proper medical care (including allopathic and/or alternative medicine) ought to be given. If you consider these afflictions to be purely psychological, this will likely damage trust and rapport— which are essential pre-conditions required to process any and all psychological trauma—between healer and client.

✦ With those who have experienced violation-type contact, the specific nature of physical and/or inter-dimensional (energy-based) wounding may generate and correlate with particular emotional dynamics. Pre-existing psychological conflicts regarding body-image will be stimulated and exacerbated, including those that are gender-specific e.g. fertility, potency, or otherwise; attractiveness, health, strength/frailty, protection /vulnerability, and physical integrity. These issues will then be mirrored at the cognitive level, often generating what can be termed "self-defeating self-talk" such as "Now I am ugly and no one will love me; now I am slowly falling apart…" Counselors need to understand this linkage between physical symptoms and mental/emotional processing.

The Emotional Level

✦ Intensification of particular emotional reactions is common to both contactees and abductees. Feelings of fear, despair, or self-pity, as well as joy, grace, or bliss may be uncontrollable. This can be understood as a normal and natural response to profound inter-dimensional events which will inevitably affect our core beliefs:

body-image, self-integrity, social adjustment, intellectual and/or spiritual world-view. A period of emotional upheaval is inevitable, and the person will need a lot of patience and self-acceptance along the way of gradual emotional readjustment.

✦ A pattern of persistent emotional disorientation that baffles the process of emotional healing and integration is equally common. UFO abductees often experience self-estrangement in many forms: depression with dulled sensitivity, vague foreboding and doom, dissociation from the feeling-life, and/or disorganized panic which may be chronic or situational. Contactees, whose experience is generally more positive, may go through feelings of messianic mission, severe self-criticism often accompanied by exaggeration of perceived spiritual imperfection, and long-term discouragement related to seeing ever more clearly their unachieved potentials. Healers need to help anchor self-acceptance, reasonable definition, and greater integration to all such potent emotions.

The Mental Level

✦ The intensity of intellectual shock will depend on prior personality tendencies and the nature of the ET contact. People who are not particularly intellectually-based may experience no trauma at all, no sense of a shattered world-view, but instead, a new vista of comprehension. For the highly analytical, whose self-esteem has been based upon their cohesive understanding of "the way things are," UFO contact can be utterly devastating, leading to long-term confusion, conceptual disorientation, and critical self-blame. With contacts that involve significant transfer of spiritual or technical information, a profusion of new ideas that demand integration is common. Cognitive-based counseling must recognize both the client's personality type and the ET contact dynamics.

✦ Many clients also experience a spiritualization of life-interests. They may show a newfound fascination with New Age subjects, religion, or studies of the paranormal. As far as possible, any material gained on these forays which the person deems important can be brought into the counseling dialogue and the healing process. Properly integrated and appreciated, they can shed light upon the person's deeper issues, and provide direction for the future. Efforts should also be made to stay true to the person's own experience without mixing in borrowed concepts that seem glamorous or sensational, but end up taking the person away from their own process. Meditation, in particular, can be a valuable tool to assist emotional balancing, self-acceptance, and the resolution of intellectual quandaries. Ideally, counselors should also have a background in metaphysics.

The Social Level

✦ As can be expected, the social ramifications of ET contact or a perceived abduction-violation can be severe. The entire network of a person's friends, associates, and family can heap scorn and ridicule upon them, leading to isolation, self-doubt, and undermining the fragile healing process. *Sympathetic social support is essential* so that people are not left alone with panic or disorientation. It may be necessary to cut adrift those social contacts that are actively destructive. *Abductees, in particular, usually cannot navigate the post-traumatic integration process alone.* An extreme need for support is usually indicative of negative-ET contact, which tend to violate central aspects of self-alignment.

✦ As an element of the cognitive dissonance generally following UFO/ET contact, a person's perceptions of human society may also be radically altered. Clients may become bitter or cynical upon feeling socially exiled, then cut themselves off from society in response. In cases of transformative, uplifting ET contact, inflated desires to "save the world" may lead to zealous dogmatism and also result in personal isolation. Counselors ought to encourage appropriate, congruent, and self-chosen social re-integration, and possibly also a period of active, soul-searching solitude. Maintaining emotional balance is essential to those who are returning to ordinary society following all such anomalous experiences.

The Spiritual Level

✦ For many, UFO contact of any sort is seen as a profound opportunity for self-development and expanded awareness of the universal order. However, for abductees, the traumatic consequences demand immediate attention and should never be glossed over in an attempt to "look at the bright side." Only *after* the healing process of personality re-integration gains momentum can the spiritual dimensions be fully addressed. Considerations of meaning and value will vary for each client.

✦ As a primary therapeutic intervention, spiritually-minded healers may support abductees in "breaking agreements" presumably made at subconscious levels with hostile aliens. Combined with careful cultivation of the client's sense of Divine Will and protection, this technique may offer one of the best long-term solutions for those who wish to terminate ongoing traumatic ET contact. However, therapists should have significant training in the theory and practice of such intervention before making any attempts in this direction, since misguided efforts can do much more harm than good. Additionally, I have had very good results teaching clients traditional Buddhist mantras for protection and soul-illumination. When these practices are done with power and sincerity, they really do work. One of the best is the traditional Tibetan Vajrayana chant: OM MANI PADME HUM (which is pronounced: "Om Ma-nee Pay-may Hoom"). This is a form of white magic, and again, counselors without background in these matters may want to get some further training.

In Conclusion

As benevolent ET contact and traumatic UFO abduction affects all levels of the individual's experience, so must our treatment considerations address the multi-layered consequences of such extreme "anomalous experience." Counselors must remain sympathetic and supportive despite any assertions and claims made by the experiencer that may be considered outrageous or unbelievable. As the primary healing does *not* emanate from the intellectual level, all debate over objectivity is generally inappropriate in the counseling, although as it proceeds, the mental level must also be addressed, as well as the client's metaphysical education through focused self-study.

In general, the basic work of self-empowerment, emotional catharsis, cognitive re-ordering, and social readjustment are essential to dealing with any personal crisis, especially in the beginning stages. Ultimately, however, the spiritual dimensions of ET contact and abduction also have to be addressed, including the need for a balanced, expanded view of the universe and human potential, as well as an understanding of the cosmic plan and the tools available for accelerated personal growth, including formal meditation practice.

THE NEW ET QUESTIONNAIRE

N EW AND REVISED, this questionnaire gives those of you who prefer the scientific method (just kidding!) a more quantitative way to decide if you are a Wanderer or ET soul. Simply answer "yes" or "no" to the following 20 questions. In my own personal experience, as well as my teaching and counseling, I've found that most Wanderers and ET Walk-ins fit the following profile:

A. YOUR CHILDHOOD

1. Did you often think about, daydream, or fantasize about ETs, UFOs, and other worlds?

2. Did you feel like ordinary things around you were somehow strange, like the human body, the color of the sky, trees and nature, human architecture, and adults?

3. Did you ever feel as if your parents were not your real parents, that you had a missing brother or sister, or a home some place far away?

4. Did you have magical dreams of flying, invisible spirit friends, or receiving special guidance and protection?

5. Did you look up at the night sky with longing sometimes and say: *"Take me home…Why am I here?"* or ask *"Why am I so alone?"*

B. YOUR PERSONALITY

6. Are you kind, gentle, peaceful, and non-aggressive—not just sometimes, but almost always?

7. Are you hurt, saddened, and confused by all the human evil and cruelty in the world?

8. Do you feel that money, possessions, and a successful career are not really that important?

9. Do you sometimes feel more comfortable with plants and animals than with people?

10. Are you generally sensitive, considerate, generous, and concerned with others around you?

C. YOUR EXPERIENCES

11. Have you felt different, out-of-place, or somewhat alienated from human society all your life?

12. Have you had dreams, visions, or sightings of UFOs that inspired real spiritual growth?

13. Have you had dramatic dreams of Earth Changes, geological and social upheaval, the end of the world, or the future civilization?

14. Are you logical, scientific, non-emotional, and somewhat confused by hot passion and desire?

15. Have you had a clear and uplifting contact with benevolent, kind, and highly-evolved ETs?

D. YOUR INTERESTS

16. Are you interested in science fiction, epic fantasy, angels, high-technology, and world prophecy?

17. Are you interested in Atlantis, Lemuria, channeling, pyramids, New Age ideas and UFOs?

18. Are you interested in meditation, alternative healing, or bringing love and light to the world?

19. Do you believe human society is ignorant of the spiritual truths that you know to be true?

20. Do you have a strong sense of purpose and feel that your mission is to help Earth and humanity?

SCORING YOUR ET IDENTITY

For each YES answer, give yourself 5 points and then total your score. (If you answered "sometimes," you can give yourself 21/2 points.)

100–75 points: In my view, you definitely *are* an ET soul, but perhaps you are not surprised!

75–25 points: You *may* or may not be a Star Person, and you would need more reflection to know for sure.

25 points or less: You probably are *not* an ET soul, but why are you interested in these matters in the first place?

Remember, only *you* can know for sure if you are from elsewhere, and knowing your cosmic roots is only the first step. After that, it is essential to consider *why you are here* and *what is your purpose*. Being on Earth gives all Wanderers a perfect opportunity to develop ourselves, to refine our understanding and expression of love and wisdom, and help the world in our own special way.

» *Appendix 4* «

INFORMATION FOR SEEKERS

1) Scott Mandelker's Web Site

Web site: http://www.universal-vision.com

E-mail: Scott@universal-vision.com

2) *L/L Research:* Carla Rueckert and Jim McCarty

P.O. Box 5195
Louisville, KY 40255-0195
Tel/Fax (502) 245-6495

Web site: http://www.llresearch.org

E-mail: rueckert@iglou.com

* Source for *The RA Material, Light Lines* newsletter, and Wanderers resource

3) Jody Boyne: *Jody's ET Phone-Home Page*

Web site: http://nic2.hawaii.net/~boyne.

E-mail: boyne@hawaii.edu

* Internet site for global Wanderers networking.

4) Operation Terra: Preparing for the Harvest

Web site: http://www.operationterra.com

E-mail: lyara@operationterra.com

* Internet site with Messages from the Hosts of Heaven regarding Earth changes, ETs, the end times, and the journey to the New Earth, Terra.

5) Ascension 2000: David Wilcock's site

Web site: http://www.ascension2000.com

E-mail: djw333@exis.net

* Information on new science and astrophysics, related to Harvest and Global Shift

A BASIC CHART ON COSMIC EVOLUTION

AN OVERVIEW OF THE PATH AND UNIVERSAL PRINCIPLES

SPIRITUAL GROWTH = Development of Consciousness, Continual Initiation to Greater Sensitivity

THE PATH OF RETURN = Returning to Source, Lessening Distortions to the Realization of Unity

7 DENSITIES ⟺ 7 CENTERS ⟺ 7 BODIES ⟺ 2 PATHS OF SERVICE TO THE ONE CREATOR

HUMAN/ET EVOLUTIONARY LINE ≠ ANGELIC/DEVA EVOLUTIONARY LINE

✦ Human Kingdom operates under Law of Free Will, making choices, exploring "good and evil"

✦ Deva Kingdom instinctively follows Divine Law, clearly sees universal plan, reproduces design

THE 7 DENSITIES

BEYOND THE OCTAVE *(UNVEILED)*

7th DENSITY—BUDDHAS/AVATARS—INFINITE SACRED/ RETURN TO FOREVER, LOOKING BACKWARDS IS FINISHED: ∞

REALMS OF ET SOULS, UFOs, AND COSMIC POLARITY (UNVEILED)

6th DENSITY—BODHISATTVA/HIGHER SELF—COMPLETE UNITY/WILL, BEING, COSMIC CHRIST, PERFECT LOVE/ WISDOM BALANCE: ☉

5th DENSITY—WORLDS OF MIND—PERFECTION OF WISDOM, CLARITY (LIGHT): ◊

4th DENSITY—WORLDS OF HEART—PERFECTION OF LOVE, KINDNESS (GROUP): ○

HUMAN 3-DIMENSIONAL WORLDS *(VEILED)*

3rd DENSITY—SELF-CONSCIOUSNESS: TRUE PERSONALITY ⇒ CHOICE OF PATH: ⊕

Beginning of Cosmic Polarity: Service to self or others (separation or unity); 75,000 year cycle (Lemuria ⇒ Atlantis ⇒ Modern Age)

2nd DENSITY—CONSCIOUSNESS OF STRIVING: MINERALS/PLANTS/ANIMALS: ⇑

1st DENSITY—BASIC MOVEMENT: ELEMENTALS OF EARTH/WATER/FIRE/AIR: □

ESSENTIAL COSMIC LAWS

1. **LAW OF FREE WILL** = LAW OF CONFUSION IN VEILED REALMS (3D Humanity), ALLOWS CHOICE OF PATH

2. **LAW OF SERVICE** = DUAL-PATH TO DEVELOP DIVINE EQUIPMENT, 7 CHAKRAS, COSMIC POLARITY FOR CREATOR

ET CONTACT AND THE FUTURE

1. **NEGATIVE CONTACT** = ABDUCTION/MUTILATION (VIOLATION, FEAR, CONFUSION)
   + ORION, REPTOIDS, GRAYS, DRACONIANS, MEN-IN-BLACK, MUTANT FORMS, ETC.

2. **POSITIVE CONTACT** = INSPIRATION, DREAMS, REMEMBRANCE / ET SOULS, SUPPORTS WORLD SERVICE
   + ANDROMEDA, CONFEDERATION, SATURN, SIRIUS, LYRA, VENUS, PLEIADIANS, ETC.

3. **EARTH HARVEST** = 2010–2012 A.D., END OF 3RD DENSITY/CHOOSING OF PATH
   + 3-WAY-SPLIT: EARTH 4D+, ORION 4D-, 3D REPEATERS (GO ELSEWHERE)

4. **MEDITATION AND PATH TO HIGHER SELF** = CONCENTRATION, CALM, INSIGHT
   + REALIZATION OF SUFFERING, IMPERMANENCE, EMPTINESS, UNITY, LIGHT

⌒CONCLUDING QUOTATIONS⌒
from the RA Material

"In each infinitesimal part of your self resides the One in all of Its power." (Vol. I, p.146)

"You are everything, every being, every emotion, every event, every situation. You are Unity. You are Infinity. You are Love/Light, Light/Love. You are. This is the Law of One." (Vol. I, p. 67)

"Each incarnation is intended to be a course in the Creator knowing Itself." (Vol. IV, p. 69)

"The root cause of blockage is the lack of the ability to see the other-self as Creator, or to phrase this differently, the lack of love." (Vol. IV, p. 110)

"The great healer of distortions is love." (Vol. III, p. 59)

"To the truly balanced entity, no situation would be emotionally charged." (Vol. II, p. 96)

"The best way to be of service to others is the constant attempt to seek to share the love of the Creator as it is known to the inner self. This involves self-knowledge and the ability to open the self to the other-self without hesitation…" (Vol. I, p. 166)

"Each entity is only superficially that which blooms and dies. In the deeper sense, there is no end to beingness." (Vol. I, p. 225)

◆OM MANI PADME HUM◆

—MAIN SEMINAR TEACHINGS—

Offered by Scott Mandelker, Ph.D.

UFOs and ET Contact: The Spiritual View—Introduction to UFO/ET research; science and spirituality; subjective and objective approaches; my personal background and conclusions; an overview of global ET contact; current events and controversies in the US; cover-up analysis.

ET Souls and the Cosmic Plan—ET groups and humanity on the path of evolution; the seven densities and two paths of polarity; world service, global change and the role of Wanderers on Earth; prophecy and prediction for the next 15 years; soul-evolution and Harvest in 2010 A.D.

Buddhist and Taoist Meditation—An introduction to Chinese Taoism and Buddhist schools; understanding mind, self-nature and enlightenment; theory and practice of Buddhist breath and mantra meditation; primary practices of Taoist Chi Kung; developing mindfulness in daily life.

Dream Analysis Group—Interpreting dreams from biological, psychological, and spiritual perspectives; soul-communication and symbolic teachings from Higher Self; collective dreams and world prophecy; trust and discernment; out-of-body experience vs. dreams; case studies.

The Infinite Self: Healing and Balance—Advanced material for developing energy centers; healing through mind-body-spirit balance and love; exercises to determine chakra-levels; Higher Self contact and alignment; using life-experience as a catalyst for growth; the adept-healer path.

Sexuality and the Spiritual Path—Relationship and intimacy as a mirror for self-understanding; sexual energy transfer and the seven chakras; positive and negative uses of sexual force; activating higher centers for joy through union; effects of unconditional acceptance; tantra, orgasm, magic.

Paranormal Experience and Spiritual Emergence—Chakras and higher bodies; kundalini and multi-dimensional awareness; understanding near-death and out-of-body experience; past-life recall and ESP; angels, guides, Walk-ins and ET contact; Higher Self and the intuition.

Seminars are arranged for local groups throughout the United States and abroad.

PERSONAL COUNSELING

SCOTT MANDELKER also offers spiritual consulting for individuals and couples by phone and in person. Covering a range of issues, our work is guided by your own unique concerns in one-hour sessions. Insight into conflicts, release of blocked energy, and greater balance in daily life are co-created through dialogue, sharing and teaching.

Counseling Themes Include:

✦ *Personal Evolution:* Knowing your own life-lessons, karmic conflicts, and spiritual challenges

✦ *Spiritual Path:* Healing energy blockages with love and wisdom, developing real empowerment

✦ *Emotional Life:* Self-understanding through the mirrors of intimacy, sexuality, and relationships

✦ *Your Purpose on Earth:* Integrating your inner path with social life, living your world service

✦ *Intuition and Higher Self:* Using meditation for insight, self-trust, peace of mind, and freedom

✦ *Paranormal Experience:* NDE and OBE, visions and channeling, interpreting your dreams

✦ *Finding Cosmic Identity:* Alienation and adjustment for Wanderers, Walk-ins and ET souls

✦ *Integrating ET Contact:* Inspiration and spiritual triggers, cosmic family and your life on Earth

Please contact Dr. Mandelker directly for more information:

PMB 201, 2130 Fillmore Street, San Francisco, CA 94115 USA

Tel. (415) 567-2190 / Fax: (415) 567-2976

E-mail: scott@universal-vision.com

SCOTT MANDELKER, PH.D.

—Biographical Statement—

Born in 1962 in New York City, Scott Mandelker completed his doctorate in East-West Psychology from the California Institute of Integral Studies (CIIS) in San Francisco in 1992. His Ph.D. combines eclectic Western psychology with intensive study of Eastern religions, and followed upon years of formal training in US and Asian Buddhist temples (in Japanese Zen and Thai Theravadan traditions).

After leaving monastic life, Scott earned a B.A. in Buddhist Studies from Naropa Institute in Boulder, Colorado in 1987. After receiving an M.A. in Counseling in 1990, he began private practice in spiritual counseling, which he maintains in San Francisco and upon his travels. He has published over a dozen essays on metaphysics, Eastern religions, and the spiritual meaning of ET contact and the UFO presence.

His interest in the phenomenon of ET Identity developed from years of meditation, personal experience, and extensive study of New Age material. Focusing on the reality of cosmic contact and human life at the turn of the millennium, his first book, *From Elsewhere: Being ET in America*, focuses on those who've uncovered their cosmic roots.

Scott Mandelker was editor and publisher of the bi-monthly *ET Journal* from 1995–1999, and has presented at numerous New Age conferences, including Whole Life Expos, Rocky Mountain and Gulf Breeze Expos, and Star Knowledge gatherings. He has appeared on over 70 radio shows including *Art Bell* and *Laura Lee*, plus network TV shows such as *Hard Copy, Strange Universe, The Other Side* and *Mysteries, Magic and Miracles*. His first book was translated into Japanese, Polish and Romanian. He offers regular teachings and counseling throughout the US, and is the Project Director of the national seminar tour, *The Time of Global Shift* (http://www.ascension2000/shift.htm). You can find more information at his Web site: http://www.universal-vision.com.

ORDER FORM

Books and Manuscripts

___ *From Elsewhere: Being ET in America* (1995 hardcover) .. $15.00
___ *Universal Vision: Soul Evolution and the Cosmic Plan* $18.00
___ *ET Souls, Cosmic Plan, and the Spiritual Path* (68 pgs.) .. $10.00

Audio Tapes

___ *A Workshop on Dreams* $12.00
___ *The Great Work* $12.00
___ *CNI News Interview: UFO/ET Update* $12.00
___ *From Elsewhere: ET Souls on Earth* $12.00
___ *Introduction to* The RA Material $12.00
___ *Global-Cosmic Dynamics* $12.00
___ *1998 Gulf Breeze UFO Conference Lecture Set*, 2 tapes ... $24.00
___ *Infinite Self: Healing & Balance*, 2 tapes $24.00
___ *Sexuality & the Spiritual Path*, 2 tapes $24.00
___ *A Study Companion to* The RA Material, Vol. I, 16 tapes . $90.00

Video Tape

___ *Soul Evolution and the Cosmic Plan*, 1 hr. 53 min. $10.00

Shipping Charges

US: $3.95 1st item, $1.25 ea. add'l. **Free shipping** on 5 or more items.
Outside US: Will charge actual cost to ship.

Name _____

Address _____

City _____   State/Province _____

Zip/Postal code _____   Country _____

Telephone _____   e-mail _____

Circle one: VISA   MasterCard   American Express   Discover

Cardholder name _____

Card number _____   Exp. date. ___ / ___

Fax to: (408) 985-1804 or (415) 567-2976 OR
Mail to: Scott Mandelker
        PMB 201, 2130 Fillmore St.
        San Francisco, CA 94115 USA